More praise for *Creative You*

"Whether you've lost faith in your own creativity or are trying to help others regain theirs, Goldstein and Kroeger provide a wealth of rich examples and practical advice on embracing— and making the most of—one's own creative style."

JANE A. G. KISE, EdD, author of *Intentional Leadership* and founder of
Differentiated Coaching Associates

"Today, your creativity is more valuable than oil or gold. It's one necessity that can't be outsourced! This timeless, fascinating book shows you how to be more creative, boost your earning power and job security, and make the world a far better place."

PATRICIA ABURDENE, author of *Conscious Money* and *Megatrends 2010*

"Finally a book that explains the two types of creativity in a well researched and logical manner. Some of us excel in "adaptive" creativity, changing a few features to make something work better. Others exhibit "innovative" creativity, generating the ideas that come out of nowhere. As an artist, writer, and seminar leader I have found that both are needed and understanding one's own strength is crucial to career success and satisfaction."

SHOYA ZICHY, author of *Career Match* and *Personality Power*

"This well thought out and articulate book cries out for us to re-examine the traditional notion of what it means to be creative. Using the frameworks of type and temperament, the authors challenge us to know ourselves, so that we can recognize and nurture our own kind of creativity. More than a theoretical work, the book is bursting with practical information on not only how to understand our creative nature, but how to implement what excites us the most."

CYNTHIA STENGEL PARIS, MBTI® Master Practitioner and president of The People Skills Group

"Over thirty years after his field-defining *Type Talk*, Otto Kroeger—with his new and wonderful coauthor, David Goldstein—has created an accessible and much needed volume on creativity through the lens of psychological type. In this age of grinding demands for creativity and change, *Creative You* empowers each of us to understand and fully realize the creativity that each of us is hardwired to have."

HILE RUTLEDGE, president of OKA

"Do you aspire to unlock and tap into your creative potential? You can by using this book's new insights and useful applications. I found it both revelatory and relevant to see my type so perfectly captured. I found it both liberating and affirming. *Creative You* has enhanced my understanding and appreciation of creative styles, and I intend to use what I have learned to paint, teach, and validate with new confidence and renewed appreciation of creative differences in both process and product."

JEAN K. GILL, AWS, NWS

"David Goldstein and Otto Kroeger have performed a valuable service by helping people of all sixteen personality types to understand and enhance their creative gifts. Creativity isn't just for one type of personality. Each of us has creative potential, and each personality type has a creative contribution to make. *Creative You* will help you find your own unique pathway to a more creative life, even if you previously thought of yourself as uncreative."

SHELLEY CARSON, PhD, lecturer in psychology at Harvard University and author of *Your Creative Brain*

"With a range of incisive, insightful, and unique metaphors, *Creative You* will assist experienced practitioners to explain type concepts more effectively and help those new to the theory to grasp it more quickly and thoroughly. Goldstein and Kroeger have made a special contribution to the type literature—from cooking to spirituality to pop art, there is something here to stimulate the creativity of all types."

KATHERINE W HIRSH, DPhil, author of three volumes in the Introduction to Type® Series

Creative You

Creative You

USING YOUR PERSONALITY TYPE TO THRIVE

David B. Goldstein & Otto Kroeger

ATRIA PAPERBACK
New York London Toronto Sydney New Delhi

BEYOND WORDS
Hillsboro, Oregon

ATRIA PAPERBACK
A Division of Simon & Schuster, Inc.
1230 Avenue of the Americas
New York, NY 10020

BEYOND WORDS
20827 N.W. Cornell Road, Suite 500
Hillsboro, Oregon 97124-9808
503-531-8700 / 503-531-8773 fax
www.beyondword.com

Managing editor: Lindsay S. Brown
Editors: Henry Covey, Anna Noak
Copyeditor: Jennifer Weaver-Neist
Design: Devon Smith
Proofreader: Claire Rudy Foster
Composition: William H. Brunson

First Atria Paperback/Beyond Words trade paperback edition July 2013

For more information about special discounts for bulk purchases, please contact Simon & Schuster Special Sales at 1-866-506-1949 or business@simonandschuster.com.

The Simon & Schuster Speakers Bureau can bring authors to your live event. For more information or to book an event, contact the Simon & Schuster Speakers Bureau at 1-866-248-3049 or visit our website at www.simonspeakers.com.

Manufactured in the United States of America

10 9 8 7 6 5 4 3 2 1

Library of Congress Cataloging-in-Publication Data:

Goldstein, David B.
　　Creative you : using your personality type to thrive / David B. Goldstein and Otto Kroeger.
　　　　pages　cm
　　Includes bibliographical references.
　　　　1. Personality and creative ability.　2. Creative ability.　3. Personality and occupation.　4. Typology (Psychology).　I. Kroeger, Otto.　II. Title.
　　BF698.9.C74G65　2013
　　155.2′64—dc23

2013005587

ISBN 978-1-58270-365-7
ISBN 978-1-4516-6904-6 (eBook)

The corporate mission of Beyond Words Publishing, Inc.: *Inspire to Integrity*

CONTENTS

Contents

To Gavin and the children of his age,
who, with any luck,
can retain their creativity as they grow up.

FOREWORD

I was honored and pleased to be invited by David Goldstein to write the foreword to this book that he authored with Otto Kroeger, as I have known, worked, and respected Otto for years.

David Goldstein, an internationally renowned artist and an MBTI® (Myers-Briggs Type Indicator®) practitioner, presented his early work at the 2011 San Francisco APTi (Association for Psychological Type International) Conference through a presentation entitled "Art in Yourself, Type, and Creativity." David had become interested in the connection between the MBTI and creativity when he was taking a watercolor class. The students, who were learning about their own painting style, were asked to fill out a questionnaire to help them determine what that style might be. Through this experience, David saw the link between MBTI personality type and art, and embarked on writing a book on the topic with Otto Kroeger. In conjunction with Otto, his research on creativity and the sixteen personality types spread from uncovering the link between painting and type to *all* areas of creativity; that is what *Creative You* is about.

Foreword

Otto Kroeger is a leader and expert with regard to the MBTI and psychological type, and has been a pioneer in the delivery, writing, and application of the Indicator. This book follows in that pioneering tradition.

When Isabel Briggs Myers died in 1980, she left the Indicator to her son, Peter, and to me—the two she trusted most to take care of her "baby." With such a great responsibility, Peter and I felt we wanted advice from others. So we put together a team to help us in guarding the Indicator's ethical use and in promoting its ongoing development. We asked Otto to join the team, and he acquainted us with a new method for presenting the MBTI assessment and psychological type to groups. This method was to use exercises for helping people to understand their type. Otto drew from Experiential Learning Theory (ELT), introduced by Kurt Lewin (1890–1947), which had led to the first National Training Laboratory (NTL) in Bethel, Maine, in 1947. The inclusion of exercises into an introductory MBTI session was a major contribution to MBTI interpretation, and it remains today as the most effective way to present type.

In *Creative You*, David and Otto have contributed something new and innovative with regard to the application of the MBTI and psychological type theory. They have used their own brand of creativity to give us insight into the area of creativity—an application that has not been thoroughly explored in the way that it is here. For example, within the type community, we tend to connect Intuition with the creative process rather than thinking of sixteen *different* types of creativity. But David and Otto accurately explore sixteen kinds of creativity in this book.

I am blessed to be the recipient of a courtesy copy of many books on the MBTI and Jungian psychological type. Any time a book like this is published, or I am asked to write a foreword, I immediately look at my type (INFP). I always assume that if the author gets my type right, he or she must have gotten everyone's right! I can say that David and Otto did a very good job of exploring INFP creativity. Their interpretation gave me a whole new perspective; I had never thought about what kind of creativity I had, and I found it interesting and enlightening. It increased my recognition that I, too, have my unique style of expressing creatively (perhaps it is writing forewords to books!).

Foreword

I invite you to take a look at your own style of creativity as well as the other fifteen types, so that you may widen your definition of creativity and its intersection with type. It might help you (as it has me) to become more aware and appreciative of what can be defined as creative, and how creativity has different expressions among the sixteen types.

Katharine D. Myers, MBTI co-owner
December 12, 2012

PREFACE

The story of how Otto and I came to write this book together began in the winter of 2001. I was taking a watercolor class from Jean Gill in Fairfax, Virginia.[1] Jean is an accomplished and talented watercolorist herself, and many of her students are professional artists who have been attending her classes for years. I had been going for about a year and a half, and like usual, Jean had a theme for the class that night; our objective this time was to gain an understanding of our own personal creative styles. To help, she gave us a worksheet with 103 questions. After filling it out, I couldn't help but notice that many of the questions seemed rooted in personality type. Since I was friends with many of the other students, I saw an immediate connection between their personality type and their creative style. For the artist in me, it was an "Aha!" moment personally, but with an MBA in innovation management, I found my professional curiosity set afire. How far did the connection go? Was there an elegant, underlying structure to all these creative differences? What were the commonalities? Did everyone have their own unique creative type?

I brought the idea to Otto, a friend and internationally known organizational consultant whose main area of expertise is the use of the Myers-Briggs Type Indicator®

Preface

(MBTI®), the personality assessment developed by Katharine Briggs and her daughter Isabel Briggs Myers to measure psychological preferences in how we perceive the world and make decisions (based on the initial work of Carl Jung). Otto, or "Mr. MBTI," is famous for his talent for bringing the wide, practical use of psychological type theory to diverse personal and professional groups throughout the world. The past president of the Association of Psychological Type, he has co-authored numerous publications and four leading books on personality, including *Type Talk*, *Type Talk at Work*, *16 Ways to Love Your Lover*, and *Personality Type and Religious Leadership*. In addition to being considered one of the most influential communicators and interpreters of Isabel Briggs Myers, Otto has also worked at the National Training Laboratories, where he developed a father-son-type relationship with renowned psychologist Abraham Maslow. If there was anyone who would be able to help me apply this new idea of creative theory to the well-established field of psychological type, it would be Otto.

Although Otto agreed with me that the intimate connection between one's psychological type and his or her own unique, core creative style was exciting indeed, and worthy of much more exploration and mapping out, we were both too busy with other work to pursue the idea further. But we kept in touch—as friends and neighbors we saw each other often—and as time went on, we continued to see more and more of a connection between people's personalities and their creative styles. We also began seeing the critical need to help others view themselves as being creative and understand their creative style (so many of us don't think we're creative, even though we're all creative in our own ways). Finally, the opportunity arose for us to work together to develop our observations and translate them into a form that can benefit everyone.

Although the idea of connecting fundamental psychology with unique creative style was initially sparked by linking personality types to painting styles, we realized it could be applied to all forms of creating art, including concerts, plays, movies, and writing. But it quickly spread beyond the arts as we noticed how entrepreneurs with different personality types created different kinds of businesses, and how different types of creative cultures exist within innovative companies. We saw differing creative types in how marketers spread their messages and how leaders use creativity to manage and govern. We even found that creative type factors into the way we solve daily problems, like whipping together a meal for the family or finding a new route to work in order to avoid construction, not to mention how we manage major life changes. What started as a simple observation of how personality type affects the way we creatively express ourselves through painting soon spread to *all* facets of life.

Whatever we choose to do, we all have an individual style for expression—a unique creative self that sets us apart from the rest, whether we're speaking, writing, painting, plumbing, dancing, singing, cooking, gardening, playing music, at the office, or using social media to keep up with friends. And when you dissect all these various acts of creation, you'll also notice that we share commonalities—preferences for gathering information, analyzing this information, making decisions about it, and then behaving based on this information; this affects the type of creations we produce.

Are you more like Norman Rockwell, who preferred to notice rich detail and have a realistic style; or are you more like Vincent van Gogh in that you see the big picture and make abstract connections? Are you more like James A. Michener, who made careful outlines before writing his books; or are you more like Ernest Hemingway, who preferred to work spontaneously? This kind of diversification of artists can be applied to every kind of creativity, in all arenas of life. Knowing your particular creative type will lend insight into the strengths of your creative style and teach you about the differences you see in others—and this will have ripple effects throughout your day to day.

In fact, understanding personality type and its connection to your creative style will help you to enjoy your life to the fullest, with more enthusiasm, excitement, engagement, and a greater ability to contribute. You will discover an exciting way to look at the world, and receive immediate tools to develop personal strategies and make you more competitive. You will also learn how to live within your true nature and how to create value by following your passions, applying creativity to your own preferences to develop a more meaningful life. These concepts will improve the way you experience the world and enrich your interactions with others. You will never watch a movie the same way or listen to music with the same ear, and every new sense will have its own wisdom. Each experience will be topped with a new layer of insight, engagement, and understanding—and you will be able to use this to solve more problems creatively.

If anyone in your life has ever told you that you weren't creative, it's time to realize that they were wrong. We're all creative; it's a facet of every human being. But the manifestations and applications of creativity are many, from writing a heartfelt letter to a friend or family member you haven't talked to for a while, to a more professional purpose, like thinking of new ways to attract more customers to your small business or building a social network around a cause you're passionate about.

What works for one personality might not be right for another, and this book will help you find what's right for you—because meeting your creative self can have far-reaching effects. Otto used to have an exercise for the beginning of his workshops where, as an icebreaker, he showed a series of posters and asked the participants which one they were most inspired by. Once people knew what they liked, they were able to learn more about themselves based on what they picked—what they liked and disliked, what inspired them, what stoked their imaginations—which, in many ways, gave them more than any art history course or trip to a museum ever could. It provided them with practical knowledge that could be put to immediate use in everyday life.

Follow these pages, and we'll provide key insights to your personal interests, style, and inborn creative talents, all of which may have lain dormant until this time. You'll learn more about yourself, along with everyone else's profiles, and you'll be ahead of the creative curve. You'll learn how to embrace the creative you.

David B. Goldstein

INTRODUCTION

Every child is an artist; the problem is how to remain an artist once they grow up.

Pablo Picasso

Ask anyone when they stopped thinking of themselves as creative, and you'll hear something like, "As a child, I used to like to sing, dance, and draw until one day in second grade, when my teacher yelled at me for coloring the sky a different color than blue. The other kids laughed, and that was the last time I tried anything creative." Variations of this story are repeated over and over again, generation after generation, as so many of us were discouraged from using our talents in the very act of thinking imaginatively just because of a teacher's creative differences.

How many of us decided that we were NOT creative while we were still children using crayons? How many of us as children or young adults were not properly taught the varied techniques of drawing, dancing, singing, cooking, or starting a small business? In light of the criticism from those who wanted us to do it in a way that was natural to them but never felt right to us—and without the right kind of instruction from someone who understood our individual creative strengths—the easy answer was to throw up our hands in frustration and say, "I can't." For many of us, this assumption came much too early.

Introduction

Our school teachers and college professors who couldn't see the mismatch didn't comprehend the level of disconnect that occurred. Without understanding that there are creative differences among different personality types, instructing us to do it their way was like forcing a square peg through a round hole, an exercise in failure and disappointment no matter how hard they tried.

In this book, you will happily discover it wasn't your fault if you've not yet learned how to fully utilize your creativity, because we're all naturally creative. The problem is that if you think you aren't creative, then you were probably not given the proper tools to discover your talents, nor the opportunity to learn how to use them effectively. You were more likely discouraged from expressing yourself and taught instead to avoid mistakes, follow the leader, and act like everyone else. If you've stopped thinking of yourself as creative, the good news is that it's never too late to harness your inborn creativity (and this is not as difficult as it might sound).

Keeping somewhat of a mystique, artists rarely tell us that their creativity comes from a combination of two parts: their ideas and their techniques. The truth is that there is a difference between ideas and techniques, and the good news is that (1) we all have unique minds from which ideas spring and (2) we are all capable of learning techniques. For instance, anyone can learn to hear pitch with the right training and then reproduce it. It has also been proven that realistic drawing is a skill that can be learned. According to Betty Edwards, author of *Drawing on the Right Side of the Brain*, in a short time, with the right instruction and practice, "drawing is a skill that can be learned by every normal person with average eyesight and average eye-hand coordination."[1] This same principle of learning applies later in life to many activities or ideas that we've perhaps never tried or have given up on because of creative differences with a teacher in the past.

In the following pages, we'll show you how every personality type can be creative in his or her own way, as well as provide targeted strategies for embracing the creative you. Dancing dinner onto the plate, sculpting the perfect memo, or drawing out the perfect business plan—whatever your own personal style of creativity, you'll be able to develop an environment of innovation at work or at home where your ingenuity and productivity can thrive. And if you already see yourself as creative, we'll show you how to optimize your talents.

Your Creative License

Have you ever wanted to pick up a brush and paint but stopped because you think that you can barely draw stick figures? Have you ever wanted to become a dancer, but you think you have two left feet? Or a singer, but you think you're too tone deaf? Or a cook, but you are too afraid because you burn toast? Perhaps you've always wanted to start a business or invent a new tool but didn't trust that your ideas would appeal to others. While there are so many different ways to be creative, there are just as many ways to feel blocked in expressing our creativity. And we ourselves are often the first stumbling blocks on the path toward a more artful and inspired life.

Whether you can admit it to yourself or not, you're creative—we're all creative. When we encounter something genuinely beautiful and unusual, we often say to its creator, "You're a real artist"; what we cannot say ourselves, others often say for us. Has a friend ever said to you, "Wow, you amaze me! I couldn't possibly do that" when describing a meal you cooked and presented, the garden you planted, the way you wore your clothes, something you hammered together?

These accomplishments are the results of creativity. You were just working on your "regular stuff," but others see it as unique, beautiful, and artsy—as you: "I could never cook a meal like you"; "I could never paint a house like you"; "There's no way I could hammer a nail correctly, let alone build something that looks so pretty." You'll hear yourself say such things when someone finishes restoring an antique table they rescued at the flea market, when someone who can't read music plays the piano beautifully by ear, when someone designs a new home addition themselves. You'll say it when a friend decorates an amazing cake, cooks the perfect chowder, or snaps a momentous photograph. And when you hear others say "I couldn't do that" to you, that's when you know you're doing something special; you're being your unique artistic self without even realizing it.

Sadly, our society makes it difficult for us to embrace our inspiration and freely call ourselves artists. We interviewed artists for this book who, although they had sold hundreds of paintings, still had trouble introducing themselves as artists. Why has our society made it so difficult to think of ourselves as creative? Instead of associating creativity with weirdness, unproductivity, and poverty, perhaps we should instead emulate the Indonesians on the island of Bali or the Australian Aborigines, who consider every adult—and child—to be an artist at heart.

The idea that we're either naturally creative or not is a myth; we're all born with personality preferences that we can use to be creative in our own way and thrive. You can acknowledge this fact by giving yourself a creative license. And be literal about it: write it on a sticky note or notepad, or find a legal form off the web that you can fill out. Then place the license where it will remind you that you have the basic human right to be yourself and to use your natural creativity.

Why We Can Learn from the Arts

With so many different channels to watch, sports to play, songs to listen to, events to attend, and hobbies to pursue, the world is fractured, but art is universal. Even if you're like most people and don't think of yourself as an artist, art is part of our common heritage, and we all have some exposure with some forms of art.

Some people label art as being complicated, even though it's not, and we certainly won't bore you with arcane art history or talk about obscure artists. The process for art is actually simple and something we can all do and appreciate. It's related to what you already do; it's an expression of how you gather information from the world around you and how you make decisions.

We can learn a lot from looking at the creative process, as it can be applied to pretty much anything we do. Even seemingly routine jobs have plenty of new problems to solve and new situations to deal with; there are always improvements that can be made to the process. And unlike other disciplines studied in school, we see through the arts that problems can have more than one solution—and many times no right or wrong answers. Art demonstrates how complicated concepts can be simplified and shown in a different light, whatever field or profession you're in.

A janitor interviewed for the book told us that he enjoyed drawing cartoons of superheroes because creating art took him away from his daily maintenance tasks, and sometimes those "Aha!" answers to sticky problems he'd been agonizing about at work would come to him while he was taking a break and sketching out an illustration. Art was allowing him to find solutions to problems in his day job.

Art shows better than anything else that there are multiple ways to solve a problem and multiple ways to be creative. This is especially handy for business owners large and small, as well as for our individual aspirations of whatever we view as success. Sports analogies are the common vehicle for explaining business-related concepts and team-work strategies: you might have little interest in literally catching a football or hitting a baseball, but you most likely know what it means to "keep your eye on the ball" while working on a project. The arts provide equally relevant wisdom and lessons about idea generation, plan execution, risk taking, and collaboration that we can all understand. And these days, being creative is more than just drawing pretty pictures; it's a basic human need essential to thriving in our ever-changing, increasingly competitive global economy. Creativity is a matter of survival. It's the key to driving economic growth.

The disappointing fact, however, is that many of us aren't exercising our creative muscles as much as we could be. According to Gallup, 71 percent of us are "not engaged" or "actively disengaged" in our work, meaning that we're emotionally disconnected from our workplaces and are far less likely to be productive or creative—and it can become a vicious cycle.[2] Only one in four people feels that they are living up to their creative potential.[3] Being creative, on the other hand, turns this unhappiness around. When acting creatively, we are actively involved and acting passionately, and this leads to better career satisfaction and overall well-being. Knowing how to leverage your creative strengths, while keeping an eye out for blind spots, will allow you to use your particular style of creativity to *engage* in whatever you are doing, whether it's collaborating on a group project at work, taking a life drawing class for the first time in years, or getting involved in your community. There is the "actively disengaged" way to live, and there is the creative, imaginative, fulfilling, *artful* way to live.

Creativity Goes Far Beyond the Arts

By taking creativity out of the art studios and laboratories, we reframe the question of what makes a creative personality. The truth is, whether you're actively trying to be creative or not, creativity is a part of daily life. Therefore, we broadly define creativity as the simple act of coming up with something new—a new interpretation, process, idea, product, service, or solution to a problem, like finding a shortcut on the way to work or substituting a few missing ingredients when making dinner. What we create doesn't even need to be currently useful. Leonardo da Vinci had a passion for flight and sketched the concept for a helicopter long before the invention of engines made air travel possible.

However, creativity is a universal currency that is increasingly valuable. From reading the personal letters of such masters as Monet, Picasso, and Dali, it becomes clear that these icons were just regular folk with regular problems, but they set themselves apart by following their passion and using their natural strengths creatively. Often, our vocational success comes from using our creativity to be innovative, and those who foster and practice creativity gain competitive advantages and rich rewards. We all know the importance of stories to illustrate complex ideas, and we value new inventions and new designs. All of this comes through creativity.

Creativity can be as beneficial for you *personally* as it is for companies and countries that cultivate creativity. Being creative helps you to save time and money, invent new solutions for old problems, and improve relationships. Seeing yourself as creative and then leveraging your creative strengths improves your life by helping you to

- Generate new ideas
- Select which ideas to implement
- Identify your optimum learning style and learning environment
- Communicate your ideas clearly and improve your relationships with others
- Remedy everyday problems with creative solutions
- Collaborate better with others
- Identify who to seek advice from and which critics to listen to
- Become more engaged and successful at your work
- Become more confident to be creative, whatever your passion
- Take a second chance to use your creativity and follow your passion

So, where do we start? Although you probably do many things well, this book is designed to help you understand your core personality and creative style so that you can do those things better and try new things too. It all comes down to understanding your own personality preferences via the time-tested Myers-Briggs Type Indicator® (MBTI®). Once you know your creative type, you can use your natural abilities to increase your capacity to generate creative ideas, improve techniques, implement practical solutions, better express individuality, and develop the power of your natural creativity.

The Myers-Briggs Personality Type System

Since humans first started drawing on cave walls, artists have been putting their personalities into their art. This fundamental relationship between personality type and creativity has been analyzed and written about in psychological journals and texts, but never before has it been laid out as a set of tools for you to use in your own life—until now.

Most people have heard of the Myers-Briggs Type Indicator, a "personality inventory" that was developed by Katharine Briggs and her daughter Isabel Briggs Myers, who based their psychological assessment on Carl Jung's theories.[4] The MBTI categorizes behavior into sixteen personality types based on how we gather information and make decisions—the same two functions that we use to be creative.

Taken by 3 million people a year, the MBTI is the world's leading personality assessment (used mostly as a tool to help people find work that will be meaningful to them). The MBTI assures us that there are no bad personality types. Every type has its own gifts, and the types are identified and affirmed to encourage confidence. Administered by trained professionals, the MBTI promotes wellness by focusing on the positive aspects of personality—something that has been shown to dramatically improve the way people live, love, and work because of the self-awareness it teaches.

How to Use This Book

This book is divided into three basic parts:

Part 1

* Chapter 1 dispels common but harmful misconceptions about creativity.
* Chapter 2 helps you identify your personal creative *preferences*.
* Chapter 3 provides full profiles of each individual preference.
* Chapter 4 discusses creative power exhibited by four special pairings of preferences—creative leanings called *temperaments*.

Part 2

This part profiles all of the sixteen creative types as they correspond to the Myers-Briggs Type Indicator. In this section, you'll learn

* Your type's strengths and weaknesses
* What blind spots to watch out for
* How to boost your creativity

You'll also be able to use the MBTI to learn more about the creative types of your friends, family, and coworkers. It's a reference tool you'll use again and again.

Part 3

In the final part, we show you the art of living creatively—how to use your type for maximum effect—including

* Techniques to heighten your creativity and productivity both at work and at play
* Tips on which groups to consider joining to increase collaborative efforts
* How to foster creativity in children
* What artistic outlets might fit you best
* How to understand the bias that all critics have—as well as how to get the most from their impressions and suggestions

At the end of the book, in the final chapters, we shed some light on how being spiritually aware helps us to be courageous at whatever we artfully apply ourselves to.

Throughout all three parts, we've included interviews, conducted specifically for this book; personal stories from our own lives as they apply to the subject matter; and wisdom from some of the world's most popular and acclaimed composers, performers, artists, writers, and scientists—all so that you can learn more about how others overcame their obstacles. You can read for yourself what they have to say about creativity and the creative process. While you're reading, keep in mind that although we use artists as teachers, the idea isn't to compare yourself to them. Instead, expect to find a few kindred spirits in those with similar personality types while being open to the others; learn from all their creative processes. Be inspired that they spent their lives developing their strengths so they could better express their ideas for others—something you can do too.

Whether you're versed in the Myers-Briggs universe or you're new to these concepts, this book is built to be a trusted reference that gets better with age—a guide to

Introduction

the Myers-Briggs matrix of creative personalities that can be revisited anytime you need to check your creative profile or look up the creative profile of a friend, family member, or coworker.

To make navigation more efficient, we've provided an expanded table of contents for easy referencing. Additionally, in the back of the book, we've also provided an at-a-glance glossary of all the different creative preferences, temperaments, and types, as well as a selected bibliography that can point you to many recommended resources if you're interested in learning more about the many facets of the Myers-Briggs methodology.

In the end, our hope is that this in-depth research into the personal writings of people with great creative achievements, coupled with the personality theories of Carl Jung and the science of the MBTI, will bring you fresh, practical insight and meaning about yourself. Let these pages lead you down a path of self-discovery in order to develop a deeper understanding of your creative self. Armed with the knowledge in this book and a profound understanding of what "your way" toward creativity is, you will be well prepared to unleash the creative you upon the world, confidently taking chances to follow your passion, being mindfully creative in your daily life, and making sure to fully self-express the creative genius that lives within.

Part I

MEETING YOUR CREATIVE SELF

1

CASTING LIGHT ON CREATIVITY

Drawing outside the lines, thinking outside the box, and driving off-road are analogies used to describe creative thinking, but they provide an incomplete picture that excludes many of us. Leonardo da Vinci, with the exactitude of his anatomical and architectural sketches, drew inside the lines; Charles Schulz cartooned whole worlds within the confines of three small boxes; and every bus driver who has weaved safely and flawlessly through traffic has acted creatively and artistically.

In the introduction, we brought up the unfortunate fact that most people don't see themselves as creative (even though they innately are), and we're here to tell you that there are many different ways to be creative—regardless of whether it's drawing inside the lines or thinking outside the box. We've mapped them all out in this book so that you can use the knowledge to discover more about yourself, and recognize the inborn creativity in you and in the people around you.

Before we can hand you your own "piece of chalk" with which to be more creative than you've ever been, we must first wipe the blackboard clean of nonsense. Over time, many misconceptions have arisen around creativity. Like the Wizard of Oz concealed behind the curtain, creativity and the creative process have been cloaked in a veil of mystery and awe, ordained only for those "touched" by the muse. It's time to burst that overinflated bubble.

Common Myths About Creativity

Thanks to modern astronomy, we no longer believe that the Greek god Helios pulls the sun across the sky in his golden chariot each day. Myths attempt to explain the unexplainable, and creativity can certainly seem beyond explanation. Even with all the breakthroughs in neuroscience these days, we're still not exactly sure where our ideas originate; the notion that our creativity is inspired by muses continues to be open for debate. However, while myths about the cosmos can be relatively harmless today, there are some commonly held misconceptions about creativity that are actually holding us back from blasting into the stratosphere of our creative stardom.

Myth #1: I don't have a creative bone in my body.

In order to be creative, you need to break self-imposed limits and think of yourself as creative. The fact is that you are unknowingly creative all the time: you create your life, and every day is different. Did you just design the remodel on your house? Lead your child's baseball team to victory? Think of a way to repair your car for half the cost quoted by your mechanic? Or combine your gift card with a coupon to get a dress practically for free? Whoever led you to believe that you weren't creative was wrong. You're creative every time you substitute an ingredient while cooking dinner, plant a garden to fit the space you're given, find a new way to organize your closet, or throw a party that accommodates all your friends' dietary needs and scheduling constraints.

Myth #2: If *I* can do it, then it can't be very creative.

These words are sometimes said when we compare our ability with what others have done, like when we see a new logo that looks like "abstract art" we could have pasted together, or when we eat a slice of bakery-made lemon meringue pie that we could have made ourselves at home. Why is our creativity so difficult to accept? When we see a design or product that we could have produced, instead of thinking it simple, why not see ourselves as creative? Try recasting yourself as creative when you see proof that you can do something other creative people are doing, especially when you know you can do better. That's what motivated James A. Michener creatively: "All I knew was that I was able to write better than a lot of the stuff I was reading, and I was going to take a shot at it."[1]

Myth #3: There is only one type of creativity.

A critical mistake many of us make is in assuming that we're all the same. Did Henry Ford have the same kind of creative style as Picasso? Ford was conservative and created within a rigid model; Picasso was much more fluid. We all have unique knowledge, can learn techniques, and are capable of creating in our own way. Give a classroom of children a topic and ask them to write an essay, then see how many variations you get. Each of us sees the world in our own way and we act accordingly. Our creativity is as unique as our fingerprints and leaves an impression on whatever we make.

Myth #4: Leave the creative stuff to the creative people.

Just as we shouldn't let others do our thinking, we can't depend on others to be creative for us. Everyone is capable, and it's everyone's responsibility to contribute through participation and support. Today, every sales person, computer programmer, and small-business owner must use their natural creativity to thrive. Adapting to our changing economy requires that we invent new ways of doing our most basic tasks—all within our budget, timetable, and desired level of quality. If you left it to others to be creative, not much would get done, and you would be left out of the new economy. According to a recent study about the global creativity gap, eight out of ten people feel that unlocking creativity is critical to economic growth, and two-thirds of respondents feel creativity is valuable to society. But only one in four people believe they are living up to their creative potential."[2]

Myth #5: Creativity can't be learned.

We all see things in our own way, and anyone can learn to recognize what they see is unique and has creative potential. We need to get past the myths and self-imposed constraints that stop many from using our natural talents. Creative sparks fly all around us like lightning bugs, and they can be captured by our hands if we don't squash or curtail them. Creativity is fragile and learning to be creative is about learning to recognize your unique perspectives and being confident enough to act on them.

Myth #6: Creative people are weird.

Have you noticed that everyone is a little eccentric once you get to know them? However, most don't have enough strangeness to prevent them from functioning in a normal, everyday life. People are generally happy when they're creating, and it's been found that neurotic people have less experiences of flow—the feeling of happiness, timelessness, and wholeness that is believed necessary to propel creativity.[3] If you're the first to create something, then by definition, what you made is outside the norm. We all go outside the norm to create, and it's fine as long as you can rein yourself in to live your life within social norms. "Normal" is a relative term anyway. The only people we know who are not at least somewhat eccentric are the ones we don't know very well.

Myth #7: Creative people are spontaneous, untimely, and unstructured.

This falsehood rests fully on personality type differences, and we will explore it further throughout the book. Creative people can be planners, deadline oriented, and orderly. One of our greatest achievements was the space program at NASA, and its work has solved unprecedented problems on a massive scale through carefully planned, scheduled, and organized program management.

Myth #8: Creativity can't be managed.

Google and 3M manage creativity by *not* managing it. They allow time for employees to follow their passions on company time. And Facebook has all-night "hackathons," where employees can try out new own ideas.[4] They manage by fostering a culture where all types of creativity are inspired and encouraged, and this has led them to success. You, too, can manage your creativity, and we'll show you how.

Myth #9: I'm too old to start being creative.

We prize child prodigies for their gift, honoring these young artists and writers for seeing things in new ways. But what if we approached these same subjects as adults, equipped with a lifetime of experiences and a deep understanding of the world and human nature? Wouldn't this give us more tools to be creative?

Many have made their greatest contributions later in life. Writer James A. Michener didn't write his first book, *Tales of the South Pacific*, until he was in his forties. Julia Child produced her first cookbook at fifty. Colonel Sanders started the KFC franchise when he was in his sixties. Grandma Moses began painting in her seventies. Many people don't discover their passion until retirement. Albert Einstein, in explaining his own "late start" creatively, aptly expresses the distinct type of insight that maturity lends to one's creativity:

The normal adult never bothers his head about space-time problems. Everything that there is to be thought about, in his opinion, has already been done in early childhood. I, on the contrary, developed so slowly that I only began to wonder about space and time when I was already grown up. In consequence, I probed deeper into the problem than an ordinary child would have done.[5]

Like Einstein says, we "probe deeper" into things as adults—much more profoundly than our younger selves could ever have dreamed. Science backs this up: research has shown that our minds are neuroplastic, meaning our brain can change itself to meet current needs. It's never too late for creativity!

Myth #10: Creativity is driven by money.

Not many people working long into the night writing or spending their early mornings in dance studios are doing it for the cash, and not many scientists are driven by the aspiration to own fast cars. Creativity is fueled by passion, not money. This is true in companies too. A study by Booz & Company found that few of the top spenders on research and development (R&D) are considered top innovative firms. In fact the top three innovative firms—Apple, Google, and 3M—weren't even among the top twenty spenders on R&D.[6]

Myth #11: Creative people are starving artists.

Art for art's sake is a tough sell, but our creative economy does not go hungry; it produces results, designs products, reaches markets, meets needs, and creates value for mainstream consumers. While there is plenty of competition for writers and photographers, there are real demands for their services. And yes, creativity is usually more about passion than making money, but there are creative people working in engineering, science, design, and marketing who can also pay their bills.

Myth #12: Creativity is inborn to a few gifted people.

This is half correct since creativity is inborn. However, it's inborn in all of us. As we discussed in the introduction, some of us have natural abilities, but it takes practice to develop technique. Take a look at Van Gogh's early paintings and you'll see he wasn't born with a masterful technique. And passion is more important than natural ability. Many singers, musicians, and actors seem to have more passion than talent, but this doesn't limit their success. Our creative process is a natural process—in *all* of us.

Myth #13: Creativity is only for artists.

Like we also said in the introduction, creativity extends well beyond the arts. We are creative when we're making jokes, leading teams, solving math problems, organizing people, and so forth. Creativity can be regained at any time, and techniques can be learned. It's never too late.

Myth #14: Creativity is only available to geniuses.

You don't have to belong to Mensa to be profoundly creative; creativity cannot be painted into a corner. Creativity manifests itself in everybody, albeit in different ways. Everyone is creative even if they don't fit the stereotypical idea of the "creative genius" type. Many great discoveries and achievements were produced by people of "normal intelligence," though this is another relative term. It's more important to be well rounded—to have knowledge in several areas that can be combined and used to meet the needs that nurture and grow your own creativity in the way that suits your own personality.

Myth #15: Creativity means reinventing the game.

Creativity doesn't have to be disruptive or revolutionary to be effective. Sometimes it's meant to simply advance your marker a few places. For example, we are continuously adapting to our changing environment by making small adjustments and optimizing our daily routines in creative ways. Adding up many small changes can have large effects—creativity is cumulative.

Myth #16: Creativity is risky.

Of course, taking a new step has some risk. With our rapidly changing environment, however, it's also risky to stand still. Like those lottery commercials say, "You can't win if you don't play." And what is risky for some isn't risky for others who are acting within their strength and experience; a normal procedure performed by a doctor could be risky if we tried it ourselves, for instance. Knowing our strengths lets us act, experiment, and gain experience from an advantageous position as opposed to a vulnerable one.

Creativity is not linear, and mistakes will happen and should be expected—for all of us. But by weighing the possible consequences against the possible rewards, risks can be managed and tested. Start by testing for seaworthiness in tide pools before being scaled up and launched into the ocean.

Myth #17: My creative process is better left a mystery.

We often hear creative people say that they don't want to understand their process, or they're afraid that knowing too much about their creativity will cause them to lose it. This is a dangerous superstition, however. Consider driving: the complexity of an automobile is something that we don't need to understand fully in order to drive a car. On the other hand, you do need to know how to use the turn signal to notify other drivers that you're switching lanes, or how to turn the steering wheel to avoid obstacles. Simply understanding that your car is powered by gas also allows you to go. Similarly, understanding the basics of the creative process will take you far.

Myth #18: You have to leave your comfort zone to be creative.

Actually, you need to be yourself to find your comfort zone. When you are being yourself, you're in a position of strength and can take calculated risks. Find the rock that balances your weight so you can stand on it and dance.

Myth #19: Creativity is personal and takes emotions

Creativity doesn't necessarily require you to draw on your experiences of suffering or joy. You can be objective as you passionately express your thoughts and dreams. Even in painting, Jackson Pollock's works weren't personal paintings; in fact, he numbered them instead of giving them names. Additionally, Moore's law, which has correctly predicted computer power doubles every eighteen months, shows a history of technological innovation that isn't driven by love or loss.

Myth #20: Personality type puts me in a box.

This last myth has to do with a misconception about personality type. Not everyone likes the idea of classifying people; they see it as a means for stereotyping and possibly discriminating. However, when used practically, categories can be quite helpful—we use them all the time to describe whether we have brown hair, live on the west side, or belong to the middle class. In fact, the more you know about your personality type, the more open you feel. Instead of thinking you're being put in a box, think about being given a present with a little bow on top. When you unwrap it, you'll find a collection of specialized tools uniquely sized to fit your personal creative style that can become part of you.

With these myths now behind us, we can move forward and focus on the basic aspects of your personality—your preferences and temperaments for certain things. This will then help you to identify your own creative type.

2

WHAT'S YOUR CREATIVE TYPE?

Have you ever traveled with another person to a foreign country? On your trip, you probably expected some degree of cultural difference, but the biggest surprises don't often come through experiencing your new location; they come instead through the discovery that your travel companion sees things in a completely different way than you! How can you and your friend be so different?

When you get to know someone better (in the way that you would from going on an international trip together), you are getting to know his or her personality intimately. But you are also getting to know your own way of "seeing" the world through your friend. Likewise, the more you understand the uniqueness in your own creative personality, the more self-aware you become, and the better you can self-manage and be creative.

So, what is your personality type and creative style? The most valid way to determine this is to take the Myers-Briggs Type Indicator®.

The MBTI® doesn't measure abilities, intelligence, skills, likelihood of success, maturity, or mental health. It is a tool that reflects your individual preferences for how you see the world and how you make decisions based on that information. This is important because everything we create, whether in an art studio, science lab, or kitchen, stems from our personality. And understanding how you prefer to gather and process new information enhances your ability to create. It's like setting all the sails at the optimum angle to catch the wind: by knowing your alignment and acting within your natural style, you can take your achievements to a whole new level.

Take a moment to write down some of the activities you enjoy most. Does your list of favorites contain items you excel in and have been praised for? Do your friends say that you are a great storyteller, that you host incredible dinner parties, or that you know more about fixing cars than anyone else? Your actions define who you are, and your personality type is reflected in the choices you naturally make in life.

Our preferences don't automatically mean we have skills; our skills develop with practice. In other words, we become good at what we enjoy doing and apply ourselves to passionately. If you spend more time on the slopes than on the court, then over time—and with practice—you probably become better at skiing than at tennis. Do you prefer to go to a museum or to a sporting event? There is no wrong answer. On a summer afternoon in New York City, you can either go to the Met (Metropolitan Museum of Art) or to the stadium to watch the Mets play baseball. If you prefer the Met over the Mets, then your interests may have led you to learn more about Andy Warhol than about the 1969 World Series Champions. Again, it doesn't matter either way. What's important to understand is that the choices we prefer to make are rooted in our personality. And when we make choices that are aligned with what we most enjoy, that's when we are most creative and happy.

Think of personality like the shoes in your closet. If you're like most people, you probably have more than one pair and use different pairs for different situations, such as dress shoes for a night out or boots for rain or snow. You might even have more than one pair for the same purpose. Chances are, however, that one pair out of all of them is the most comfortable—the most broken in. It's the pair you love to wear. Is it any surprise, then, that these are the shoes that get used most of the time? Like your favorite pair of shoes, your personality type can be identified by figuring out where you are most comfortable in these four situations:

1. How you gain and focus your energy
2. How you gather information from the world around you
3. How you make decisions
4. How you prefer to appear in public

In the following sections of this chapter, we will help you identify your type, and show you how these four personality preferences are the drivers of how and what you create. And while it may seem like we're asking you to leave your comfort zone, we are instead showing you how to find your comfort zone. You are most creative when you are freely acting within your preferred personality type—the most natural, enjoyable use of your most developed skills.

Since so many people have already taken the Myers-Briggs assessment, it's possible that you may already know your type. If you don't know it, however, you can begin to understand it by answering the four simple questions in the sections that follow. Each has two basic choices, and like the choice between the Met or the Mets, there are no wrong answers. Your personality type comes from how you observe the world and the individual decisions you make from your perceptions. Observing and making decisions is how we function in life, and they are the same mechanisms that we use to be creative. This is the amazing connection we will explore.

The Four Questions of the Personality Indicator

By answering four easy questions, you can learn more about yourself than in any other way. It's an abbreviated method of understanding your personality type that gives you a behind-the-scenes look at how you prefer to (1) focus your energy, (2) gather information,

(3) make decisions, and (4) interact with the world. Your answers will be used in upcoming chapters to confirm your choices and show you how to maximize your unique creativity to reach new levels of success in life and work.

For ease of use, your four preferences, or answers, are abbreviated as letters. Since millions of people take the Myers-Briggs assessment each year, you may already be familiar with the shorthand. If not, it's easy to follow, and allows you to plug into a large community and existing network of knowledge. "Once you have mastered a technique, you barely have to look at a recipe again," described Julia Child, and once you understand these symbols, they will become second nature to you.[1]

In addition, to assist you with answering the questions, we've provided each with a list of words to choose from. The lists originated from Otto's book *Type Talk* and have been used for decades to help people determine their type.[2] You will notice the word pairs throughout these sections aren't exact opposites, as they are designed to provide positive options and prevent bias. You will also see that each personality type has its own unique strengths, so answer the following questions by being honest with *yourself*. Don't answer them as your boss, client, or spouse would expect you to answer them, and don't answer as you *think* you should. Instead, answer *as you are*. There is no right or wrong answer; just choose what you prefer most.

So, let's get started!

The first question about your personality has to do with your basic orientation toward the world and, when it comes to your creative style, whether you look inward or outward for energy and inspiration.

Energy Flow

When your car gets low on fuel, you find a service station, but when you feel worn down, where do you get your energy? Sometimes, even with a good night's sleep and enough food, we can feel tired. Knowing how to recharge effectively prevents a personal energy crisis, because when we are most energized, we are most creative. And when you are actively cranking the wheel of your creativity, you keep the momentum going. Answering this first question will be a key to unlocking insights into the way you interact with the world and how you prefer to create.

Question #1: Are You an Extravert or an Introvert?

Do you become most energized when you are with a group of people (E) or when you have time alone (I)? For more help, look at the following lists of words to see the column with which you most identify:

Characteristics of Extraversion and Introversion

Extraversion (E)	Introversion (I)
Sociable	Territorial
Interaction	Concentration
External	Internal
Breadth	Depth
Extensive	Intensive
Multiple relationships	Limited relationships
Energy expenditure	Energy conservation
External events	Internal reactions
Gregarious	Reflective
Speak, then think	Think, then speak

Either "E" or "I" is the first letter in your four-letter creative type profile.

Next are the two ways we can gather information.

Gathering Information

While the last question had to do with how you fundamentally interact with the world, this next question relates to your preference for gathering information. The starting point for understanding ourselves is learning the way we collect data from our environment. Information gathering is the input that provides raw materials for all our human interactions and for everything we create. There are two opposite ways of gathering information, and everyone uses both processes. Here, we ask which one you like to use most.

Question #2: Do You Prefer Sensing or Intuiting?

When gathering information, do you prefer to look for the details of what is practical (S), or do you prefer to look at generalities and consider theories (N)? Use the following lists of words to help you figure out which column resonates the most:

Characteristics of Sensing and Intuition

Sensing (S)	Intuition (N)
Direct	Random
Present	Future
Realistic	Conceptual
Perspiration	Inspiration
Actual	Theoretical
Down to earth	Head in the clouds
Fact	Fantasy
Practicality	Ingenuity
Specific	General

The letter you pick, either S or N, becomes the second letter in your four-letter combination.

Now comes the forking road that we take when processing this information that we've just gathered. The understanding of your choice will make all the dfference for you.

—∿∿∿∿∿—○

Making Decisions

Have you ever been shocked when two people with the same information make completely different decisions? Some of the reasons those two people make different choices have to do with their individual personality types. After you gather data using either Sensing or Intuition, your next step is to make some decisions based on one of two different mental frameworks.

Everyone uses each mental framework at times, but tends to prefer one over the other. Creating involves making countless decisions involving materials, structures, messages, subjects, and many other elements. With every brushstroke, ingredient, theme, musical note, word, and dance step, you are making decisions, and every time you choose what clothes to wear, your decision process plays a role in developing your personal creative style. Answering the following question will help you understand how you prefer to make decisions and give you more insight into how you make creative choices.

Question #3: Do You Prefer Thinking or Feeling?

When you are making a decision, is it more important for you to consider what is logical and fair (T), or do you foremost consider how the decision will affect people and promote harmony (F)? Of the following lists of words, which column do you identify with most of the time?

Characteristics of Thinking and Feeling

Thinking (T)	Feeling (F)
Objective	Subjective
Firm-minded	Tenderhearted
Laws	Circumstances
Firmness	Persuasion
Just	Humane
Clarity	Harmony
Analytical	Appreciative
Policy	Social value
Detached	Involved

Place this third letter, either T or F, in the third spot of your four-letter combination to signify how you prefer to make decisions.

Finally, we'll look at the last letter, the final opposing pair that represents the completion of your personality combination—the face that you show others. This determines the last letter of your personality combination.

Outward Orientation

Do you project an image and create an environment that is structured, organized, and punctual (J), or do you appear to be and create an environment that is spontaneous, scattered, and doing things in your own time (P)? There are no right or wrong answers, of course, and you will see that both types have their own ways of being creative.

Question #4: Are You a Judger or Perceiver?

Do you prefer to make final decisions and reach closure (J), or do you prefer to continue to gather information and leave things open (P)? Neither way is better than the other, and both types can be creative. Again, for more help, review the following lists of words to see which column rings the most true for you.

Characteristics of Judging and Perceiving

Judging (J)	Perceiving (P)
Resolved	Pending
Decided	Wait and see
Fixed	Flexible
Control	Adapt
Closure	Openness
Planned	Open-ended
Structure	Flow
Definite	Tentative
Scheduled	Spontaneous
Deadline	What deadline?

After considering the terms in the left and right columns, if you still aren't sure which you prefer, you may be a Perceiver, since Judgers tend to make up their mind before they even finish reading the question. This should help you add the final letter—a J or a P—in your personality combination.

Putting It All Together

Please record your answers to the four questions:

1. Extraversion (E) or Introversion (I) _____
2. Sensing (S) or Intuition (N) _____
3. Thinking (T) or Feeling (F) _____
4. Judging (J) or Perceiving (P) _____

Once combined, your four letter choices determine your creative style. We'll examine each four-letter combination and its unique creative profile in part 2.

The Sixteen (Four-Letter) Creative Types

ISTJ (The Organizer)	ISFJ (The Facilitator)	INFJ (The Inspirer)	INTJ (The Visionary)
ISTP (The Crafter)	ISFP (The Dreamer)	INFP (The Muser)	INTP (The Idea Mill)
ESTP (The Adventurer)	ESFP (The Entertainer)	ENFP (The Socializer)	ENTP (The Brainstormer)
ESTJ (The Realist)	ESFJ (The Teacher)	ENFJ (The Persuader)	ENTJ (The Commander)

If You're Still Not Sure

If you're not sure of your type, this an appropriate point to explain a common misconception. Your answers don't indicate degree but instead show how sure you are of your decision. For example, if you identified with every word in the column that describes Extraversion, it doesn't make you more of an Extravert than others; it only makes you certain that you're an Extravert. Furthermore, if you identify with both Extraversion and Introversion words, it doesn't make you a little of each. It just means you're unsure of which one you prefer more.

One other thing to consider is that society pulls us toward the letters E, S, T, and J. If you're borderline, then your environment may be influencing your true self, and your preference may actually be among the letters I, N, F, and P (and T if you're female). Secondly, read the profiles in the following chapters and see which one fits best with your behavior. Generally speaking, EJs are the most certain and EPs are the most uncertain of their type. Another good way to solidify your type is to read the profiles and eliminate those that aren't you.

It is important to note that, although understanding your personality type is a tremendous tool, it is no panacea for all of life's problems, and it doesn't explain all of the complexities of our personalities. This method of looking at personality type to understand one's creative style is only one set of measures; your personality is made up of many additional qualities that are both inborn and come through your experiences. The key is to use this as a starting point to learn more about yourself, what works best for you, and how you are most creative. If you become aware that we're all different and have different strengths to contribute, then you're already well on your way to being more creative, productive, and engaged in the way you live your life.

In addition, type should never be an excuse for unproductive or bad behavior. Don't ever say, "I'm a Thinker, so it's okay to not consider others," or "I'm a Feeler, so I don't have to follow logic." You can't say, "I'm a Perceiver, so it's okay that I'm always late," "I'm an Introvert, so I'll let other people speak for me," "I'm an Intuitive, so I don't have to pay attention to the details," or "I'm a Sensor, so I don't need to think about the future." Don't use your type to box yourself in or other people; instead, use it to understand your strengths and weaknesses, as well as the natural creative differences that make you—and everybody else—unique.

Moving Forward

Once you're armed with your four-letter profile—or you think you've at least got a good idea of your type—you're ready to move to the next level. But before you do, know that there are different ways you can approach the next few chapters.

In chapter 3, each of the eight preferences just covered—Extraversion (E), Introversion (I), Sensing (S), Intuition (N), Thinking (T), Feeling (F), Judging (J), and Perceiving (P)—gets a full creative dossier. Essentially, we show how our inborn preferences express themselves effectively, how they innovate best, how they can avoid tripping over creative blind spots, and how we can use their strengths to the fullest. Keep in mind as you read, however, that this book is meant to be used over and over. So if you're not inclined to read every single profile in one sitting, you can move slowly through all eight, taking your time with each preference and letting it all sink in gradually. You can also just look at your four preferences first and then come back later to the other sections you skipped the first time—perhaps when you want to discover, for example, more about the creative profile of a loved one, acquaintance, or coworker.

From chapter 3, we move into chapter 4—from the one-letter *preferences* to the two-letter *temperaments* (pairs of various preferences that exert their own powerful influence in our personalities, creations, and lives). Here, you'll find out which of the four creative temperaments fits you best (and later, in part 2, you'll explore the sixteen creative type profiles). In perusing these two- and four-letter profiles, the same rules apply: feel free to skip around, coming back to various profiles when you want to learn more about yourself or the people around you.

CREATIVE PROFILES OF
THE EIGHT PREFERENCES

In the previous chapter, you identified with the words in the right or left side column. In this chapter, you will learn that those preferences tell you more about how you see the world and make decisions than any other way. Everyone leans most of the time toward one or the other, but we can't stand at both ends at the same time. To clarify which side you prefer, the following profiles dive further into the intricacies of the eight preferences and should help you to determine which ones suit you best.

In this chapter, you will see how we use these eight preferences to act creatively and in very different ways through our daily activities—at both work and play. Understanding these preferences will help you identify core strategies for using your strengths so you can lay the groundwork for your creations, including the best practices for boosting your creativity and ways to be on the lookout for blind spots that form when you're focusing too much in one mode. You'll learn to turn blind spots and other challenges into advantages, allowing you to refine what you create to better communicate with your audience.

Extraversion (E) or Introversion (I)—Your Energy Flow

How do you prefer to celebrate your birthday? One Introvert interviewed for the book (who preferred to remain anonymous) told us that her favorite way of celebrating this special occasion was going for a walk with her husband to a small, quiet tapas bar.

Otto, on the other hand, is a known Extravert, and as you can expect, his idea of the perfect birthday is something else entirely. For his sixtieth birthday, Otto held a weekend-long party at his lakeside home. It started with shrimp and champagne on Friday and went for sixty consecutive hours, complete with a church service on Sunday morning at his home. The celebration didn't end until late Sunday evening! And because the party also coincided with the Kentucky Derby, the theme involved derby hats, colorful dresses, and mint juleps. There were endless buffets of food, and the cake, which was baked by a cooperative effort in many kitchens, was so big that it had to be transported by boat and supported on a wooden door. Otto included everyone, and since he traveled often, he invited virtually everyone he'd met along the way. Officially, 524 people signed in, but many more attended. People still talk about the extravaganza.

Are you thinking "How fun!" like an Extravert and wondering if that sounds like just the thing for your next big day? Or are you thinking like an Introvert—"How exhausting!"—since you gain pleasure from the idea of celebrating your special occasion by going for a walk with your partner to a small, quiet restaurant?

Of course, not every Introvert wants an intimate celebration and not every Extravert wants a three-ring circus, but when you are looking for creative energy in life or focusing your creative juices, there are two solutions: one is right for you and the other makes you fatigued. Just as you can't use the power adapter for your digital camera to recharge your cell phone, you need to know how to plug yourself into the right charger. And to know how to do that, you first must know if you are an Extravert or an Introvert.

The answer is not as obvious as you may think. Talkative hosts or people speaking about their expertise or passion sometimes appear as Extraverts even though they may not be. More than being a talker or a nontalker, the real defining question is, "Where do you get your energy?"

Energy flow is typically described by different cultures in many spiritual and physical ways; here, we look to whether you're an Extravert or an Introvert to determine your mental source of power. You may say that sometimes you like to be with people, and other times, you enjoy alone time. "Everyone possesses both mechanisms," described Jung, "but only the predominance of one or the other determines type."[1] Introverts become drained when they spend time in the external world with people, and Extraverts become tired from time alone. Each of these two opposite poles represents about half of the population.[2]

When you think of a Caribbean vacation, what do you have in mind? Casinos and nightlife or deserted beaches? On a business trip, after a long day of meetings, do you look forward to dinner with your colleagues or do you prefer to head back to your hotel for room service?

Some Extraverts say they are refreshed by having some alone time, and some Introverts say they are energized by people; however, this charge is usually short lived. It's like the energy you feel from jumping into cold water: invigorating for a few moments but then tiring, and eventually, you want to get out.

How do you refuel? We know that periodic breaks allow us to renew, but what we do during those breaks matters. For Extraverts, being with people and with engaging objects in your surroundings is your source of power; when you get drained by working alone, you should find time to engage with others. If you're an Introvert, your power comes from having time to reflect in your inner world, so find a way to get some time alone to reflect.

There doesn't have to be a stigma associated with either Introversion or Extraversion, as each type has individual strengths in the way that they interact with their environment and how they approach the creative process. Creativity is a form of communication, and Extraverts and Introverts simply express themselves differently. When we talk about inner world or outer world, we are thinking about the happenings either inside or outside our minds. We are energized when we are in the environment that we prefer, doing what we love. For inspiration, Introverts focus their energy inward, using their imaginations for building virtual inner worlds. Meanwhile, Extraverts focus their energy outward, making direct actions in their outer world for building real cities.

Extraverts (E)

Have you ever been told that creativity is about getting lost in your imagination, and then you decided it wasn't for you? Ironically, Extraverted creativity is in plain view, yet it's often overlooked. It involves engaging with people and items, like arranging people by height for a group photo so everyone's face shows; weaving through a crowd to reach the front of a stage; telling a story at lunchtime and making it up as you go along; leading a group in brainstorming to improve a product; or finding a solution to a schedule conflict by talking through the problem.

Alone in their dressing rooms, performers may seem lifeless, but when the curtain goes up on the stage, the audience cheers for their dynamic display; this is how Extraverts come alive. Wide rivers flowing with clear water, the visible Extravert surface takes up vast amounts of physical space and moves swiftly. If you're an Extravert, you gain your thundering currents—your steam—from the people, objects, and activities you encounter and engage with in the outer world. You also say what you are thinking, and just as blind people navigate by touch, you navigate by talking.

Extraverts think out loud, cook out loud, build out loud, and paint out loud. You may hear one say, "There's the turnpike," "Needs more basil," "Too much yellow," "Where's my hammer?" or "Have I told you the story about . . ." As campers, they tell stories over the fire. As musicians, they play at full volume. As painters, they are inclined to work big and bright, with bold colors. As actors, they fill the stage with their presence. As managers, they gather teams together for staff meetings. For Extraverts, creativity comes through focusing energy on external action.

Extraverts *have* to be there! And the first step to begin a project is to gather the "usual suspects." Michener would travel to the location in which his novel was set to interview the locals. Extraverts are inspired by bouncing around ideas and interacting with people, but real objects matter to them too. Robert Motherwell, an Extraverted abstract expressionist, said, "I couldn't work in an empty room."[3] He filled his studio with items that served as triggers, and described his creations as collaborations between artist and canvas. Innovation takes teamwork and requires that we get out and talk to people (such as our customers, suppliers, manufacturers, and marketers) to learn their current needs, the problems they are experiencing, and how they actually use their current products.

All forms of expression take Extraverts out of their heads. For example, sketching or writing takes a mental activity and makes it a real-world experience, as does molding a lump of clay or striking piano keys to sound out a melody. "The only way to see it is to build it," said Jeanne-Claude, who collaborated with her husband, Christo, on large art instillations, like the wrapping of the Reichstag in Berlin and "The Gates" in Central Park.[4]

The lives of Extraverts are often open books, as they publicly express their most personal ideas and intimate feelings. Salvador Dalí explained what set him apart from the other Surrealists: "I was the only one who went out and was received in society."[5] Dalí revealed his most intimate secrets and audaciously named his writings with attention-grabbing titles, such as *The Secret Life of Salvador Dalí* and *The Unspeakable Confessions of Salvador Dalí*.

If you are an Extravert, do you sometimes say more than you want as you are talking through a problem? Nevertheless, with plenty of contact with people and much practice talking, Extraverts tend to develop strong verbal skills. They discuss what they are doing while they are creating, and this allows them to demonstrate their process to others.

Extraverts engage with their physical environments as a form of narrative. Looking at a scene, Monet engaged his surroundings by analyzing forms with his pencil. Journalists embed themselves in the field and interview sources in person; portrait painters work from live models; and directors look beyond the scripts to work with their actors, props, and sets.

For many creative activities—whether it's writing, painting, quilting, or gardening—our alone time helps us to be productive, but Extraverts find this challenging. Extraverts often resort to locking themselves away in a quiet setting to limit distracting outside stimuli; however, time without the stimulus becomes tiring for them. One Extraverted novelist said that sitting alone to write for a half hour is worse than going to the gym alone, and she wishes she could dictate her story to someone else to write for her. Just as she is energized by exercising with a friend, she finds inspiration by teaming up with another writer to sit across from her for support and encouragement as they work.

Extraverts enjoy praise, depend on feedback, and become energized by group interactions. Extraverts enjoy working in teams, painting in groups, acting as part of an ensemble, teaching, and sharing ideas with others as they focus their creative energy outward.

Extraverts, You Innovate Best By . . .

* Interacting with people and objects
* Talking through solutions
* Openly sharing expertise
* Telling stories

Extraverts, Reduce Your Blind Spots By . . .

* Listening to others
* Reflecting upon lessons learned
* Pausing before speaking

Extraverts, Use Your Strengths to Boost Your Creativity By . . .

* Sketching your ideas on paper
* Leading discussions and brainstorming
* Leaving your office/home and going outside
* Testing your ideas in the real world

Introverts (I)

Let's begin by dispelling some myths about Introverts. Introversion doesn't mean anti-social. Some of the most social people we know are Introverts, throwing big parties, participating in clubs, and enjoying public speaking. Choosing the letter "I" doesn't mean you're shy either; anyone can feel shy. In fact, some Extraverts feel social anxiety since they worry about having someone to listen to them and fear awkward pauses in conversation.

Contrary to the wide, rushing rivers of Extraverts, Introverts are like deep and narrow canals, flowing slowly and quietly while concealing their contents with a shield of cloudy water. If you are an Introvert, others may notice you drifting off into your own world of daydreams, as you gain and recharge your energy from reflecting in your inner world; you find yourself most at home within your mind, where your imagination is free to generate ideas. Introverts are generally quiet people who enjoy the peace of working alone, and creativity is the result of focusing their energy through this internal process of reflection.

Although they need time "alone," Introverts don't need to get away from it all. If they find themselves in an unpleasant situation or unsuitable location, they slip away into their own mind to create a more pleasing world. Solitary creative pursuits are energizing and especially satisfying since it gives them time in their inner world of dreams. They become drained when bombarded by the demands of interacting with people for too long, and once tired, being creative becomes a challenge.

Do others think you are unengaged and say to you, "Why so quiet?" If you're an Introvert, people may not understand that you have a lot going on below the surface, in your mind. Introverted creativity is often nonverbally expressed through painting, writing, and dance, allowing Introverts to communicate ideas that would otherwise go unsaid. "I found that I can say things with color and shapes that I couldn't say in any other way," described Georgia O'Keeffe.[6] While creating and adrift in their own minds, Introverts find it difficult to talk, since communicating drives them back to the outer world. And afterward, they often cannot explain their choices in words. Many ideas cross their minds, but most never get expressed.

Introverted creativity takes time too. Introverts prefer to think before acting, which causes them to react somewhat slower than Extraverts, often having the thought afterward, "I wish I'd said that." As dancers, they do mental rehearsals beforehand; as authors, they think before writing; as painters, they imagine the next brushstroke in their mind's eye. Extraverts are sometimes astonished to learn that Introverts know what they are going to say before they open their mouth.

As they gather information, Introverts are most comfortable observing and sharing from a distance. Being private, Introverts create without exposing too much of themselves. When a critic asked to see Paul Gauguin's drawings, he replied, "My drawings? Never! They are my letters, my secrets. You wish to know who I am; my work is not enough for you? I only reveal what I want to reveal."[7] Concealing their work, Introverts create their own codes, preferring to indirectly express or abstract their innermost thoughts. They typically avoid showing their creations publicly, opting instead to share their work among small groups of trusted friends. And when Introverts share, they are letting you see a glimpse of their private world—a true honor. Overall, Introverts make a small footprint on physical space, desire working in a modest scale, and tend to use more muted colors, attracting less attention than Extraverts.

As preferences are combined, we start to gain insight into how our personality influences our creative process. Like everyone, Introverts enjoy praise, but kind words can be uncomfortable for them, especially if they are also Thinkers. According to actress Helen Hayes, known as the "First Lady of the American Theatre," accepting honors and awards was embarrassing: "Why single me out just for doing what was asked of me?"[8]

In a classroom, in a meeting, or just with a gathering of friends, Introverts keep much to themselves and take time to consider their thoughts before speaking. Even if they have done great work and have incredible ideas, without voicing those ideas, Introverts are often misunderstood and seen as nonparticipating. With many of their thoughts unsaid, they are underestimated and lose out to others who are more vocal. Worse, it's common to hear an Introvert say, "Nobody asked me."

If you're an Introvert and you've got a good idea, make sure to speak up. If you have difficulty getting a word in, try to summarize the points at the end. Without sharing your ideas, others get the wrong impression of your capacities. And your ideas can't be accepted if they aren't first communicated. Sharing your ideas is necessary to gain the support of others.

While innovation can attract attention, there is plenty of competition, and what's new can still go unnoticed. This can be a problem for Extraverts, who are driven by attention, but Introverts are undeterred since they don't want to stand out. They are happy to toil away alone and unnoticed.

When Extraverts rely on the reality of their physical surroundings by studying actual objects, Introverts are more likely to focus inward and reflect on what they have already perceived. Edvard Munch conjured up memories when he worked: "I don't paint what I see but what I saw." He was thought to "paint in his head."[9] True to the Introvert way of creating, Munch demonstrated through his artwork that reflecting on his experiences could be as effective as working from live models.

Introverts, You Innovate Best By . . .

* Contemplating and imagining
* Processing ideas
* Being alone or with a trusted few

Introverts, Reduce Your Blind Spots By . . .

* Getting out of your head to experience life
* Allowing enough time to reflect
* Bringing other people into the equation
* Saying what you're thinking
* Sharing and collaborating

Introverts, Use Your Strengths to Boost Your Creativity By . . .

* Developing nonverbal means of expression
* Taking time to daydream
* Working in private

Summary: Extraversion (E) and Introversion (I)

Jung wrote about a bridge between the unconscious and the conscious mind. He urged his patients, including Salvador Dalí, to paint their dreams and use the act of creating, as well as the action of dance, as a means of therapy. It's worth mentioning that some think crossing this consciousness bridge and creating in the "real world" (the conscious world) allows people to solve conflicts in their unconscious mind, possibly reducing neurosis.

While our unconscious mind is difficult to study, we can still make worthwhile observations about it. The boundary between our inner and outer world, while murky, plays an important role in creating. Ideas originate in our mind (the preferred realm for Introverts), and we must take action in the outer world (the preferred ground for Extraverts) to convert ideas into tangible creations that can be shared, like paintings, poems, pottery, or product design. Introverts tend to spend more time mulling over ideas and less time physically creating, while the opposite is true for Extraverts. Extraverts spend less time contemplating and more time actually creating.

To bring our conceptions to life in the real word, we have to cross the consciousness bridge at some point. Extraverts cross upstream at their first opportunity, so they can spend more time in the external world. Introverts, on the other hand, cross downstream, after first spending more time in their inner world.

Of course, these are only signposts pointing to our deeper personas; everyone has the capacity to be gregarious or reflective, especially when it involves a subject of interest. And though we all tend to prefer one world over the other, understanding the other side—and having the ability to function in both the inner and outer worlds—is a true advantage.

Sensing (S) or Intuition (N)—The Complete Picture or Big Picture

Whether you're an Introvert or an Extravert, your preference influences the way you energize and express yourself creatively. We discussed energy flow first, but not because it's most important. It's the order in which Jung first presented his theories and the pattern from which Myers-Briggs is typically discussed. Next, as we continue through the preferences, you will see the Sensing and Intuition pair is even more powerful in lending insight into your creative self.

We begin again with another real-world example from the time David moved to Asia. In his first few days living in Hong Kong, he stayed in temporary housing that had a common area where new people gathered to have breakfast. One morning, he met a woman from South Africa and immediately realized she knew much more about the city than he did. To him, she was practically a local, since she had been living in Hong Kong for a whole week. He jumped at the chance when she offered to show him around.

They walked down a very foreign-looking street, and she pointed out the post office, dry cleaner, hardware store, fabric stores, expat grocery, local grocery, trolley station, and the pharmacy where you could buy medicine without a prescription. She explained in detail the bus and train systems, and showed him the flower market, goldfish market, jade market, and snake market on the map.

At the end of the street, David asked if she knew where he could exchange money, and she said, "What, are you blind? We just passed nine banks!" While she noticed everything, the only thing he noticed on the short walk were some general connections of what they had in common: they were both uprooted, she was also an artist writing a book, and her spouse also worked in finance. Clearly, she had a very different perspective of what they had just experienced.

How do you gather information? Do you mostly notice specific facts or a general theme? One type of person, like David's friend, is called a Sensor. She uses her five senses to gather every detail of sight, smell, sound, taste, and touch for reasons artist Roy Lichtenstein explained: "Looking without touching would uncover for you none of the world's structure."[10] If you are a Sensor, you view the details of the world directly, realistically, and as a collection of the facts as they exist right now.

The other type, like David, is called an Intuitive. If you're an Intuitive, you don't have to see or touch anything; instead, you prefer to rely on your sixth sense to gather information that is indirect, random, abstract, conceptual, and theoretical. You see meaningful coincidences all around you, just like Sir Isaac Newton, who conceived the notion of gravity from such an ordinary incident as an apple falling from a tree. As an Intuitive, you see meanings and connections but only notice what you need to know. In David's story, he didn't notice the banks because he didn't know he needed them, while his friend noticed them whether she needed them or not.

Our differences in perception are evident everywhere. Consider Google and Apple, two giant innovators that incorporate opposing methods to gather information. Every time we enter keywords into Google or click on the links we find there, Google's founders use the data to glean a detailed look at how we're using the service. On the other hand, Apple's Steve Jobs wasn't interested in collecting data. He was known to dismiss market research and focus groups, relying on his gut instead.

How do you see the world? Knowing how you prefer to gather information is the most important factor in understanding how you create. Whether you prefer Sensing (S) or Intuition (N), we will give you your own set of tools for building.

Here's an exercise to get you started.

Find a sheet of paper and a pencil, and describe the following:

- Your childhood home
- The environment outside your window

Your descriptions in this exercise reveal how you take in data. Though everyone sees things in their own way, we all select from two channels for gathering data: on one channel, we see all the details of the "complete picture," as it is today; and on the other channel, we take a step back for a broad view of the "big picture," as things could be. Do you mostly notice specific facts or a general theme? Over time, like everything we practice, the more we use either Sensing or Intuition, the stronger that function becomes. And our information-gathering function uses this input from the world as rocket fuel for the creative process. (We'll revisit your descriptions further in the Intuitive section below.)

"The way that art and beauty are sensed by different individuals differs so widely that one could not fail to be struck by it," observed Jung in his book *Psychological Types*.[11] According to surveys, Sensing types make up 70 percent of the population[12] but only 31 percent of them are professional artists and entertainers.[13] This often leads us to describe creativity as an activity exclusive to Intuitive types. This myth is far too limiting since Sensors, too, are successful in creative fields. It also leaves out the majority of the population while ignoring 31 percent of artists and entertainers.

There are two ways that creative ideas can originate: they can come either *ex nihilo*, a Latin term meaning "from nothing"; or *creatio ex materia*, meaning the idea came from something, so this is a good place to start. "To inspire and develop children to think creatively" is the mission of Lego.[14] If you've been to a toy store lately, you probably noticed that the Lego pieces are packaged in two ways. Some kits contain collections of bricks used to build anything you can dream up "from nothing." And the other kits come "from something," with a theme and instructions for building specific things, such as train stations, vehicles, or animals.

Those of us with the Intuitive preference, such as Thomas Edison, are more likely to create in the space where nothing existed before, such as the light bulb or phonograph. These were completely new inventions that were not derived from anything previously known. Though others with the Sensing preference are inventive too, they prefer to create as Henry Ford did—"from something." This can come in the form of improving an existing process in which modifications and incremental improvements are made on what already exists. Ford did not invent the automobile, but his introduction of the assembly lines certainly improved the manufacturing process.

How do you generate ideas? Inspirations for the Sensing types come largely from what currently exists and can be verified by fact and experienced through their senses.

Even ideas generated in the imagination have some kind of starter seeds that originate from specifics of the environment. Pablo Picasso claimed, "There is no abstract art; you must always start with something. Afterward, you can remove all traces of reality."[15] Like Picasso, Sensors create by building on previous experiences or ideas while Intuitives prefer to consider possibilities where nothing existed before.

Most of us have experienced a time—taking a shower, driving, exercising—when an idea suddenly jumped into our minds like a flash. Ideas can come from anywhere and everywhere. Perhaps your idea to create a character for your novel was sparked by an interesting encounter you had with a person at the gym, or maybe a friend's health scare spurred you to invent a new medical alert system. Or maybe you don't even know where your latest idea came from.

When we have these flashes, there are two ways to react to them. Sensing types are grounded in reality and tend to disregard unsubstantial thoughts; their flashes are often ignored. In contrast, the Intuitive types are unconcerned with the source of the spark. They have learned from experience to recognize and trust these impulses, and use them to leap to new ideas. Although Intuitives don't disregard reality, catching these sparks are a favorite way of gathering data, providing a rich source of inspiration. All types have ideas that flash into their minds, but the big difference is that Intuitive types trust their flashes while the Sensing types tend to dismiss them.

What Do You Perceive?

Sensing (S)	Intuition (N)
Every detail in your environment	What you need to see
What is immediate	Future possibilities
Omissions	Information between the lines
Facts/specific details	Patterns/connections

What's the Most Natural Way for You to Generate Ideas?

Sensing (S)	Intuition (N)
From the five senses	From flashes of inspiration
From memories of stored facts	From infinite possibilities
Through convergent thinking	Through divergent thinking
From dependable sources	Sparked from seemingly irrelevant sources
By "rolling up my sleeves" and "getting my hands dirty"	By brainstorming
By putting ideas together without mixing	By melding ideas together, like the flavors in a stew

If you identified most with the word choices in the left-hand column of the two tables, you probably have a preference for Sensing. If you identified most with the word choices on the right, you probably have a preference for Intuition. You'll get an even better grasp of these two information-gathering methods in the next two sections, where we'll take a closer look at each of them individually.

Sensing (S), The Complete Picture: What You Need to Know

Now, before the Intuitives skip ahead, there is value in continuing to read about Sensing since it's your occasionally used nonpreference. It's also worthwhile to learn about Sensing behavior because it describes a large portion of the population.

An essential part of innovation comes from scanning your current environment. If you prefer to gather information through Sensing, you tend to gather data in sequence, discerning every detail as a separate fact. And you create best by being descriptive, engaging the senses. Sensors are concerned with specifics, are grounded in reality, and experience the world "as it is," in a very practical, literal fashion. "My aim has always been the most exact transcription possible of my most intimate impressions of nature," described the realist Edward Hopper in his "Notes on Painting."[16]

As a Sensor, you make a realistic scan of your environment by detecting all the sights, sounds, smells, touches, and tastes, making note of all the details. You learn to trust your senses to tell you about the world. "If you don't know how an especially fine dish is supposed to taste, how can you produce it? Just like becoming an expert in wine, you learn by drinking," described Julia Child.[17] In this manner, Sensors look to immediate sensations for inspiration, and when they create, they try to replicate, relive, or engage their experiences. If you are a Sensor, your strength comes from solving existing problems with information that is immediately available and by using your experience from what has worked in the past.

When you thought back to describe your childhood home (a few pages ago), were you specific? It was said of Ernest Hemingway: "He kept no notebook or journal, but his phenomenal recall kept places, names, dates, events, colors, clothes, smells, and who won the 1925 six-day bicycle race at the Hippodrome."[18] Author Truman Capote also relied solely on his memory to recall his interviews.

If you are a Sensor, your strong memory for facts is a strength you draw from in the details you express. Whether they stop or not, Sensors really do smell the roses and remember what they smelled. They notice and remember everything, making them the people a police sketch artist loves to have as witnesses. Sensors observe eye color, clothing, and the exact time of day. Like journalists, they gather information by being sensory, specific, and keeping to the facts. And though they may not always tell you, Sensors notice if you have a different haircut, a missing button on your shirt, or an untied shoelace.

A Sensing preference also leads you to notice omissions and differences, so try creating by *adding* what you see is missing. If you are an accountant, try including a new column to your spreadsheet, such as cost savings that no one else noticed; if you're an engineer, build bridges that complete a route. Or if you're a passionate cook and entrepreneur, open a food cart on a corner where you noticed there were none.

Trusting what is tangible and creating what is tangible, Sensors have a "believe it when they see it" attitude, disbelieving until they can see it and touch it for themselves. Seeing the world in a literal way, they make realistic work. Hemingway wrote in a style that was "so real that people . . . think the stories really happened to [them]."[19] If you're a Sensor, try defining problems by laying out your tools and materials so they can be touched; try building a scale model to see how the pieces can fit together. Roll up your sleeves, put your hands into your work (whether carpentry, masonry, or knitting), and construct something real, like a cabinet, patio, or scarf. When you face a problem, try drawing or sculpting it out. Both mediums have a tactile quality, and many Sensors find the mere texture of the paper or the coolness of the clay to be a stimulating means of finding solutions.

"All painting is fact, and that is enough," said Andy Warhol.[20] When the Sensing types take in stimuli, they discern them as individual facts that usually do not need further analysis. The sky is defined as the sky, and the earth is the earth. If you are a Sensor, are you inspired by music where the notes are distinct and the lyrics are recognizable? And do you like reading books where the authors make it clear who is speaking and when the scene changes?

A great way to understand how Sensors use the information they gather in their creative process is to look at how Sensing painters compose their work. They often isolate elements by setting them apart with outlines. Look at a portrait created by a Sensor; are the eyes outlined? Is the hair separate from the face? Is the red skirt delineated from the blue blouse? Is the figure isolated from the background? If you look at a Sensor's landscape, are the mountains separate from the rivers? Does the horizon line make it clear where the earth ends and the sky begins? If you are a Sensor, is this the way you see the world? Do you see each element as an individual piece?

The unique way Sensors perceive boundaries fits with one of two profiles described by Heinrich Wölfflin. As a pioneer in art psychology, Wölfflin explained that some of us perceive tangible qualities of objects, such as surfaces, and use outlines to isolate the objects. For Sensors, the touch of the surface matters, such the feel of grass between their toes, the texture of a weathered piece of driftwood, or a smooth silk dress. Whether you're a Sensor fashion designer or a Sensor who likes to shop for clothes, touching the fabric to your skin matters. If you're a top chef or like to cook at home, thumping the melons and smelling the strawberries in the market matters.

If you're a Sensor and see objects as stand-alone nuggets, then try to design by juxtaposing elements together. Just like moving into a new apartment and arranging your lamp, table, and couch; the individual items are combined to make up the whole room (but the couch doesn't merge with the lamp or table). Sensors create by describing the buildings, not the city; the people, not the crowd; and the individual flowers, not the garden. When they plant a garden, each shrub is given its own space. In the kitchen, the meat and potatoes don't mix; however, they are served on the same plate as one meal—the whole.

Remember that, for you, being hands on and experiencing the process is important. Start projects by tasting the ingredients, smelling the paint, feeling the fabric, and listening to the music. Your gift for noticing detail is one of your greatest assets, and sharing with others who don't see what you do is one the greatest ways for you to innovate and contribute. As creative individuals, you innovate best by being practical, making actual items that meet immediate needs and fit within existing systems. "You say I started out with practically nothing, but that isn't correct. We all start with all there is; it's how we use it that makes things possible," described Henry Ford.[21]

Sensors, You Innovate Best By . . .

* Taking small steps and making incremental changes
* Improving a process
* Using resources that are present
* Solving immediate problems
* Making improvements that are physical
* Combining facts to build a whole
* Considering immediate needs

Sensors, Reduce Your Blind Spots By . . .

* Taking a step back to consider the big picture
* Thinking about future implications and considering long-term effects
* Accepting and using data that's incomplete or out of sequence
* Challenging your assumptions (some "facts" may be conditional or false)
* Examining the overall purpose
* Trusting unverifiable flashes of inspiration

Sensors, Use Your Strengths to Boost Your Creativity By . . .

* Considering and verifying the facts
* Concentrating on the immediate/the present
* Inspecting the situation
* Carefully defining problems
* Using your tremendous attention to detail
* Filling in missing blanks
* Considering the process (the process is your purpose)
* Remembering what has worked before
* Laying out problems so the pieces can be touched
* Steadily implementing ideas in a practical way

Intuition (N), The Big Picture: What You Need to Know

If the Sensing preference is the South Pole, then the Intuitive preference is the North Pole. The Sensing type notices a wide swath, while the Intuitive's awareness is a deep and narrow cut. Intuitives walk around unaware that their shoe's untied or that they have ketchup on their shirt because they are occupied with something bigger. In the last section, if you identified more with the words in the right columns of the table (the Intuitive side), you see the big picture and generalities, and have a preference for gathering information through Intuition.

While Sensing types see the world "as it is," with their eyes guiding their minds, Intuitive types know the world "as it seems," and the mind tells the eyes what to see. People with an Intuitive preference are said to use their sixth sense to "perceive things that are not and never have been present to their senses," according to Isabel Briggs Myers in her book *Gifts Differing*. Intuitives notice what they want and need to notice as it relates to their own frame of reference. Chefs skip steps in recipes that don't seem relevant. Entrepreneurs observe procedures in order to learn but later leave out parts that don't seem to have meaning. When a director focuses on the performance of one actor, the rest of the cast becomes invisible. In fact, everything that isn't directly relevant is invisible. As an Intuitive, do you modify and simplify by ignoring? Give yourself the license to confidently ignore and omit what you find irrelevant.

Intuitives make up only 30 percent of the general population[22] but 69 percent of the population of artists and entertainers.[23] If you're an Intuitive, your strength is making connections—finding relationships from seemingly random occurrences that trigger meaningful coincidences. It helps for you to be aware that you are best at considering possibilities and taking the long-range view.

What Intuitives create is often designed with multiple layers of meaning. Where do the meanings originate? Some believe their ideas appear by design, coming from a muse or God, while others don't know where their ideas come from but have learned to trust their instincts based on successful past experiences. If you are an Intuitive, you often stumble upon relevance, attributing meanings to whatever you encounter. Once you have an idea or a question, answers seem to fall into your lap from unpredictable sources. Though it is believed that some linking of ideas comes from the subconscious, it is tough to observe and goes beyond our scope.

When you described the view out your window a few sections back, did you describe what is most meaningful yet omit the details? While the Sensors among us concentrate on specifics, Intuitives often gloss over details that seem unimportant or obvious while they emphasize others; they automatically self-edit and simplify. They look at complex scenarios and readily carve out what they see as relevant. Have you listened to someone tell a joke who skipped so many parts that the punch line wasn't funny? When Intuitives take leaps and leave out details, Sensors especially don't understand what the Intuitive sees as obvious. A challenge for Intuitives is to clearly communicate with others. "I frequently fail to make my point with the average reader," admitted author James A. Michener, who continued, "I am no longer surprised when readers fail to grasp what I have been trying for hundreds of pages to say."[24] Even Michener would have benefited from glancing toward his blind spots and dropping a trail of breadcrumbs—details—for his readers to follow.

Enjoyment and satisfaction for this type comes from theorizing and processing possibilities. Seated in a theater, watching a play, the Intuitives focus on relevant action within the spotlight. They can become oblivious to much of the environment around them, and the details of the actual scene, such as the costumes or the stage design, may not register. This is a marked difference from Sensing types, who keenly observe everything. Instead, Intuitives focus intently on the particulars of their area of interest and frame their own contexts. As they look beyond the current moment, a phrase or song may stimulate them to jump to all kinds of scenarios and directions outside of the script, and they may predict an alternative storyline. Be open to this idea if you're an Intuitive, for watching a love story could strangely lead you to develop a new economic model for hedging inflation, or going for a jog around the lake could lead you to develop a new loop in the code for the app you are writing. Playing basketball with some friends could spark an opening joke for the speech you're making this afternoon, and watching a squirrel bury an acorn could give you an idea for marketing your business for next winter.

Your best creative work comes from what you enjoy, and as an Intuitive, you are most entertained when you have the opportunity to connect unrelated themes, assign meanings, and use theories. Put yourself into the position to be inspired by seeking out diverse experiences that you can connect together. Focus and be aware that entertainment can spark ideas that are in no way related to what you're watching or doing but are still useful in solving unrelated problems.

Like fast forwarding through the frames of a movie, Intuitives analyze the big picture along a time horizon, looking beyond today to consider what will happen next. They look toward future possibilities and observe the world, developing long-range strategies based on expectations, interpolations, and predictions. However, as they become preoccupied with foretelling how things *could* be, Intuitives are often blind to current happenings. And when they do consider what is current, it's usually held in a past-and-future context as they share what they foresee. If you're an Intuitive, your creativity comes through your vision of intended and unintended consequences in the future, and you show how the world could be with some improvements.

The method is less important than the idea. Claude Monet described his process as "[creating] without worrying too much about the process," and further expressed, "I want to grasp the intangible."[25] Whether it's a broad concept like beauty, comfort, or death, Intuitives look for patterns and relationships. If you're an Intuitive, have confidence when making sweeping generalizations and revealing connections that others don't see. Use your connections to create intangibles, like the look and feel of concepts in product design or marketing; indistinct cues and vague notions can express the essence of an idea. Think of watching a horror movie and feeling the imminent danger by the tempo of the music and tone of the dialog alone.

Mozart is often quoted as saying, "The music is not in the notes but in the silence between." Intuitives have strength in joining what is seen and unseen together, even if they don't have a physical connection. For Intuitive-type artists, light and shadow can become part of the composition; for example, the folds in a cast-off piece of clothing can form shadows and shapes that look like something entirely different than a jacket or pair of pants.

A good way to understand what Intuitives see is to look through their eyes. Imagine a forest scene where all the trunks, branches, and leaves merge together to form a single mass. The Intuitives see the forest, not the trees; the ocean, not the waves; the field, not the blades of grass; and the city, not the bricks. When they create, they meld ingredients together, like combining flavors in a stew, keeping an eye on the overall flavor profile.

Solving problems as if they are puzzles, Intuitives create by considering how each part fits into the entire assemblage. "I do not consider my studies in isolation but always think of my work as a whole," wrote Van Gogh.[26] When elements are seen as approximations, work can look messy. The exact colors, lines, dollars, or measurements aren't as important as achieving the big picture. Just as some entrepreneurs don't follow their business plans to the letter and some chefs don't follow their recipes, Intuitives painters tend to use their sketch as a rough guide, then proceed to paint loosely "outside the lines." They find it perfectly acceptable for the blue from the sky to run into the green trees. "One doesn't want a picture to look 'made' . . . since precision belongs to the world of machinery," described the abstract expressionist painter Robert Motherwell.[27] If you go through the trouble to cook a tray of appetizers from scratch and they look too uniform, too perfect, your guests may assume they are store bought and not appreciate your artistry.

"How?" and "Why?" are the type of questions frequently asked by Intuitives, and the answers allow them to understand and then predict. While the Sensing types like specifics and definiteness, the Intuitives embrace ambiguity. If you are an Intuitive, try to apply your abstractions and theories to solve real problems. For Intuitives, your creations can take on the complexity of chessboards, with every element contributing to the overall impact.

Like linking stars to form constellations in the sky, Intuitives form unions with their creations, connecting the dots to make something new where nothing existed before. If you have this preference, it helps for you to realize that you miss a lot of details and instead view the world as blurs and impressions that make up the big picture. As Henri Matisse explained, you "sift rather than accumulate detail."[28] As you seek meaning and gather information to make connections, each link becomes solidly welded knowledge that serves as a foundation upon which to build.

Intuitives, You Innovate Best By . . .

* Starting with a vision (details may follow)
* Breaking the mold

- Assigning meanings and developing symbols
- Developing and applying theories
- Improving a system
- Designing complex models
- Approximating and predicting
- Seeking diverse experiences
- Connecting dissimilar ideas
- Finding patterns in abstract data
- Working in spurts when inspired
- Considering future needs

Intuitives, Reduce Your Blind Spots By . . .

- Noticing, gathering, and considering all facts
- Identifying immediate problems
- Solving real issues
- Making quick fixes without reinventing the system
- Showing your work, including all the steps
- Offering practical solutions
- Acting on your ideas
- Remembering to look, listen, touch, taste, and smell

Intuitives, Use Your Strengths to Boost Your Creativity By . . .

- Considering meanings and purposes
- Noticing patterns and making connections
- Looking toward solutions of analogous problems
- Developing theories
- Seeking alternatives and possibilities
- Considering the context of the issues
- Predicting what may happen

- Considering how all parts affect the whole
- Identifying drivers
- Ignoring the irrelevant and emphasizing key elements

Summary: Sensing (S) and Intuition (I)

To understand wet, we must know dry. Sensing and Intuition each chisel out the facets of the other to bring into focus both the complete picture (the details that make the whole, in the present) and the big picture (the whole and their potential). If you understand the difference between these two vastly different ways that we all use to gather information, you will have more control of your creative process; you will know how to best use your strengths. And you'll see next that creating takes more than just gathering information; decision making and idea selection need to be done too.

When Intuitives and Sensors go beyond their first impressions with prolonged concentration, a shift occurs. Over the years, some of us have learned that the more a group of Intuitives beat an idea for its meanings and possibilities, the more they get into some really good details—past the big picture to the smaller elements. Likewise, the more Sensors beat the details, the more they begin to look at the big picture and ask, "What are we missing?" They begin to see the meanings and possibilities of the whole.

It's important to think of the information-gathering function as a separate unit from the decision-making function. The information-gathering function is like the nurse who draws blood samples, as opposed to the lab that does the testing; the nurse (Sensing and Intuition) is only concerned with collecting data. Processing data to make decisions uses the judging function through either Thinking or Feeling, a completely different process that will be explained next.

Thinking (T) or Feeling (F)—Decision Making with Your Head or Your Heart
On a bus heading along the Nha Trang Bay in Vietnam, Carl noticed something about the passengers: when they loaded the bus, some took seats on the left and some grabbed

the ones on the right. Our friend wondered if they made this decision based on a simple preference of one of two views on the coastal road—the view of the water, docks, boats, and distant islands, or the view of the land and the local people along the seaport. Of course, there were times some of the passengers would crane their necks to look across the aisle through an opposite window, but for the most part, they kept to looking out their own window. This said everything about our inborn decision-making process: we are all on the bus together, but we all make decisions in one of two ways, based on which "side of the bus" we prefer to sit.

Making decisions can be much more challenging than which side to sit on in the bus. With so many choices—yet limited time and resources—how do you choose in which ideas to invest your efforts? This next pair of opposites relates to our process for making decisions using either our preference for Thinking (T) or Feeling (F). By under-standing your process of whether you prefer to make decisions with your head or with your heart, your decisions will be stronger and come easier.

We all like to think that our decisions are logical and that they reflect our personal values, and although we consider both, our final choice is made mostly using one or the other. It's important to note that while our decision-making and information-gathering functions work together, they are wholly independent of each other. So it doesn't matter whether our inbox gets filled using Intuition or Sensing; all that counts here is that our inbox has data we are going to decide upon.

We don't define "Thinking" and "Feeling" the same way as Merriam-Webster. If you're a Thinking decider, you obviously still have feelings. And if you are a Feeling decider, of course you think. Thinkers simply prefer to make determinations based on objective criteria that promote clarity, such as selecting a plan with the largest market potential. Feelers tend to decide using subjective criteria, preferring to choose outcomes that make people happiest and engaged. Both may ultimately come to the same conclu-sion via different methods. When we create something new, we are faced with unprecedented decisions regarding what needs to be done: What ideas to select? Which materials to use? When will it be completed? And who will perform various roles?

Making Decisions By Thinking or Feeling

Thinking (T)	Feeling (F)
Objective	Subjective
True or false	Better or worse
Asks: What? Where?	Asks: Who?

Priorities When Making Thinking or Feeling Decisions

Thinking (T)	Feeling (F)
Expressing universal truths	Expressing personal values
Seeing scenes and objects as primary subject matter	Seeing people and relationships as primary subject matter
Influence of logic	Influence of friends
Filtering out emotion	Absorbing and projecting emotion

As you can see from the tables above, if you have a preference for Thinking, then you tend to elect to make choices in a true-or-false, yes-or-no manner. As a Thinker, Paul Cézanne saw art as either good or bad, for example.

Thinking deciders are objective and often seen as impersonal, while the Feeling deciders put people first. If you have a Feeling preference, you give priority to the needs and concerns of others, and weigh the circumstances of a situation when making decisions about whether a choice is better or worse. Thinkers seek the truth, and Feelers seek to be true to themselves.

To some, being told to be authentic means showing your emotions. Though this may be natural to Feelers, who show their true selves, Thinking types aren't built this way. Of course Thinkers may tell personal stories, but their feelings aren't often at the forefront of their decision making. When asked to express how they feel, it often requires them to unnaturally stretch beyond who they truly are as people.

This is the only one of the four personality scales that differs widely by gender. The different ways that men and women make decisions are widely observed and have been the subject of much research, and many popular books and movies. Men are 60 percent likely to have a Thinking preference and 40 percent likely to have a preference for Feeling. Women, on the other hand, are 75 percent Feeling deciders and only 25 percent likely to be Thinking deciders. Generally speaking, the process of decision making accounts for a major difference between men and women.[29] In addition, society teaches female Thinkers to act more empathetic—as Feelers—in certain circumstances, while the male Feelers learn to make tough decisions to be like the Thinking majority. Thinking women often find themselves swimming upstream, against these cultural expectations, as do Feeling men.

If you're a Thinker, you ask questions that start with "What?" and "Where?" If you are a Feeler, however, your questions frequently begin with "Who?" Two artists whose personality types differed in their decision-making process were Edward Hopper and Norman Rockwell. As a Thinker, Hopper's subjects included places and buildings, and when he included people, they were often stiff and unanimated. By contrast, Rockwell framed stories of the human experience. As a Feeler, Rockwell expressed his personal values as they related to his friends and family. This difference translates into how we make decisions when we are creating. What do you consider first: the problem or the people?

A Thinking-type CEO of an information technology company said he finds decision making to be easy, since he has clear priorities. He considers the firm's mission first, followed by organizational structure, and then people. In contrast, his head of sales, who is a Feeler, considers relationships with their customers first, the company's brand second, and product last. Both are great at their jobs.

How do you prioritize your decisions? How do you decide on the color for a new logo, for example? A Thinking decider may first consider which hue our eyes are most sensitive to and how it provides differentiation from the competition. One Feeling decider, who is a designer, explained that she first considers "how the color makes me feel and relates to the image I want to express."

Thinkers (T)

Has a creative writing teacher ever told you to put your heart into your work by expressing your emotions, but it didn't seem natural for you? This may have been because a Thinker's type of creativity comes from being objective and detached. The "concern for justice," explained John F. Kennedy, "must motivate any true artist."[30] Creative people with a Thinking preference seek truth and logic, and become inspired to correct injustices. In the words of Sir Isaac Newton, "My greatest friend is truth."[31]

Thinking deciders often create through the accurate stories they tell, the precise words they choose in their writing, and the proportional drawings they make. Thinkers make decisions by comparing and contrasting from known standards.

"If you just set out to be liked, you would be prepared to compromise on anything at any time, and you would achieve nothing," stated Margaret Thatcher.[32] Without sugar coating, Thinkers are known to "tell it like it is," as it's not about making friends; being right is more important than being liked. At best, this detachment allows for honest debate without hurt feelings. However, it translates into a willingness to choose subjects that are controversial or inadvertently offensive to others. Thinkers don't try to offend; they just don't always consider others' reactions as they weigh truths over popular opinion. "If I had asked people what they wanted, they would have said faster horses," Henry Ford quipped.[33]

Thinkers prefer to limit the weight of their emotions in decision making. As artists, this detachment allows for the expression of a sense of mood and place without being clouded by personal feelings; they express how it feels without injecting how *they* feel. By filtering out their emotions, pilots keep a level head during trouble, entrepreneurs make tough choices necessary for survival, and stockbrokers remain calm during market crashes. Unrattled, Thinkers don't allow their own happiness or sadness to affect their decisions.

With a greater interest in objects than people, Thinkers choose to paint landscapes more often than portraits. As authors, their characters are second in importance to the setting, as illustrated by this statement: "The chief character in this narrative is the Caribbean Sea," described James A. Michener in his book *Caribbean*.[34] Though significant to them, Thinkers choose subjects that may seem impersonal to others, but this is a misconception. The subject is just not meant to be personal. They often think of statistics or objects rather than living and breathing beings. "Whether it be an apple or a face," Paul Cézanne explained, "it is a pretext for a play of lines and colors, nothing more."[35]

Thinkers are interested in the dynamics of a system, and seek to understand cause and effect. Andy Warhol, who was fascinated by machines, called his studio "The Factory." And he removed himself from his subjects, expressing that they are all the same—even his prints of Marilyn Monroe, which, in his opinion, "are about as sentimental as Fords coming off the assembly line."[36]

If you have a preference for Thinking types, then you desire the truth and prefer to use cool logic to formulate your decisions.

Thinkers, You Innovate Best By . . .

* Evaluating problems from an arm's length
* Considering the logical consequences of your actions
* Keeping issues in perspective
* Setting a clear mission

Thinkers, Reduce Your Blind Spots By . . .

* Thinking about how others will react
* Knowing when to bend a rule
* Letting others be right, even if they aren't

Thinkers, Use Your Strengths to Boost Your Creativity By . . .

* Keeping a cool head
* Making clear and consistent decisions
* Seeking truth and justice
* Looking at cause and effect

Feelers (F)

Your feelings matter, and you can use them to make powerful statements. As Feeling painter Mark Rothko said, "I'm interested only in expressing basic human emotions—tragedy, ecstasy, doom."[37] Feelers make subjective decisions based on relative circumstances and their personal values. According to Isabel Briggs Myers, people who are "conscious first that . . . ideas are pleasing or displeasing, supporting or threatening [those] ideas already prized," have a preference for Feeling.[38] If you are a Feeling decider, then every decision is personal.

The personal belief system is the command center for Feeling deciders, and Feelers innovate best when their work promotes their personal values. Their beliefs develop by absorbing ideals held by the people they admire in their communities, such as mentors, friends, and contemporaries. "My strongest sympathies in the literary as well as in the artistic field are with those artists in whom I see the soul at work most strongly," said Van Gogh.[39] Since there is no telling which groups of people someone is going to get swept up with, our sources of influence are somewhat of a wildcard that make for an unpredictable range of beliefs and potential styles.

Whether Feelers create products or services, stories or songs, it's often autobiographical, as they inject themselves into what they make. "My work is like a diary," noted Picasso,[40] and Matisse considered every painting to be a self-portrait regardless of the subject (he was known to destroy his work if it didn't represent him). If you're a Feeler, whatever you create says something about you as a person. As Jung said, Feelers "want to feel their own life in the object" as they express their love, hate, fear, anger, joy, and hope.[41]

"It makes no difference what . . . the proportions [are], if there is feeling," explained Matisse.[42] Feelers rely on their beliefs as they decide by agreeing or disagreeing with a proposition; for example, they may agree that a color could be darker and disagree that it could be warmer. Unlike Thinking types, who make absolute, black-and-white decisions, Feeling deciders choose from the grey areas, choosing harmonious colors. And Feeling types tend to express their emotions and attitudes toward their subject with color choices, just as Dr. Seuss described times that are "happy pink" and others that are "sad and purple" in *My Many Colored Days*.[43]

Feeling authors create characters that mirror humanity in the same manner that songwriters and poets write about what is personal; Feelers can't help but inject themselves into whatever they create—just as sculptors can't help but project their own identity into the stone figures they create. Through molding, carving, and chipping, Feelers bring their creations to life with their own breath and blood.

Empathy and affection for people help Feelers thrive within teams. In performing arts, they shine as part of an ensemble, and they are unlikely to undertake controversial or offensive subjects, as they strive to promote harmony. As part of an ensemble or acting along, Feelers project their values, beliefs, and attitudes into what they create, whether it's portraits they paint, the fictional characters they bring to life, or the products they develop.

Are you influenced by the people in your life that you admire but consider rivals? Two creative people who influenced each other were Pablo Picasso and Henri Matisse, and both were Feelers. They peeked over each other's shoulders out of jealousy—but also to learn. The intertwined nature of their styles, subjects, and techniques is a testament to their longstanding yet friendly competition. Like a ping-pong ball bouncing back and forth between the two giants, their reactions to each other's work served as a dialog that inspired masterpieces. If you are a Feeler, do you have people in your life who influence you—whose ideals rub off on you and inspire you?

Interested in developing and understanding personal identity, Feelers use their creative expressions and appreciation to better define themselves. Do you put yourself into what you create or buy? Whether it's a pot roast you cooked or a jacket you purchased, do you ask, "Do I like this? Is this what I believe? Is this what my life is about?"

Empathizing helps us relate to others. Jung explained that "both empathy and abstraction are needed for any real appreciation of the object, as well as for artistic creation . . . both are present in every individual."[44] Feeling artists especially empathize with their subjects, wondering things like "What is it like to be a horse pulling a heavy cart? How would my life be if I had the lead in a Broadway show? Does the poor mountaintop get lonely when it's lost in the fog?" If you can relate to the struggle of the horse, are pleased with the notion of life as a Broadway performer, or even resonate with life on a lonely mountaintop, then what you create represents your alignment with these views. If you're unhappy with what you see and it doesn't coincide with your values, then as a Feeler, you tend to create by abstracting the view to make it fit with what you would like to see.

By empathizing through representing or abstracting, it's no wonder that Feeling deciders put people first, or that people are an important theme in whatever they create. Feelers are successful actors who draw on both their own emotions and those of their audiences. "I have feelings too," said Marilyn Monroe. "I am still human. All I want is to be loved, for myself and for my talent."[45] Feelers are also artists who paint portraits or make sculptures with facial expressions that represent human nature. In their creative quest, Feelers search for their own identities and find themselves in what they create.

Feelers, You Innovate Best By . . .

* Being autobiographical
* Gaining support from others
* Accessing and expressing emotions

Feelers, Reduce Your Blind Spots By . . .

* Considering other people's values
* Knowing when to keep feelings to themselves

- Keeping your feelings in check so they don't distract from the issues
- Not trying to please everyone
- Considering logical arguments: circle = πr^2 (whether you like it or not)

Feelers, Use Your Strength to Boost Your Creativity By . . .

- Understanding interpersonal relationships
- Gathering insight into how decisions affect people
- Considering your values

Summary: Thinking (T) and Feeling (F)

Have you ever heard a no-nonsense mechanic say, "Skip over how it felt when your car stalled, and just tell me about the noises you heard"? Or have you heard an emotional music teacher say, "You need to put more of yourself into your songs." A ten-year-old boy we interviewed said, "I used to like art class but not anymore. The teacher says we have to draw faces of people, and all I want to draw were planes and trains" (both of which he is really passionate about). These are Thinking and Feeling differences. If you are a Thinker, you prefer to decide using your head; it's unnecessary to say to you "don't take it personally" since you rarely do. And if you are a Feeler, you prefer to decide—and create—using your heart. To you, *everything* is personal.

Judging (J) or Perceiving (P)—Your Public Face

Sitting in a Georgetown restaurant and finished with his first drink, (coauthor) David started to wonder if his friend Peter was really going to show up. Many of you probably have a friend like Peter, who has good intentions but also the habit of getting distracted. Once, he came knocking on the door seven hours after David's party had ended. Other times, he was a no-show. So even though Peter had spoken to David that afternoon and the two were scheduled to meet for drinks, David had his doubts. After Peter failed to show, David found a payphone and checked his answering machine (this was before cell phones). Sure enough, there was a message waiting for him from his friend: "Hi, it's Peter. Guess I can't make it. I'm on an Amtrak to New York; just remembered school started three days ago. Oh well, I guess I'm going to be late this semester."

While Peter often got distracted by new information, David's other friend John always stuck to his plan. He would say, "Next Wednesday, 5 AM, let's drive to the beach." When the day came, there he was in David's driveway at 5 AM on the dot, regardless of the weather.

These are extreme examples, but we're sure you have friends who are spontaneous like Peter and friends who plan like John. Of course, we all can be spontaneous and we all can plan, but we prefer to do one over the other. And both of David's friends act creatively, by the way: Peter is a successful designer, and John is a resourceful engineer.

We have already explored which way your energy flows, how you gather information, and how you prefer to make decisions; now we will look at our last set of polar opposites, which represent our outer-world orientation. What face do you show others? Do you project an image of buttoned-up structure or shirt-untucked spontaneity? Do you appear organized and punctual or somewhat scattered, doing things in your own time? When you create something new, do you spend more time planning as a Judger or more time doing as a Perceiver? (Remember, there are no right or wrong answers.)

Every day, we are drenched by a deluge of new information. How do we keep from getting saturated? If you like having set decisions, you are using your preference toward Judging; you make decisions quickly and close the case to move on. Judgers extinguish the fire and turn off the hydrant. Alternately, if you are a Perceiver, you prefer to continually collect information. You make decisions but don't consider them fixed, as you readily change your mind as new information warrants. Perceivers also put out the fires, but they leave the valve open so new information can continue to flow. Our preference is an important distinction between whether we tend to follow a plan or improvise as we create.

Like a billboard, this is the part of your personality that others see through what and how you communicate. If you're a Judger, then you share your decisions (as a

Thinker or a Feeler); and if you're a Perceiver, you share with the world the information you're gathering (as either a Sensor or an Intuitive).

How Judgers and Perceivers Communicate

Preference	Express to others	Example
Judging (J)	What they decide (Thinking or Feeling)	The leaves are beautiful.
Perceiving (P)	What they gather (Sensing or Intuitive)	The leaves are red and yellow.

Judgers (J): The Planners

Creativity doesn't need to be spontaneous. Those with the miscast notion that all creative people are disorganized aren't considering Judgers. As a man who painted while wearing a coat and tie, Matisse reinforced this idea. "Spontaneity is not what I am looking for," he said, and "Painting requires organization."[46] Paul Cézanne echoed this sentiment: "A powerful ability to organize represents the most precious collaboration [that] a sensibility can have in its efforts to realize a work of art."[47] Judgers bring their sense of order to what they make by deliberately organizing every sight, scent, and sound. They classify their thoughts and feelings, as well as objects and people.

If you're a Judger, you keep your goals in sight, and you prefer to have a structured, ordered, deliberate, meticulous, and controlled outer persona. Whatever you create exhibits the same qualities as well. A studio in disarray or a messy desk isn't for Judgers, as they organize their workspace for utmost efficiency. Anyone who has ever tried to organize their garage knows that putting everything into its place is a creative act. If you're a Judger, your persona shows in the orderly compositions you create, the punctual dinners you serve, the prim gardens you plant, the dapper clothing you wear, and the conclusions you reach in the stories you tell.

Real life isn't always so organized. Before gleaming skyscrapers are raised, there are noisy, chaotic messes of mud and materials. Similarly, the creative "work in progress" is full of ambiguity, distractions, blind alleys, and moments of uncertainty. Judgers may be tempted to stray but are driven to follow their blueprint.

We respect Judgers for being confident and decisive; however, sometimes quickness comes at a cost when decisions are closed and the flow of new information stops. Rapidly changing circumstances require new issues to be considered, and without a real-time flow of information, decisions are made on stale information and creations appear stiff. Backed by absolute convictions, Judgers use language with little leeway, such as "always," "never," "should," and "must." What they lack in adapting to changing circumstances, they gain in executing plans and seeing them through to the finish. A Judger we know is steadfast in never accepting any of those flyers that people try to hand out on the street. One day, when he was looking to buy a newspaper to read since he expected a long wait for an appointment, a person tried to hand him a free *Daily News*. The Judger automatically said "no thanks" and continued to look for a place to buy a paper.

Judgers stick to their decisions, and this makes them rather slow to accept new ideas and techniques—even if they are improvements. When Judgers are willing to consider something new, expect that they'll still follow a formal process to determine whether to reject or integrate these new ideas.

The Judging types have a firm sense of time and speak of specifics—for example, "I got the 7:15 PM train and arrived at the theater by 7:45." When you mention the possibility of an upcoming event, they usually know if they are free or not, and they are on time to meetings, having planned their route in advance. Whatever they are about to do, they prepare for, making note of the duration and bringing the necessary equipment. Unexpected changes that deviate from this plan cause them problems and stress. Not everyone likes a surprise, but this is especially true for Judgers.

All the possibilities posed by a blank page or an empty stage can be overwhelming to anyone, but don't let it keep you from being creative if you're a Judger. Contrary to what's often written on working outside one's limits, Judgers are inspired by bounds and perform well with some constraints. Judgers can get overwhelmed by their need to process and categorize too many possibilities, but by setting limits on their resources—a fixed number of colors or a particular theme, budget, beat, word count, or deadline—they gain traction. Later, in chapter 9 ("Art in Yourself: More Creative Outlets"), we offer unique suggestions tailored to help either Judgers or Perceivers overcome creative blocks.

Judgers fill their mug to the brim without spilling coffee over the sides, but working within bounds doesn't necessarily mean "inside the box." Bounds can be as wide as a football field or as large as an ocean, and boundaries can provide guidance. If you are designing a house, the building codes, number of bedrooms, size of the lot, location of the easements—all provide limits, and limits like these form the canvas on which a Judger freely creates.

As photographers, Judgers show up with all the right lenses, backdrops, and lights; as Judgers, they plan. Do you schedule your time, even on your day off? Do you plan what tools and materials you need? Do you amaze your friends by getting everything to complete your project with only one trip to the hardware store?

So, can you be a planner and also be creative? The answer is positively *yes*. Many visual artists consider subject, composition, colors, media, and size in advance, and it is also common for authors to begin by developing a theme, outline, and character profiles first. Michener would plan his outline, profile his characters, and know the ending before starting a novel. Scientists plan their experiments, and business people plan their cash flow. In any form of creation, if you are a Judger, you are persistent and make the appropriate plans to ensure that you finish.

Achievement for Judgers is the result of finishing, and this drives them to a high rate of completion. What is left unfinished is uncomfortable. "At each stage," described Henri Matisse, "I reach a balance, a conclusion."[48] With an endpoint in mind before beginning, Judgers plan the resources and time to reach closure; they calculate if the project can be completed with the available resources and make adjustments accordingly. And Judgers are diligent, sticking to the program and measuring how closely they achieve their preconceived objectives. "Nearly all of these various features had been planned in advance. That is the way I have always worked. I draw a plan and work out every detail on the plan before starting to build," described Henry Ford in *My Life and Work*.[49] Happiest with their performance, Judgers attribute their success to strong organizational skills and careful planning. Their finished work represents a completed statement.

Judgers, You Innovate Best By . . .

* Selecting ideas
* Carefully planning and organizing
* Following through to completion

Judgers, Reduce Your Blind Spots By . . .

* Seeing that every deadline is not fixed, every decision is not final
* Withholding your judgment until a decision is necessary
* Staying open to new ideas
* Questioning your assumptions
* Accepting when something is beyond your control
* Playing without an end product in mind
* Trying new things (sit somewhere new)
* Exploring new ideas (read something different)

Judgers, Use Your Strength to Boost Your Creativity By . . .

* Persisting
* Staying neat and organized
* Controlling your resources

Perceivers (P): The Improvisers

When the Australians say, "No worries," they are talking as Perceivers—people with an outward persona of being easygoing and flexible. With many ongoing projects, few are completed. If you're a Perceiver, you prefer endlessly modifying, editing, repainting, and revising since there is an unlimited and continuous flow of data to consider. Your creative output looks spontaneous, playful, loose, and full of free-flowing curves; fluid ideas are driven by your open-ended curiosity. You may wonder if subjects, themes, or objectives have to be defined or if projects ever need to be finished. If you are a Perceiving type, you make decisions but tend not to view them as final; you choose to keep your options open. By continuing to collect information, Perceivers don't settle with the first solution to a problem, as they are on the lookout for a better way.

Picasso made it clear that he had a preference toward Perceiving when he said, "A picture is not thought out and settled beforehand; while it is being done, it changes as thoughts change." As he continued, he made a proclamation that can be thought of as an anthem for the Perceiving types: "To finish a work? To finish a picture? What nonsense! To finish it means to be through with it, to kill it, to rid it of its soul."[50]

Creating provides an avenue for Perceivers to express their inquisitiveness because they typically start projects without preconceiving an endpoint. This makes them well suited for innovating since they enjoy entering unchartered waters without defining a destination. "All my books started as short stories . . . I never sat down to write a novel," said Hemingway.[51] He suggested starting with a true sentence and seeing where it leads. Whether they're working on a novel, a painting, or a dance routine, Perceivers don't know where their character's composition—or feet—will lead; they don't even know whether their experiment will ever become a product. Distractions are part of the process, and surprises and risks are welcome. Without a finish line, every move provides a new opportunity and direction on which to pounce. Perceivers continuously gather information, with every new sentence, brushstroke, dance step, or experiment inspired by the last.

Perceivers often consider it wasteful to prepare for things that may never happen. By either favoring Intuition or Sensing, they continue to collect new information, even toward the end of a project, and finish only when they reach hard deadlines. Seeing the world as open and full of endless possibilities, Perceivers reprioritize in real time and use incoming data to ad lib when unexpected situations arise. The eraser on their pencil, the delete key, the forgivingness of oil painting, or the improvisational nature of jazz all allow for trials without permanent consequences.

If you are a Perceiver, you are happiest when you have no strings that tie you down. As Marilyn Monroe described, "I am invariably late for appointments—sometimes as much as two hours. I've tried to change my ways, but the things that make me late are too strong and too pleasing."[52] A Perceiver's versatility allows them to quickly switch from one topic to the next without first finishing their previous thought. And if invited to an event taking place in a month, they could be excited and look forward to it whether they're actually able to attend or not.

For Perceivers, there is nothing worse than a fully booked day. They don't like the constraint of making firm reservations for dinner in advance since they have no idea what kind of food they will be in the mood for when hunger strikes. And being curious, they like to press all the buttons on a new television remote control, just to see what happens. Led by their inquisitiveness, Perceivers create by trying every color, style, phrase, song, and joke, without limits or commitments.

"Don't be afraid of perfection; you will never attain it!" advised Salvador Dalí.[53] If you are a Perceiver, you may appear to others as unorganized and sometimes messy at times, but this is only because you prefer to talk about the information you are gathering rather than about decisions you made. When Perceivers talk about their advance preparation, they often use the phrase "last night."

Everything is a work in progress for Perceivers. They usually have lots of started projects, but only a few get completed. Each start provides excitement—unlocked potential, unlimited choices, and unexplored possibilities—and even when pieces of work are finished, questions are left unanswered. There are times, however, when completion is necessary. As one entrepreneur explained, "The most important thing I learned was to decide what matters and what can be put off. I avoid procrastinating by doing the hardest, most important thing first."

Perceivers are limitless in their use of resources, like the number of colors, quantity of fabric, or amount of time for a project. And like a herd of buffalo stampeding through fences, Perceivers are not stopped by the edge of the canvas, the number of pages in their books, or the confines of any stage. With a Sensing preference, Perceiving artists outline individual objects and freely arrange them, while Perceiving Intuitives see no boundaries on objects or anything else.

When Perceivers are happy with a performance or creation, they attribute their success to a loose organizational style and a responsiveness that allows for capitalizing on the unexpected. If Perceivers are displeased with their work, they may feel too much structure or schedule has squelched their creativity. In the words of Andy Warhol, "When I have to think about it, I know the painting is wrong. If you don't think about it, it's right. As soon as you have to decide and choose, it's wrong. And the more you decide about, the more wrong it gets."[54]

Perceivers, You Innovate Best By . . .

* Producing without a known outcome
* Responding to new information
* Managing change
* Just starting (ideas will follow)

Perceivers, Reduce Your Blind Spots By . . .

* Watching schedules
* Focusing
* Setting some limits
* Completing what you start
* Sticking to your decisions

Perceivers, Use Your Strengths to Boost Your Creativity By . . .

* Maintaining openness to change
* Staying flexible
* Encouraging curiosity

Summary: Judging (J) and Perceiving (P)

Whether you're a Judger or a Perceiver, you create by using a mix of discipline and playfulness. While Judgers tend to answer questions with a resolute "yes or no," Perceivers are more comfortable with an answer of "maybe." Judgers finish their painting, sculpture, or novel to bring closure, and Perceivers leave things unfinished to keep their options open. Judgers plan their spontaneity while Perceivers may only plan certain elements in advance to achieve desired results. The creations of Judgers often look serious, structured, and linear; Perceivers' creations often look fun and loose, and may have more curves. Judgers and Perceivers can be quite successful in either method of expression, but they are most comfortable with their inborn preferences.

4

THE FOUR TEMPERAMENTS OF CREATIVITY

During an eye examination, optometrists ask their patients to cover one eye at a time to read the chart. Afterward, when both eyes are opened, a much clearer image is seen. Thus far, we have covered the four individual pairs of preferences, functions, and attitudes that make up our personality. Next, we'll uncover a clearer, more nuanced picture of ourselves by combining two of these preferences to form particular temperaments. This is the precursor to eventually putting all four preferences into dynamic play with one another in your creative style profile in part 2.

So, what is a temperament? "Painting is nature seen through a temperament," noted Paul Cézanne, but he wasn't the first to make this observation.[1] Since Greek times, different temperaments have been connected to how and what we create. And although there have been many classification systems of temperaments, most essentially function under the same principle: people with similar behavior grouped together.

With the MBTI assessment, when we lean toward or away from a two-letter pair, it can say a lot about our personal process and style. So, knowing these temperaments is like putting on special glasses that help us predict group behavior while also showing us how we relate to our own creative processes and styles.

There are twenty-four possible combinations, but we have chosen to concentrate on the four that cover more behaviors in the scope of human nature with greater accuracy than the other sets of pairs (the idea of looking at these four particular pairs originated with MBTI pioneer David Keirsey and his graduate student, Marilyn Bates):

- NFs (Intuitive Feelers) are poetic and personal.
- NTs (Intuitive Thinkers) are experimental and complex.
- SJs (Sensing Judgers) are realistic and traditional.
- SPs (Sensing Perceivers) are dramatic and flexible.

In many ways, the four combos can be thought of as having similar characteristics to four US cities famous for their distinct personalities:

- *The NFs are all about people.* San Francisco, with its Haight-Ashbury section, is an NF city of love and ideas, and a promoter of social causes.
- *The NTs are all about ideas and systems.* Boston is an NT town, where innovation flows between academia and high-tech startups.
- *The SJs play by the rules.* Washington, DC, is an SJ city, where new ideas are implemented within the guidelines of a rule-based system, such as the procedures to get a new bill passed into a law.
- *The SPs play for thrills.* Detroit, the Motor City, is a purely SP haven of tangible creativity. Where cars are built to be trendy, speedy, and exciting, this industry town has had its ups and downs. Now an influx of creative people are staging the next comeback. According to a 2011 *New York Times* article, "Not unlike Berlin, which was revitalized in the 1990s by young artists migrating there for the cheap studio space, Detroit may have this new generation of what city leaders are calling 'creatives' to thank if it comes through its transition from a one-industry [town]."[2]

Of course, it's important to remember that each of these cities has diverse neighborhoods with plenty of their own variety—just as temperaments have room for individuality. Furthermore, there are obviously more than four types of people and cities, so you don't let it seal you into a box. Our hope is that this two-letter shorthand will not only show you the fascinating and compelling dynamism it plays in your own creative style, but it will also give you a quick advantage when collaborating with others who have similar and/or different temperaments.

Intuitive Feelers (NF)—Poetic and Personal

If you have a preference for Intuitive Feeling (NF), you use your creativity largely as an outlet for self-expression. But to truly understand NF creativity, it's valuable to first look toward Otto Rank, the Austrian psychoanalyst, novelist, poet, and playwright. As a young man, Rank was a member of Sigmund Freud's inner circle and became like a son to Freud, but rebelling against some of Freud's teachings caused Rank to be ostracized and ignored by history.

As both a psychoanalyst and an artist, Rank is especially interesting. He intimately understood creativity, and described his experiences and process in his book *Art and Artist*. In it, Rank echoes the philosopher Max Dessoir that a pure form of artist rests within actors, since the subject and material used to create this art are joined within their own body.[3] Acting epitomizes the creative experience NFs have, as NFs empathize with their subject and personally embody their creations. Rank described such an individual as having a rich emotional life by way of his or her connection to others: "His outlet and satisfaction comes in identifying himself with the emotions of the other."[4]

From closely reading his work, Rank certainly appeared to have an NF temperament and seemed to write about what he knew most—himself! While his ideas may not apply to everyone, if you're an NF and interested in creativity, you may find looking further into his work enlightening, perhaps genius.

An associate of Rank's was the author Anaïs Nin. As an NF, she wrote extensively about her personal life and relationships in her journals, and is often attributed with saying, "We don't see things as they are, we see them as we are," though some believe this statement may have originated with the Hebrew Talmud. Whatever its origin, the quote aptly sums up the way NFs at times create their own reality related to themselves: life is a projection that may say more about yourself than it says of the world.

Contemplating the meaning of life and desiring to help others are two characteristics of this temperament. Edvard Munch, the painter of *The Scream*, said, "In my art, I have tried to explain to myself life and its meaning; I have also meant to help others to clarify their lives."[5] For these reasons, NFs are most likely to become involved in promoting social causes that support their personal values, because they are inspired to make creations that enrich the lives of others or persuade them to see their point of view. As actors, they get involved in championing and raising awareness for social programs for the betterment of humankind. As business owners, they establish a volunteer program in their company that donates some of its time to charity. As physicians, they go to give medical aid after natural disasters. As musicians, they share their philosophies and inspire others through the songs they write.

If you're an NF, you also prefer to make personal connections by gathering information in an abstract and theoretical way that you can then use to make value-based decisions. As an Intuitive, you see the big picture and make connections, and as a Feeler, your subjectivity is supported by a lifetime of accumulated personal values and meanings taken to heart. "We belong to our time, and we share in its opinions, its feelings, even its delusions," said Henri Matisse, in true Intuitive Feeler fashion.[6]

Those with the NF temperament make up about 19 percent of females and 13 percent of males in the general population,[7] and when they choose their favorite subjects in school, their first pick is art, followed by English and music over science, history, math, and practical skills.[8] Seeking personal identity and relevance, NFs ask: "What is the reason?" and "How does this affect me?" "The buzzing noise means something," said Winnie-the-Pooh, whose thoughts jumped to bees, then honey, whereupon he concluded, "The only reason for making honey is so *I* can eat it."[9] In the way that Pooh described the *reason* for the sound—food for him—NFs seek meaning that is personally geared.

If you're an NF, you're future oriented, and your ideas and actions relate to possibilities in people and relationships. You enjoy interacting and collaborating with people, and you consider how ideas can affect others, helping them to reach their full potential and benefit the group. NFs are cooperative, aim to please, care deeply about others' feelings, and are especially encouraged by praise and recognition—especially when it comes from people they admire, such as teachers, parents, and spouses. Accolades reinforce their self-image more than other types, and as children, early recognition of their creative accomplishments helps build their personal identity.

Intuitive Feelers are idealists, and as David Keirsey wrote, "their communications are laced with metaphors, ascribing features to people and things that belong to other people and things—animate or inanimate, visible or invisible."[10] They express abstract concepts using a "gift for language" that is most appreciated by readers of the written word. NFs make complex connections in their poetry and literature with layers of embedded meanings.[11] Otto Rank described what he called the "purely creative side of poetry" as a side that is concerned "with that subjective expressive capacity which we have called the language of the soul."[12]

Everything is personal if you're an NF, and as you describe what is meaningful to you, others relate. As performers, NFs draw on their own emotions while responding to the feelings of an audience, and as visual artists, they tend to create artwork with personal interpretations. As Matisse said, "I do not literally paint that table, but the emotion it produced upon me."[13]

It's a creative act to see possibilities in people. NFs are here to help by using their ingenuity to build and maintain human relations. As such, NFs develop skills in making the right introductions, incorporating words and other forms of expression to inspire, motivate, support, encourage, and recognize people. They also find inspiration at the intersections where different cultures come together.

In their creations, Intuitive Feelers empathize and personify objects, animals, and people with their own being. If they create a product, the product has a soul; if they create a nonobjective or abstract work, it expresses an intangible thought or feeling.

Whatever their means of expression, their friends, lovers, and family are frequent subjects of their works. Interpersonal relationships are often the subject of their creations, and characters are shown alive, full of emotions and attitudes.

If NFs also have a preference for Introversion, they tend to look inward to create self-portraits in their continuous journey to better understand themselves. Intuitive Feelers seek identity and put themselves into whatever they make. Van Gogh created dozens of self-portraits in his search for his own identity, showing himself in varying stages of heath as a form of status update. When NFs are Extraverts, they often project their feelings outward into their subjects. NFs create what they feel, and what they make has deep personal meaning that relates to their lives.

NFs often value individual uniqueness within the greater whole. When they create, they strive to be harmonious by avoiding conflict and controversy. At times, however, to promote the common good, they may create what is heinous or scandalous to gain attention and support. And according to type specialist and author Marci Segal, "For them, creativity is the process [that] unleashes personal expression . . . [and] in so doing, [makes] the world a better place."[14] This is especially true when Intuitive Feelers have a preference for Perceiving; they may bounce from medium to medium and technique to technique, all in an effort to better understand themselves. Regardless, if NFs express themselves through their creativity, it's because it makes them happy, first and foremost. These are the people who are a part of what they create, the ones who surely must have invented the concept of the "artist statement."

NFs, Use Your Strengths to Boost Your Creativity By . . .

* Aligning your personal values with a mission
* Surrounding yourself with people who inspire you

NFs, Reduce Your Blind Spots By . . .

* Looking beyond yourself (how would someone else solve this problem for themselves?)
* Balance group harmony with workable systems

Intuitive Thinkers (NT)—Experimental and Complex

If you're an NT, you probably realized you were different from an early age. This combination of preferences is found in 15 percent of males, and only 6 percent of females.[15] NTs are found in the deep end of the pool, so when a creation looks complex, it may have been made by someone with this temperament. If you're an NT, what you create is meaningful and also impersonal. Looking at one thing and seeing another, the Intuitive part of you absorbs information in an abstract and theoretical way, and then the Thinker part of you processes the information to make objective decisions, often by keeping an arm's length and filtering out the personal. Developing knowledge and skills to build competence is what drives an Intuitive Thinker.

Instead of seeking personal meanings like NFs, if you are an NT, you look for universal meanings in the laws of nature or mathematical formulas. "It seems to me that art makes one feel the essence of something, turning the ordinary, everyday object or scene into a universal one," said Paul Mellon, a benefactor to the National Gallery of Art in Washington, DC.[16] For NTs, creative pursuits provide an avenue to explore ideas in their search for meaning.

Placing high importance on the competence of themselves and others, Intuitive Thinkers strive to develop proficiency by seeking out the best teachers and sources of information. Constantly learning, challenging, and growing, they often find that the written word is an ideal source of knowledge, and they surround themselves with nonfiction books.

There is a marked difference in the way NFs and NTs express themselves. While NFs are on a quest for self-discovery, they may use self-portraits as one way to explore their own identity. As we mentioned in the last section, Van Gogh, an NF, painted self-portraits (thirty-seven, in fact) to understand himself in various states of health, almost like a status update today acts as a way for us to express ourselves by describing our sickness and well-being on social media. In contrast, J. M. W. Turner only painted one self-portrait. He did this as a student to prove his competence, and as an NT, once he completed it successfully, Turner never felt the need to do it again.

Intuitive Thinkers see what they create as an experiment and an opportunity for development. The prospect of learning something new leads them to accept change and even endure discomfort. For example, NTs will make it especially difficult on themselves by holding their own carrot just out of reach. As a milestone is about to be achieved, NTs will push their own carrot further away, setting a new higher standard to which all future work is compared. "After all my years in the theater, I can look back on only a handful of moments that met my own standards of perfection," described Helen Hayes.[17] Frequently self-critical of their abilities, NTs wonder if their creations are good, original, and nonobvious enough to be shared, displayed, or sold; however, this endless uphill climb toward competence takes them to ever higher achievements.

If you're an NT, you strive to understand systems by frequently asking questions that start with the words "how" and "why": *How does inflation affect the price of bonds? Why is cornstarch added to soup? How come customers are more willing to wait longer at a drive-through window than they are inside at the counter?* Questions seek to understand causes and predict effects. Looking to optimize systems, NTs study the dynamics of each component to determine the drivers. As photographers, NTs go beyond taking photos to study the relationships between shutter speeds, f-stops, focal lengths, depth of field, and sensitivity. One father said of his NT son, "He doesn't break the rules . . . but probes the edges of the rules to solve problems." NTs learn the rules before inventing their own rules and techniques, like customized spreadsheets, tools, color systems, sentence structures, genres, and formats. They invent products, services, and systems for every aspect of their lives.

Do you often find yourself intrigued by theories and concepts, where your expressions are a way to share your revelations through teaching others what you observe and contemplate? If you are an Intuitive Thinker, you challenge others to stop and think about what you create, just as Cézanne explained of his artwork: "Its aim is the elevation of thought."[18] With your interest in complexities and your goal of making others think, it's useful to remember this isn't always what your audience is seeking.

While NTs are exceedingly ideological, they aren't very hands on. People with the NT temperament often develop ideas only to lose interest before getting their hands dirty. Especially as Introverts, NTs often have to remind themselves to actually create something in the real world and not just in their mind. Suppose, for example, an NT wonders about woodblock printing. She researches the technique by reading about it or by arranging to see a demonstration. Afterward, she is satisfied with acquiring the knowledge as an end in itself and finds it purposeless to get ink on her fingers. If NTs are Introverts, they think about new knowledge, and as Extraverts, they talk about it, but neither is inclined to break ground, especially if they are also Perceivers. Of all the NTs, the Extraverted Judgers are most likely to produce in the real word.

Doubting, debating, searching for flaws, and developing solutions are part of the NT process as they turn a problem on its head. For them, "Their creativity invents new levels of understanding, often through problem redefinition."[19] Innovative approaches yield new solutions and serve as learning experience.

Intuitive Thinkers are often competitive, independent nonconformists who push and test the competency of colleagues and question authority—even family members—as they challenge the status quo. And while NTs may be good at building teams, they have to work at being team players. Their challenge as they innovate and lead is to avoid alienating the people around them.

Proud of their inventiveness, NTs are quick to point out the innovative features of their creations, which they see as their real achievements. Monet, for instance, was proud to show his friends the one-of-a-kind gardens he planted, just as singers who are also songwriters may be most proud of a novel lyric they wrote. NTs seek to express the novel and nonobvious aspects of what they create.

NTs tend to see future possibilities in science (unlike NFs, who tend to see future possibilities in people). They innovate by reading between the lines, connecting ideas, and finding patterns in dissimilar items. Often found in the lab or experimenting at home, NTs use and develop technology for innovating.

Innovation doesn't need to be high tech, however—even though Intuitive Thinkers are often drawn to it. Consider Impressionism, which was partially the result of technological change. At the time, tubes of paint were a new invention that gave the Impressionists portability, enabling them to leave their studio and explore a world of new subjects out in the countryside (much like Wi-Fi for us). Technological advances give us new capabilities and new worlds to explore, and this inspires NTs.

NTs are lifelong learners who strive for competence, exploring their visions as they seek universal meaning. Attempting to see the reasoning behind multistep processes, NTs skip steps where they don't see relevance. Being future oriented, they look past the popular fads to create what is timeless instead. Putting minimum effort toward a maximum result, NTs put efficiency ahead of conventions and traditions.

NTs, Use Your Strengths to Boost Your Creativity By . . .

- Finding patterns
- Integrating unrelated ideas
- Gaining inspiration through theorizing
- Challenging authority

NTs, Reduce Your Blind Spots By . . .

- Asking, "Is this simple enough for people to understand?"
- Considering, "How will people use it?"
- Actually building it
- Being practical

Sensing Judgers (SJ)—Realistic and Traditional

The biggest added value from social media didn't come through cutting-edge hardware or ingenious software; the simple "like" button was an innovation that transformed an industry from merely sharing photos and status updates into one that gave advertisers instant feedback on the sentiments of their target market, creating astronomical valuations for the companies that use it. This incremental improvement came through thinking within the box to enhance an existing system. Heart buttons and finger pokes already existed, so the thumbs-up button was a natural extension—and this is SJ creativity at its finest. The problem is that Sensing Judgers don't see themselves as creative, even though they can be and often are.

Somewhere along the line, many accept the myth that creativity is weird and wild. If you like to take one step at a time to gain your footing before taking the next step, you may be a Sensing Judger. Creativity for SJs is grown up and responsible—more methodical. While NTs read between the lines, the SJs are the first to notice when a line is missing. As they move to correct these minor discrepancies, they make discoveries that others overlook. If you're an SJ, you prefer to innovate by adapting and improving what already exists. You prefer to play by the rules, color inside the lines, and consistently produce perfection.

Because Sensing Judgers play by the rules, they like to make realistic work that represents life as it exists today or as it was in the past. Whether a writer, painter, actor, or historian, SJs are masters at creating illusions of reality, using carefully crafted details to make their audiences believe they can actually reach out and touch the puffy clouds, smell the salty air, hear the army marching into battle, or taste the freshly baked cookies. In fact, John J. Audubon, the well-known painter and cataloger of birds, created paintings so real that buzzards were fooled into eating his canvases as part of an experiment to prove the birds hunted using sight instead of smell.

Being hands on, SJs enjoy producing tangible output. They implement ideas by filing off rough edges to fit them within workable systems. "Almost anyone can think up an idea," said Henry Ford in *My Life and Work*. "The thing that counts is developing it into a practical product."[20] SJs solve problems by generating new procedures through cutting and pasting from tried-and-true methods. As Ford further explained, "If an old idea works, then the weight of the evidence is all in its favor."[21]

Like Ford, Sensing Judgers understand that, while new ideas often come by chance, innovation results from hard work and discipline. Corporate R&D departments rely on

SJs to continuously and consistently make deliberate innovations. The systematic repetition of trial and error using small variations takes patience, and they "seem able to take routine more philosophically than any of the other types."[22] SJs find "new and improved ways of doing things" and "demonstrate their creativity through taking something already done and improving it for a practical payoff."[23] Making hundreds of batches in a test kitchen, for example, a Sensing Judger chef will vary one ingredient at a time to perfect the consistency, aroma, taste, and calorie count of her newest culinary creation. The hits and misses of each trial are carefully recorded in a notebook and used to refine the tests.

As Sensors, SJs prefer to gather facts using their five senses, and as Judgers, they use their sensations to form rapid conclusions and then implement plans. "I have tried to present my sensations," said Edward Hopper of his paintings.[24] SJs make up 43 percent of the male population and nearly 50 percent of the female population.[25] Developing their perspectives from past lessons, SJs are considered more "old school," and interestingly, many elementary school teachers have this temperament.

When it comes to creativity, SJs tend to put their responsibilities ahead of activities like hobbies, especially if creating isn't part of their full-time occupation. As a result, creative pursuits are often postponed until commitments are met and chores are finished. If you're an SJ looking to increase your creative stance, then consider taking creativity seriously. Regard it as your duty, and allow yourself to give it priority.

When they create, Sensing Judgers generally have a style that is traditional, clear, clean, and neat. Though they excel at arranging facts in categories, they are less likely to make up entirely new categories, as they prefer to create within pre-existing systems. For this reason, SJs organize by collecting stories and then adding them together to make composites that are interesting and clear. They perfect reusable routines for accomplishing everyday tasks, mixing and matching like building blocks to make a functioning whole. As performers, they develop repertoires that can be added when appropriate, allowing them to use time-tested methods in ways that appear spontaneous.

The Four Temperaments of Creativity

If you have an SJ temperament, you may be like the schoolmaster who learns, complies, teaches, and enforces the rules. You create using the "right" procedures to make beautiful work that is technically precise and rich in detail. And you are critical of other's work when it's sloppy or when procedures are not followed.

As with John Audubon's realistic paintings, SJ creativity in the form of visual art tends to be logically organized as compositions that look as they are "supposed to look" in nature—classic color systems, with blue skies and green grass, where the rules of perspective, scale, and direction of lighting are followed. Nature itself is expressed with unabridged splendor, including the warts and weeds. Starting with a careful drawing, SJs usually paint within the lines to make precise geometric shapes with distinct edges and smooth gradients, the details uniform and in sharp focus. To set the head apart from the hat in their compositions, SJs like to outline individual objects. Their exactness and attention to detail is the standard of SJ creativity, whether in a painting, flower garden, or business plan.

Being nostalgic, Sensing Judgers recall the past in an accurate and appropriate way, making them the perfect historians for family history or corporate memory. As authors, they write grammatically correct, granular descriptions; as moviemakers, they produce documentaries; as photographers, they show it like it is; and as journalists, they report the facts about real places and real people.

Being dependable, SJs collaborate as dutiful members of a cast, band, or team. They seek affiliations with established institutions, and through the societies, orchestras, theater groups, or dance companies that they join, SJs feel responsible to continue and protect traditions. One example of this comes from a Chinese artist who is a student of a last master of the Lingnan School of art (a school that combines elements of Western and Japanese realist painting). As an SJ, he feels a sense of loyalty and duty to continue the school's legacy.

SJs work through procedures in the proper order without getting distracted. As teachers, they rarely deviate from the lesson plan; as actors or musicians, they carefully follow the script or score and repeat a performance night after night with consistency; as dancers, they keep time with the music; as painters, they build up the pigment, layer by layer, until it's "right"; as chefs, they follow recipes and cut vegetables with precision; as bakers, they make exact measurements and decorate cakes meticulously. SJs are rarely thought of as wildly creative. However, they are *endlessly* creative in their everyday lives as they work to keep their part of the world turning.

SJs, Use Your Strengths to Boost Your Creativity By . . .

* Defining problems
* Scanning your environment, gathering details of present surroundings
* Remembering what's worked before
* Mixing and matching tried-and-true procedures
* Making incremental improvements

SJs, Reduce Your Blind Spots By . . .

* Being open to change
* Seeing creativity as your duty
* Recognizing the procedure could be wrong
* Questioning orders and tradition
* Not waiting for all the facts before acting

Sensing Perceivers (SP)—Dramatic and Flexible

What SPs create is excitement! And they are vastly different from SJs. For SJs, going to see lions and tigers at the zoo is enough adventure, but SPs are completely different. As Dr. Seuss wrote, "You see things like these in just any old zoo. They're awfully old-fashioned. I want something new."[26] While both SJs and SPs gather concrete facts, SPs tend to be unstructured, undisciplined, nontraditional, action oriented, and spontaneous. They resist corporate cultures and boundaries, as they are freestylers who creatively seek instant thrills to avoid boredom. SPs are alive, pulling from what is around them in the moment and reacting to what is happening now. Even mistakes are seen as opportunities.

As daredevils, ski jumpers, and monster-truck drivers, SPs innovate by sizing up rivals and allies, and noticing what they are or are not doing. When facing a ski slope, a golf course, a stage, or a boardroom, they read the ground in search of immediate opportunities. Sensing Perceivers develop and use new tactics to beat out the competition by creating the "wow factor." While NTs (Intuitive Thinker) generally use long-range strategies to win wars, SPs are the lieutenants on the frontlines, using tactics for winning battles.

People with the SP temperament are "verbs" since they embody action and seek thrills. By seizing the day without ties to the past or presumptions about the future, those with an SP temperament are captivated by the here and now. The impact of what they create is far more important than why it was created, and it's the activity—not the final outcome—that matters most. Echoing the issues of the day into their creations, they are the ultimate contemporary artists, absorbing and reacting to their current environment. And with this intense focus on the immediate without much regard for the consequences, SPs make an impression as risk takers.

As Sensors, they see the particulars of the world through aromas, sounds, textures, tastes, and sights. As Perceivers, they are flexible and responsive to their immediate environment. How else could anyone hit a ninety-five-miles-per-hour baseball? Whether it's a fastball or some surprising news, SPs sense the reality of the situation and react accordingly. And although they avoid tests or surveys, it's believed that SPs make up about a quarter of the population. If you are an SP, you are seen as smooth, agile, optimistic, bold, exciting, and easygoing. You are the firefighter who heroically charges into the burning building to rescue children and then helps put out the blaze.

Sensing Perceivers "put the art before the course," which means that they take action without first learning the background theory taught in school. Keeping current with what is new and having an eye for what is practical, SPs are often well versed on the use of cutting-edge technologies; however, they don't bog themselves down with underlining theories like NTs do.

SPs try to "affect the course of events by defying, shocking, or mocking the estab-lishment."[27] They risk climbing to the top of water towers to spray graffiti, and they make contemporary art to create impact—to give society a jolting new way of seeing current issues.

Sporting a free, nonconformist spirit, the SP temperament doesn't readily socialize into norms. Without wanting to come into the fold or be poured into a mold, SPs have the temperament most likely to reach adulthood with their childlike enthusiasm intact. For SPs, creating is the process of their life. While other types are motivated by the prospect of the final product, SP artists maintain youthful exuberance for the act of creating. Having fun is the point, and the process is their purpose. Whether they're acting, taking photos, painting, or sculpting, they're truly enjoying it, and if their activity is no longer exciting, they move on to invent something else.

Sensing Perceivers innovate by solving today's problems. Jackson Pollack had a canvas that was taller than his ceiling, so out of necessity, he developed the unorthodox technique of painting it on the floor. He was called an "action painter" and craved the fun of dripping and splashing paint. His wife, Lee Krasner, explained, "He never stopped being a figurative painter, but his figures were . . . airy nothings that existed only momentarily in midair loops of paint then disappeared, leaving behind their vacated skin on the canvas."[28] Pollack called these "memories arrested in space," and his creations were a byproduct of his playing.[29]

If you are an SP, you try things and travel down avenues others are afraid of. And though you are likely to find some dead ends, you also discover some shortcuts that lead to valuable destinations. As an SP, you take the extra step after playing to look back and see if you've created something of lasting value. You look at your methods and ask if you have developed an improved process to share.

Almost every kid dreams of traveling in space or to the bottom of the ocean, but billionaire Richard Branson actually created these realities through his extreme space-tourism company. Speaking in the SP voice, he says it's more than just a joy ride: ". . . the fascinating thing about adventures like that [is when people] push the limits [and see] what they're capable of, other byproducts come that they hadn't even thought of at the time."[30] By turning boredom into excitement, SPs try what has never been tried before, sometimes creating value in the process but always making entertainment for themselves and others.

Change is a chance for excitement, and Sensing Perceivers gamble—take risks—to make the most of it. "I have no fears about making changes, destroying the image, etc., because the painting has a life of its own," noted Jackson Pollack.[31] Throwing paint is exciting, random, and fun, and when SPs abstract, it's often without deeper meaning.

SPs start many projects but often lose momentum and complete few. When engaged, they go to great lengths, expending whatever time and materials are necessary to achieve the effect they desire. Paul Gauguin wrote, "I am not in the habit of giving up a project without having tried everything, even the impossible, to gain my end."[32] His book *Nora, Nora* was written in fragments over a period of ten years. SPs are the filmmakers who go over budget and blow deadlines, whether they create blockbusters or disasters.

Creating is spontaneous and unpredictable for SPs, who don't care to ask why. They are driven to create by the exciting moment when the brush hits the canvas, not for what will be framed later. For example, an SP painter may not care if the media is acid free, archival, or resistant to fading. As performers, Sensing Perceivers care only for today's performance, not how it will be remembered. As graphic designers, they create logos for today, without concern for shelf life. And as photographers, they enjoy instant results, like those that Polaroids used to provide or the preview images on digital cameras today.

Resourceful, grounded in practicality, hands on, and technique oriented, SPs are tactical, finding relevance in immediacies (much like James Bond). They combine whatever resources are available—begged, borrowed, or stolen—to creatively solve problems. This includes ordinary items, spare parts, trendy or tarnished icons, or even trash, all of which they remix, reduce, reuse, and recycle to make something new. SPs "make aesthetic and practical use of existing items and ideas, juxtaposing them in ways others rarely imagine."[33] If you're an SP, surround yourself with supplies of all colors, textures, shapes, and materials to provide inspiration.

Sensing Perceivers don't like to sit still or be on the clock. Charles Schulz found himself "fighting the schedule" and explained that he was "not one who can work steadily at the drawing board"—that he "gets jumpy" and needs to "get up and move around, and do something else."[34] If you're an SP, try to build flexibility into your day and allow for outlets to stretch your muscles with a new task or change of scene.

"I have never been able to foresee the hysterical and preposterous course of my conduct and, even less, the final outcome of my art, of which I am often the first astonished spectator," explained Dalí.[35] Creating without planning, SPs let their projects guide the way as they respond to each new mark as a springboard—like jazz musicians reacting to the notes, actors improvising from the last spoken word, painters adjusting for changing weather, and writers allowing their character's actions to lead the plot along. Similar to a game where one person makes up the beginning of a story and the following players make up the next part from where it leads off, each new brushstroke, dance step, note, or sentence flows to the next.

SPs are especially sensitive to visual and auditory stimuli, such as color, line, and texture. David Keirsey calls people who prefer the SP combination "artisans," as they are particularly drawn toward an education in fine arts, painting, sculpture, and performance arts.[36] He goes on to say that they have an "ear for sound" and have a sense for "harmonic coherence, or what sounds good."[37] "To me, the greatest pleasure of writing is not what it's about but the inner music that words make," described Truman Capote.[38] Just as NFs (Intuitive Feelers) have special language talents, SP authors have special talents with dialogue. They excel at producing stories with natural conversations, like those in screenplays or page-turning adventure novels.

Like sharks, Sensitive Perceivers have to remain in motion. They are driven by the need to avoid boredom through stimulation and pleasure, and as a side benefit, this is how they learn. By launching thousands of trial balloons in their experiences, SPs learn to notice—and benefit from—those that float and those that sink.

SPs use their life experiences to be nimble. For example, they may briefly try many forms of expression using different techniques and media, like going from oil painting to sculpture to watercolor to acrylic to dance and then back to oil. In whatever mode they choose to work, they quickly learn to use the necessary tools and techniques. They are more impulsive than the other temperaments and are often drawn to buy the latest materials or tools, expecting these items will change everything for the better. If the new toy doesn't work as they had hoped, however, it's abandoned.

The Unique Writing Strengths of SPs and NFs

Sensitive Perceivers (SP)	Intuitive Feelers (NF)
Gift of dialog	Gift of language
Writes what sounds good	Writes what reads well
Rhyme, wit, fun	Multiple meanings, entendre,
Screenplays, limericks	inspirational
	Literature, poems

Sensing Perceivers' creations often look spontaneous, playful, stylized, stenciled, illustrated, or cartoonish. When portraying people, SPs notice body language and mirror these observations. They simplify by using the fewest marks, seeking the shortest path with the least resistance—the fewest lines to represent an object. As Pablo Picasso explained, "Art is the elimination of the unnecessary."[39] SPs are also interested in playing sports, taking adventures, and encountering wild animals or the dangers of armed conflict. Hemingway, a likely SP, wrote about all of the above.

SP workspaces are laid out in whatever way seems most practical, with items left wherever they were last used. Then the next time they work, SPs choose tools and materials from whatever is close at hand. Picasso once said, "Wanting to use a blue, I didn't have it. So I used a red instead . . ."[40] In the kitchen, instead of continually keeping staples in stock, SPs will use whatever *is* available and in season.

If you are an Sensing Perceiver, then follow Dalí's lead: "My capacity to profit from everything is unlimited."[41]

SPs, Use Your Strengths to Boost Your Creativity By . . .

* Seeing what's needed now
* Improving how it's done today
* Surrounding yourself with material that inspires you
* Disrupting the status quo
* Identifying current trends
* Sending up trial balloons
* Keeping things fun by creating what stands out
* Borrowing from many sources

SPs, Reduce Your Blind Spots By . . .

* Looking beyond the present
* Being patient with what seems boring
* Finishing what you start

Other Pairs of Preferences

We have seen that NFs are poetic and personal, NTs are experimental and complex, SJs are realistic and traditional, and SPs dramatic and flexible. But like we stated at the beginning of the chapter, there are many other possible combinations. Here are some brief insights on fourteen additional types of pairs, starting with the SP's polar opposite, NJ.

Intuitive Judgers (NJs)

If you are an NJ, you are a lightning rod—a dreamer with a grounded side. As an Intuitive, you trust flashes of inspiration, and as a Judger, your ideas are quickly grounded by your decision process. Unlike SPs, who are often unstructured and undisciplined, NJs are all about structure and results, having a clear vision of the whole from the start. This type bounds and grounds the possibilities: "I use photographs to limit the field of my imagination's potential," described Matisse.[42] Future oriented, they are happy to know their creations will survive for generations.

Extraverted Sensors (ESs)

When the sign says "Do not touch," it's written for ESs, because they want to engage with the current reality of their surroundings. If you have an ES preference, your sleeves are already rolled up, and you are a "super sensor" who notices every detail. Changing your surroundings is a prime way to become inspired, as you are sensitive to your physical environment. And what you create is often spontaneous, practical, and full of specifics.

Introverted Intuitives (INs)

With an IN preference, your hands are in your pockets since you have little need to physically touch anything. You seek meaning and are sensitive to what is unsaid. People with an IN preference are most at home contemplating abstractions. They drift away into daydreams where they imagine how the future could be. An IN we interviewed said, "I need lots of thinking time. Television time can be thinking time for me. I can totally tune it out, especially commercials, even when I'm looking at them." INs are inspired by reading and reflecting on visions, and they need time to mull things over, let their subconscious work. Jung suggested that the creative artist truly embodies the IN temperament: "[This individual] reveals strange, far-off things in his art . . . beautiful and grotesque, sublime and whimsical . . . If not an artist, he is frequently a misunderstood genius."[43]

Extraverted Feelers (EFs)

If you are an EF, you are people oriented, inspiring, uplifting, dramatic, in touch with your emotions, and open to sharing your feelings. Being natural on stage, ENFs are inspired by their connections to people and may use acting to discharge emotions (such as grief or aggression) and to confront fears. In contrast, ESFs (Extraverted Sensing Feelers) act out their five senses. Either way, EFs want to please others, especially their heroes. Humorous and entertaining, EFs seek affirmation and praise that allows them to shine. They project their feelings, empathizing with their subjects. In some cases, however, EFs privately internalize their feelings, becoming their own subjects.

Introverted Sensors (ISs)

If you have an IS preference, you have a constructive imagination, where you contemplate the practical, and you have a nonverbal "felt sense" that provides you with an inner knowing about the properties of things. It comes from stored memories. Take this quote from Georgia O'Keeffe: "When I do anything with material—paper or plastic— I know its density; whether it will stretch, give, or tear; and how to move it or work with it."[44] People with these preferences need time to digest the realities of their sensations.

Feeling Perceivers (FPs)

With an FP preference, you roll from style to style like a tumbleweed blowing in the wind, looking for your identity and following your heart, your mentors, and kindred spirits, whether they exist in the past or the present. If you are also an Intuitive, your search for a style is also a search for personal meaning. If you are a Sensor, you're particularly apt at observing, replicating, and mixing and matching the styles of others.

You try on styles like you try on shoes: looking for what feels right, and you like finding a pair that fits perfectly. There is synergy for Feelers when their role models have a similar type as themselves.

Thinking Judgers (TJs)

If you are a TJ, you hold your creative style at an arm's length from your sense of self. You may believe your style isn't a part of you, believing instead that it results from a culmination of learning. Like a flag swaying in the wind that remains fixed to a pole, your style wavers but does not change much. Slow to change, TJs stay with the style that works best for them.

Intuitive Perceivers (NPs)

Original and flexible, if you have an NP preference, you are an endless lightning storm of ideas, but the bolts don't often strike the ground. You thrive in chaotic environments and see the possibilities in everything, as you are always stumbling upon something that is surprisingly relevant. Even when you find a solution to a problem, you do not stop looking for a better solution. Working from a broad framework, NPs improvise the rest as they leave their creations open for interpretation.

Introverted Feelers (IFs)

Although the Feeler in you is empathetic and sensitive to interpersonal relations, as an Introvert, you often prefer to be alone. This creates a stark contrast with ETs (Extraverted Thinkers), who like engaging with people but aren't particularly empathetic. This proves challenging for both IFs and ETs.

Introverted Perceivers (IPs)

If you're an Intuitive Perceiver, you have a boundless imagination. "Isabel Briggs Myers suggested that higher levels of creativity require the preference combination of intuition and perception."[45] So, when you have a preference for IP, beware that without developing a strong judging piece, you tend to endlessly reflect upon your ideas with a limited interest in implementing them.

Extraverted Intuitives (ENs)

ENs are often outspoken as they seek out and promote new possibilities. Inspired by external events, they derive their big and often abstract ideas from the activity around them. If you're an EN, you like to share your visions and are adept at motivating others to act.

Extraverted Judgers (EJs)

As an EJ, you tend to assert your position to control the space around you. This includes positioning external objects or organizing people, whether it's laying out the schematics for a skyscraper, planting flowers in a garden, or leading a marching band.

Extraverted Perceivers (EPs)

EPs are fast and flexible, and most reactive to their environment. If you're an EP, you're the first to open your mouth to answer a question and prefer to think on your feet as you talk through the answer in front of a group, whether it's composed of friends or new acquaintances. EPs often must start a project to determine if it's worth continuing.

Introverted Judgers (IJs)

Needing time to reflect and compose, if you're an IJ, you may be slow to change as you contemplate your movements—but you finish what you start. Before beginning to answer a question, IJs prefer to formulate a complete statement, much like one of Edward Hopper's paintings, which he "planned very carefully in [his] mind before starting."[46]

Encounter a Happy Accident

Francis Bacon once wrote, "All painting is an accident, but it's not an accident, because one must select what part of the accident they choose to preserve."[47] Many great discoveries have been made in science as the result of accidents. When Alexander Fleming saw that the penicillin mold growing in his petri dish was killing off the flu that he was studying, he took notice. Velcro and Post-it Notes were also inadvertently discovered at 3M while aiming to discover something else.

When we are in the chaos of creating, inadvertent things happen, and when they are favorable, they are known as "happy accidents." Happy accidents are often the catalysts for innovation, but as we end this chapter and move on to part 2 of the book, it's important to understand how each of the four temperaments approaches these happy accidents differently.

- NFs (Intuitive Feelers) are naturally experimental, but being deeply individual, they're most attuned to value in accidents that have personal meaning to them. Van Gogh provides the perfect example: when discussing an accidental hole that ended up in a painting, he wrote to his brother Theo, "By a curious chance, an accident to

Delaroche's portrait has left it with a hole in the middle of the forehead. It looks good and actually seems to belong there."[48]

- The scientific and experimental NTs (Intuitive Thinkers) analyze why the accident happened and then see if it can be repeated, since they understand that innovation often arises from mistakes. Robert Motherwell believed all creation originates in the subconscious: "There is no such thing as accidents, really . . . [but] I accept them if they seem appropriate."[49]

- If the accurate and orderly SJs (Sensing Judgers) have an accident, they see it as a blunder because the error wasn't part of the original plan. Even if they find the mistake interesting, it's carefully corrected to resume course. Henry Ford explained, "Every accident, no matter how trivial, is traced back by a skilled man employed solely for that purpose, and a study is made of the machine to make that same accident in the future impossible."[50]

- The action-oriented and spontaneous SPs (Sensing Perceivers) expect the unexpected. They depend on chance happenings, always ready to capitalize on the unplanned. As Dalí said, "Mistakes are almost always of a sacred nature. Never try to correct them."[51]

Of course, we all handle happy accidents in our creative lives a little differently. We all have an individual style for adapting to changes, whether it's in our art or in life—speaking, writing, painting, dancing, singing, cooking, gardening, playing music. Next up is part 2, which examines your creative type and the profiles of the fifteen others. Armed with these profiles, you'll have a better understanding of yourself, your creative style, and the other styles around you.

Part II

THE SIXTEEN CREATIVE TYPES

5

YOUR CREATIVE TYPE: FINDING YOUR GLASS SLIPPER

In the last part, we covered the basics of each element in your creative profile, and you can think of this part as a time-release pill—a potent cure that addresses many of your creative ailments in regulated doses over time. This section of the book shows you the heart of your creative style via profiles and examples of various personality types, showing you how you can be creative in your own way. But it can be difficult for anyone to absorb all of this at once. From our experience, the value of this section continually seeps in as you find more and more reasons to revisit passages about yourself and about the profiles of those around you, as you contemplate life's defining moments, and as new people come into your life.

It's true that you can color a picture using four colors and get some good results, but with a bigger box of crayons, you have more possibilities. While the temperaments we just looked at are useful, people are multifaceted, and we quickly see limitations when using only half the scales. Now, we'll extend our range by combining all four letters to form sixteen unique personalities.

Like combining reactive chemicals, the letters don't only mix but interact to form unique solutions that are more than the sum of their parts. We gain a greater understanding of how the people of each personality create and appreciate in their own way. And as you read the profiles, just as Cinderella slipped into her glass slipper, look for the profile that gives you the most comfortable fit.

We don't have to say this for the Intuitives (because they're already skipping around), but for the Sensors, don't feel as though you need to read this section straight through. People are mostly interested in understanding themselves, and they get the most from reading their profile first. Then they typically look at the profiles of a few of their close friends, relatives, coworkers, and even some adversaries, to try to understand them better.

With so many different ways to be creative, you can learn more about yourself by finding a profile that resonates best with you. The more you understand your ways, the more confident you can be as you create.

Dominant, Auxiliary, and Inferior Functions

Before we get into the profiles, there's something else to cover: the dominant, auxiliary, and inferior functions of each of the sixteen types. These functions affect all of us and can be a good starting point for further exploration as you learn more about your type. Understanding how they work together gives you insight into yourself and how others see you.

The *dominant* function is our strongest and most trusted function while the *auxiliary* function is what Isabel Briggs Myers called our "second best." We also have an *inferior* function, which is the opposite of our dominant, since it's the least used and therefore the least developed and least trusted (often approximate to the skill level of a child). The way these functions are derived is nuanced, so to make it easy, we provided a chart that lists the dominant, auxiliary, and inferior functions for each four-letter creative type.

Your Creative Type: Finding Your Glass Slipper

The Three Main Functions of the Sixteen Creative Types

Creative Type	Dominant	Auxiliary	Inferior
ISTJ (The Organizer)	Introverted Sensing	Extraverted Thinking	Extraverted Intuition
ISFJ (The Teacher)	Introverted Sensing	Extraverted Feeling	Extraverted Intuition
INTJ (The Visionary)	Introverted Intuition	Extraverted Thinking	Extraverted Sensing
INFJ (The Inspirer)	Introverted Intuition	Extraverted Feeling	Extraverted Sensing
ISTP (The Crafter)	Introverted Thinking	Extraverted Sensing	Extraverted Feeling
ISFP (The Dreamer)	Introverted Feeling	Extraverted Sensing	Extraverted Thinking
INTP (The Idea Mill)	Introverted Thinking	Extraverted Intuition	Extraverted Feeling
INFP (The Muser)	Introverted Feeling	Extraverted Intuition	Extraverted Thinking
ESTJ (The Realist)	Extraverted Thinking	Introverted Sensing	Introverted Feeling
ESFJ (The Teacher)	Extraverted Feeling	Introverted Sensing	Introverted Thinking
ENTJ (The Commander)	Extraverted Thinking	Introverted Intuition	Introverted Feeling
ENFJ (The Persuader)	Extraverted Feeling	Introverted Intuition	Introverted Thinking
ESTP (The Adventurer)	Extraverted Sensing	Introverted Thinking	Introverted Intuition
ESFP (The Entertainer)	Extraverted Sensing	Introverted Feeling	Introverted Intuition
ENTP (The Brainstormer)	Extraverted Intuition	Introverted Thinking	Introverted Sensing
ENFP (The Socializer)	Extraverted Intuition	Introverted Feeling	Introverted Sensing

The Dominant and Auxiliary Functions

Why do we underestimate Introverts and sometimes overestimate Extraverts? The way Extraverts and Introverts use their dominant and auxiliary functions are markedly different. An Extravert's dominant function is like a cruise ship crossing the ocean in plain view, its white decks visible for miles. Meanwhile, an Introvert's strength is more like a submarine—mostly hidden beneath the waves, only making contact with the world above by raising its periscope.

If you're an Extravert, you're straightforward. As such, Extraverts publically show their dominant function by laying their highest card—their strengths—face up on the table for all to see. For example, if your dominant is Feeling, your expressions are loaded with personal values. If your dominant is Sensing, you notice everything and express these details.

In contrast, if you're an Introvert, you are more guarded, concealing your dominant function's strengths by covering your highest card. What you show instead is your second-best function—your auxiliary. Without putting your best foot forward when you communicate, you are often underestimated. If you saw comic book characters Clark Kent, the mild-mannered reporter, and Bruce Wayne, the discrete philanthropist, walking down the street, it wouldn't be obvious that their real strength resides within their secret identities as Superman and Batman. By showing their second-best faces in public, Introverts reserve the driving force of their personality—their dominant function—for themselves and a few close friends.

Ultimately, everyone must live their life in the outer world, and it's important for Introverts to acknowledge that all the demands and stimuli put a strain on them. Though Introverts usually prefer to live in their own head, using their minds to create allows them to recharge, giving them the opportunity to use their dominant functions. At these times, when they create something tangible, a rare window is cracked opened for others to see into their private inner world—and catch a glimpse of their amazing strengths.

The Inferior Function

Concerning the inferior function, this is the least developed of the three functions, and it only starts to emerge as we mature (also known as type development). Some suppose that our inferior function is the secret to our creativity, but how can this be? While leaning on our weaknesses does provide some balance, our weaknesses will always be inferior to our strengths. If you are right handed, you prefer to throw with your right hand; however, when you are driving, you sometimes have to throw coins into toll buckets with your left hand. Even though your least favorite hand—your least favorite strength—is perfectly capable, using it isn't the secret to becoming an all-star pitcher or unlocking your greatness. Although it adds some value, your inferior function cannot compare to what you can achieve by using your strengths.

─────∿∿∿∿∿─────○

There is, of course, much more to say on the subtle interplay of one's dominant, auxiliary, and inferior functions—so much so that it could be its own chapter. If you're really interested in MBTI and wish to explore the topic of functions further, *Gifts Differing* by Isabel Briggs Myers, et al. is a wonderful source to consult. Please see the bibliography at the back of the book for details.

Up next are the sixteen creative profiles.

The Sixteen Creative Types

The Organizer (ISTJ)—Introverted, Sensing, Thinking, Judging (page 102)

The Facilitator (ISFJ)—Introverted, Sensing, Feeling, Judging (page 106)

The Visionary (INTJ)—Introverted, Intuitive, Thinking, Judging (page 110)

The Inspirer (INFJ)—Introverted, Intuitive, Feeling, Judging (page 113)

The Crafter (ISTP)—Introverted, Sensing, Thinking, Perceiving (page 116)

The Organizer (ISTJ)—Introverted, Sensing, Thinking, Judging

A watchmaker experiments in private to make a mechanical watch from scratch that is more precise than any quartz model. Like the dependability of a ticking clock, if you're an ISTJ, you can be counted on to be austere, objective, realistic, and traditional. There are 16 percent of men and 7 percent of women who are represented by this type.[1]

For the Organizer, creativity involves solving today's problems using practical solutions from the memory of what has worked before. Often, creativity takes the courage to be first. George Washington, as the military leader of the American Revolutionary War, was known for his bravery, unwavering character, and administration skills. As the first president of the United States, Washington's brilliance came through in his implementation of the ideals held by the founding fathers, setting precedents, and creating a culture of service in government that still exists today.

When ideas originate from a respected source, ISTJs add value by stepping in to carry out the ideas in a practical way. If you are an ISTJ, you don't need an endless supply of new ideas to be creative; you just need one. Ford said in *My Life and Work*, "It is better to concentrate on perfecting [an existing idea] than to hunt around for a new idea. One idea at a time is about as much as anyone can handle."[2]

If you're a traditionalist and a planner, how do you act creatively? ISTJs show that creativity can be found in routine, and can involve following the rules and fulfilling requirements. An Organizer mom didn't want her brownies to be too fudgy or too much like cake, so she mixed together fudge and cake recipes to get the consistency she wanted.

Most discoveries and innovations aren't glamorous but come about by combining technologies or making small improvements on what we already have. Henry Ford, for example, was a tinkerer whose creativity literally took off when he invented the first self-propelled vehicle—a proto-automobile called the Quadricycle—by combining four bicycle wheels with the tiller of a boat for steering. By combining individual items to make something new, Ford's device retained the look of the individual items, in this case looking like a pair of bicycles with the tiller of a boat. Another way to break this down is that the difference between N and S innovation is that Intuitive innovation tends to add a 1 and a 2 to get something completely new, like a 3, while a Sensing innovation tends to add a 1 and a 2 to get 12, like Ford's vehicle is made of parts added together.

Like Ford, ISTJs prefer to be creative within a system by combining different components; making improvements to processes and quality; and reducing costs, time, and the amount of required materials.

ISTJs are able to create within systems because they excel at gathering large swaths of detailed facts and cataloguing them, from the streets on a map and the times on a bus schedule to the fluctuation of gasoline prices and the cost of corn. Colors, textures, sounds, and aromas are absorbed and reflected upon. When they think of the old house at the lake, they recall the worn tire swing and the creaky white Adirondack chairs. They notice and remember the grass-stained footprints that marred the wraparound porch in the foreground but also the details of the hillside and maple trees in the background. Isabel Briggs Myers said that, when relaxed and free of responsibility, sometimes ISTJs share a "vivid private reaction" that is "all their own and unpredictable."[3] The strength of the creative process comes from using their storehouse of memories to solve today's problems.

Using his attention for detail and meticulous memory when he is being creative, an Organizer engineer interviewed for the book explained that he enjoys improving on what already exists, but it takes time getting the process right. He starts a job by reading the directions and thinking through each step, and he won't start until he has the whole procedure worked out. He recalls being criticized once at work for taking too long in the design stage and not enough time in the construction phase. It later became evident that his careful attention in these early planning phases created designs that used existing facilities in ways that were less expensive and quicker than gutting and starting from scratch.

ISTJs keep much of what they observe to themselves until it's ready to share. The face they show the world comes from their Thinking preference, so they tend to express detailed descriptions of facts in a clear and organized fashion. This tendency is also evident in their creations. ISTJs are driven to maintain calmness and stability and in our chaotic world, this takes creativity.

If you're an ISTJ, you are among the most private of the sixteen types. And as an Organizer, you don't like it when people come along and change your systems. However, because you are also the most dutiful, it's your sense of responsibility that drives you out of your shell. When it's expected, you'll leave your comfort zone to become an outgoing host, speaker, actor, or performer.

ISTJs re-create memories of sensations, like cooking delicious lasagna from their memory of eating in a classic Italian restaurant. Through their process of Introverted reflection, their mind wanders from reality as they prioritize and simplify (necessary ingredients, balance of flavors, homemade versus mass produced). With some details becoming more important than others, their daydreams are quickly reined in by their TJ (Thinking Judger) preferences. And what they ultimately express—the finished dish—is so authentic, you wouldn't know the tomato sauce came from a jar.

For an Organizer, creativity is very real. Most known for his iconic painting *Nighthawks*, Edward Hopper, who seemed to be an ISTJ, was a realist American painter who depicted stark urban landscapes, empty streets, isolated figures, and the architecture of old buildings. With little success until late in his life, Hopper earned his living by teaching and working as an illustrator. As a teacher, he maintained a serious classroom atmosphere and was known to dismiss students when they were too silly or insincere. As an illustrator, he disliked self-promotion and was frustrated by clients who asked him to alter facts. One time, when designing a movie poster featuring the Napoleonic wars, Hopper illustrated the soldiers in French uniforms of that period only to be instructed (much to his annoyance) to cater to popular American taste by repainting them to look like US soldiers. "Catering to the mass market would never be [Hopper's] forte," noted Gail Levin in *Edward Hopper: An Intimate Portrait*.[4] Hopper took plenty of time selecting his subjects before he simplified, organized, and expressed the facts—all very characteristic of a devout ISTJ.

ISTJ creativity looks like an accurate and detailed description of facts that record experiences in a straightforward way. It is brief and purposeful, expressing a sense of neatness, order, and seriousness through the details. An Organizer sees individual objects such as gears, nuts, and bolts as separate pieces of information, and seeking clarity—in artwork, for example—they prefer to show each piece as separated, outlined, and clearly identifiable, making it clear what is an apple and what is an orange. Then, in keeping with their fastidiousness, ISTJs veil their process: they file their blueprints, clean and put away their cookware, erase their pencil marks, and smooth out their brushstrokes. Any trace of their creativity is eliminated beyond the final product itself.

ISTJs tend to appreciate the plain over the glitzy, where "personal property, price, and durability are of primary concern," and "classics, antiques, and heirlooms are especially valued."[5] Attracted by nostalgia, ISTJs include places and events as subjects in their creations, more often than people. And when figures are included, they're often isolated and rigid, like the people in Hopper's paintings.

If you're an Organizer, more than doing what you want to do, you do what you think *should* be done. You cautiously and objectively evaluate which ideas to implement and which projects to undertake. Once accepted, you carefully plan and follow procedures, and persistently push through to completion.

ISTJs don't create "just for the sake of art"; creativity fills a need for them, such as fixing a squeaky door, commemorating an event, decorating a wall, or finding a faster route. Even their artwork has utility, and their purpose for creating may simply be to make a living. ISTJs are attracted to the hands-on nature of working with crafts, and they enjoy tangible output. They may be especially attracted to photography for its accuracy, equipment, and processes. For example, in his down time, the Organizer engineer mentioned earlier also enjoys photography and photo manipulation on his computer, where small changes—cropping, altering contrast, tweaking color balance—make pleasing improvements. He says he isn't as interested in making big changes, but he is proud of his ability to split and recombine images to add missing people to a group shot, for example.

As comedians, ISTJs have a literal sense of humor. Johnny Carson, remembering high school, said, "People might say, 'Oh, he's conceited, he's aloof.' Actually, [I] was more shy. See, when I'm in front of an audience . . . , it's a different thing. If I'm in front of an audience, I can feel comfortable because I'm in control."[6] Carson was able to separate his professional life from his personal life, and after he retired, he disappeared from public view. As authors, ISTJs write accurate descriptions with details galore; as musicians, they play sheet music to precision; and as actors, they follow the script and take whatever role is asked of them.

If you're an Organizer, some of your biggest challenges in being creative occur when doing something new requires you to abandon tradition—your process. Operating without a clear objective and having too little time to plan causes discomfort, but your awareness of challenges like these helps to keep them in check.

Over time, ISTJs have one of the most consistent creative styles since they are continuously assessing their current work with what they completed in the past. ISTJs create classics that are realistic and rich in detail. Ford sounded like an ISTJ when he advised, "The man who will use his skill and constructive imagination to see how much he can give for a dollar, instead of how little he can give for a dollar, is bound to succeed."[7]

The Facilitator (ISFJ)—Introverted, Sensing, Feeling, Judging

It's difficult to see ISFJ creativity since so much of it happens behind the scenes. Humbly serving the poorest of the poor, the sick, and the dying, Mother Teresa was guided by her faith to found a worldwide family of missions that continues to help millions in need. Much like an ISFJ, she said, "Don't look for big things; just do small things with great love."[8]

For this type, like ISTJ (the Organizer), creativity comes through reflecting on today's problems to solve them with practicality and a sponge-like memory of what has worked before. As an SF (a Sensing Feeler), you gather great storehouses of detailed information, mostly about people. You remember faces, conversations, how grateful your friend felt, what flowers were blooming, what the air smelled like after the rainfall, and that the park bench you sat on felt damp.

Although gathering information through Sensing is their greatest strength, as Introverts, ISFJs conceal this, showing others their second-best strength of Feeling. As a Feeling decider, they pour all their data through a filter of personal values. So, if you're an ISFJ, your creativity reflects your dearest-held values, whether you are baking cookies to celebrate your friend's promotion or making scrapbooks of your family's history.

Making the world a nicer place to live, ISFJ is the most frequent type, accounting for 20 percent of women and 8 percent of men.[9] ISFJs are loyal, dependable, and dedicated to serving the needs of others, especially friends and family, and they have a sense of obligation to others—as well as themselves.

If you're an ISFJ, your creativity is inspired by the act of helping others. You're practical, reflecting on ideas that you can apply concretely to make tangible products; and you're a Facilitator, striving to promote harmony by being supportive of others while fostering a nurturing environment where creativity can thrive. Expressing your personal values in an agreeable, unassuming way, you tend to also express subtle messages to the benefit of others. An ISFJ chef, for example, may prepare a wonderful meal of foods he or she thinks others should be eating.

All parents are thrust into a role of being creative, but if you're an ISFJ parent, you will do what it takes to make things happen. Perhaps your child has her heart set on a crazy idea for a Halloween costume. Even if costume designing isn't your thing, you'll gather the necessary materials, tools, and talents to have the costume ready in time for trick-or-treating. Driven by your strong SJ sense of duty when it comes to serving to your family and promoting harmony, if your kids are bored, struggling, or upset, you will find ways to engage and support them.

As a Facilitator with the goal of doing what is most appropriate, you cautiously weigh your personal values to evaluate which projects to undertake. Once accepted, your procedures are carefully planned, and you are persistent in following through the steps to completion. Combine this with your powerful memories, and you are especially good at creating by recalling details, copying from others, and combining facts about people and events. A sense of neatness and order predominates your ISFJ creations, and your favorite subjects are often sentimental.

Two artists with a one-letter creative difference were Edward Hopper, an ISTJ (a Thinker), and Norman Rockwell, an ISFJ (a Feeler). This seemingly small difference in their personality preferences is clearly seen in the way they depicted people in their paintings. Hopper expressed deserted landscapes and lonely, stiff-looking figures; Rockwell depicted family life—everyday life—by illustrating the warm interrelations among people. As an ISFJ, Rockwell was known largely for his nostalgic images of life in small-town America, He was also a natural storyteller who, instead of talking before an audience, told his tales through pictures. Using mostly friends and family as subjects, and with his particular insight into human emotion, he mastered the facial features of his figures, showing what they were feeling.

Although Rockwell was a realist, he projected himself and his own values into his work by painting "life as I would like it to be."[10] Reserved and introspective, Rockwell was observant of details—particularly in relation to people—and carefully planned his work. He said, "I paint what I do the way I do because that's the way I feel about things."[11]

ISFJs are clearly inspired by people, but they prefer to observe from afar. Even though Rockwell used his friends as subjects, he still preferred working from photographs rather than from real life. Rockwell especially aimed to flatter, and this was seen when he created a portrait of President Johnson "as he would like to think he is."[12] Through his process and his paintings, Rockwell demonstrated how Facilitator creativity is planned, on time, aims to please (serve others), and follows the rules.

When they create, ISFJs put themselves in the audience's hearts and minds, asking themselves what the observer feels. As actors, they follow the script and enjoy character studies, role-playing, imaginative parts, reenactments of historical events, revivals of classic performances, and fantasy. Whether in the theater, an orchestra, or a business, ISFJs are excellent team players and take whatever positions are needed of them. As comedians, they have a literal sense of humor, laughing at and telling jokes about subjects like happiness and interpersonal relationships.

ISFJs tend to have consistent styles, as they are always comparing their current work with what they completed in the past. They play the role of curator well, as "they are honored to care for collections of rare old things, books, paintings, china."[13]

As we've already discussed, ISFJs create to fill a need; they are Facilitators who coordinate past experiences and current requirements to successfully honor a family member's birthday or fill an evening with entertainment for friends. As teachers, ISFJs mix and match lessons while following the curriculum. As writers, expect them to be straightforward, with accurate descriptions and details galore. As musicians, they play sheet music with precision and feeling. To that end, it was Johann Sebastian Bach who modestly pointed out, "I play the notes as they are written, but it is God who makes the music."[14]

ISFJs' biggest challenges occur when they must abandon tradition, operate without objectives or outside of their value systems, and have too little time to plan. If you're an ISFJ, being aware of this helps to keep things in perspective. You must also remember to respect your own thoughts and value yourself as much as you value the people you serve. Stand up and share your ISFJ ideas, even if they seem inconsequential. As Mother Teresa has shown, small acts matter and can make a tremendously positive contribution, especially when coming from a genuine, well-meaning place.

The Visionary (INTJ)—Introverted, Intuitive, Thinking, Judging

Do you know people who quietly follow their "plan A" but always have a series of "plan Bs" for every imaginable scenario? Inwardly focused, complicated, theoretical, and strategic, INTJs are imaginative wizards who direct and control from behind the curtain, and always have a contingency plan. People of this type are Visionaries who are future oriented but paradoxically have a practical side as they strive to execute plans.

If you're an INTJ, you generally keep your greatest strength—your Intuition—to yourself and publically express what sounds logical through your secondary Thinking, outwardly conveying confidence, competence, and decisiveness. You are vastly independent and are likely to be drawn to the freedom that can be obtained through creative activities. You're rare too, accounting for about 3 percent of men and less than 1 percent of women.[15]

Do you prefer to gather intangible concepts and spend your time contemplating, dreaming, and visualizing as your way to relax? INTJs take each piece of data and rotate it like squares on a Rubik's Cube to see how it can relate to information they have previously classified. It's a never-ending game of matching ideas and looking for patterns, as their minds are always churning. Surprisingly, the results they produce appear original, without resembling the elements that provided the inspirations. With so much processing required for new information, however, INTJs often get overwhelmed by their diverse interests and ideas, and the many sources they're collected from.

Since INTJs monitor many channels for new information, inspiration can come from seemingly everywhere, such as magazines advertisements, songs, travel, or a change in season. In quiet moments, INTJs periodically experience visions that strike like lightning bolts. As Thomas Edison said, "The first step is an intuition and it comes with a burst."[16]

As Visionaries, INTJs may have a creative process that involves starting with many "wild" ideas from their Intuition. INTJs innovate by leaping ahead, generating flashes of ideas that pass through their strong logical filter before making any hasty judgments. Then, after some reflection, their TJ (Thinking Judger) side gives clarity to their ideas, polishing them and making them presentable. Paul Cézanne explained the grounded side of an INTJ's creativity: "Imagination is a beautiful thing, but one must also have a firm base."[17] In time, with a foundation of making many leaps with successful landings, INTJs learn to trust their instincts and develop confidence in themselves.

Predicting what will happen next—as photographers, for example—INTJs anticipate where the action is likely to occur. However, while occupied with finding the best vantage points to test their predictions, they can miss what is currently happening. As these Visionaries innovate for the future, INTJs are reminded to look toward the details of what's happening in the moment to meet today's needs.

When you have a hammer, every problem looks like a nail; similarly, for INTJs, it's much like something Thomas Jefferson said: "The moment a person forms a theory, his imagination sees in every object only the traits that favor that theory."[18] If you're an INTJ experiencing stumbling blocks in your creative process, make sure that you're considering all the tools and options available to you. Thomas Jefferson was one who, by using all the means of his creative personality, was able to apply his diverse knowledge and interests to invent everyday items, and to help lay the foundation for an innovative form of government.

In fact, throughout the years, many INTJs have developed theories that have benefited humankind—something that may be particularly appealing to other INTJs. Abraham Maslow's theory of self-actualization is an INTJ type of model that values aloneness and independence. Another example is the strategic management model called SWOT: Strengths/Weakness and Opportunities/Threats, which formalizes the ways INTJs think.

Like other TJs (Thinking Judgers), INTJs have a need for exactness; and like other NTs (Intuitive Thinkers), they strive for competency. Decisions are evaluated based on logic. Selective rules and customs are followed under the condition that they are meaningful and reasonable. Because INTJs envision possibilities and see traps well in advance, they are quick to dismiss unproductive ideas and thereby experience a high rate of completion for what they start. On the other hand, they miss opportunities from seeds that are never planted. The projects INTJs select often involve complex ideas used for practical applications that are prioritized and optimized to meet future needs. Steve Jobs explained it this way: "Innovation . . . comes from saying no to one thousand things to make sure we don't get on the wrong track or try to do too much. We're always thinking about new markets we could enter, but it's only by saying no that you can concentrate on the things that are really important."[19]

Competence is important for this type, yet skills like drawing or playing a musical instrument take time to develop. Without having a necessary skill level, INTJs often decline to express their ideas if they cannot reach the high standards they expect of themselves.

INTJs are primarily strategic. For them, the arena for innovation is like a chessboard, where each move represents a purposeful choice that advances their position to an end. Every word in the novel, every gesture on the stage, and every brushstroke on the canvas is essentially one piece carrying out the mission of the whole.

Even though INTJs are creative, their type is rare, and they don't readily share their creations. Unless you frequent libraries or laboratories, you don't often see what they make. Furthermore, since they project an image of orderliness (and because creativity is so messy), they don't typically show their work until it's completed—just as Apple keeps its products quiet until they are launched. At its best, Visionary creativity looks like a sleek mobile phone on the outside, with all its immense complexity hidden inside its modest exterior. Again, in the words of Steve Jobs, "Some people think design means how it looks. But of course, if you dig deeper, it's really how it works."[20]

Do you prefer to work alone with ideas more than you like to work with people? Do you frequently use analogy and metaphor for describing your ideas, and do you decline to state what you consider obvious? If you're an INTJ, what you create is often carefully planned, complex, and serious. Like a controlled fire, INTJ creativity is controlled by figuratively roped-off safe areas for play—areas that leave room for the unexpected in a way that can be contained and managed. And although INTJs are independent and inclined to do everything themselves, they must still remember that to amplify their projects and allow their innovative ideas to spread, they must cooperate to gain the support of others.

Envisioning products or future events, INTJs ask, "What path is necessary to get there? What events need to happen for these two companies to merge? What technologies need to be developed for this satellite system to be viable?" Furthermore, INTJs reverse engineer what they see, and wherever they look, they wonder, "How did this come about?"

INTJs wrestle with the dilemma of balancing their need for completion with their inclination to improve everything, as there simply isn't enough time or energy to do both. They also must come to terms with how they define success. Often, their triumphs are fleeting because they raise their own standards as they are about to finish; when climbing the apple tree, just as they pull themselves up on the limb they were trying to reach, a higher branch becomes visible that bears more desirable fruit and a better view. INTJs need someone close to them to point out and celebrate their milestones—to teach them to give more value to what they attained and to have pride in their laurels. Otherwise, INTJs "are motivated by inspirations, which they value above everything else," and they build on their successes to climb higher and higher.[21]

If you're an INTJ, you are most creative in developing theories that can be applied to solve future problems. To increase your effectiveness, you are reminded to occasionally think about people's reactions and to consider the details of today's issues. As Cézanne explained, "You have to create your own vision . . . create a perspective of your own, to see nature as though no one has ever seen it before."[22] He also is known to have said, "In my thought, one doesn't replace the past; one only adds a new link to it."[23] The INTJ Visionary links concepts and theories to create unique visions of how things could be, and then works tirelessly to make those visions a reality.

The Inspirer (INFJ)—Introverted, Intuitive, Feeling, Judging

Inspiring others, INFJs are contemplative visionaries whose creative style is driven by the possibilities they see in people. INFJs are the rarest type, making up about 1 percent of the population and having equal numbers of males and females.[24]

INFJs' strength and inspiration for their creativity comes from their rich imagination of fantasy and theory through their dominant Intuition, while they persistently and outwardly express their own personal values using their second strength, Feeling. "There is an indefinable, mysterious power that pervades everything. I feel it, though I do not see it," described Mohandas Gandhi, who continued, "It transcends the senses."[25] Gandhi used nonviolent civil disobedience to lead the independence movement in India. In true INFJ form, Gandhi internalized his message by using his own body to endure hunger strikes and imprisonment—a bold, creative act of passionate defiance that sent ripples throughout the globe *and* history.

If you're an INFJ (an Inspirer), you may agree with philosopher and poet Ralph Waldo Emerson when he said, "People only see what they are prepared to see."[26] As an IJ (Introverted Judger), you contemplate and plan, and as an NF (Intuitive Feeler), you see what is meaningful and corresponds with your values. Furthermore, your reflectiveness and Intuition allow you to visualize ideas without requiring an actual stimulus to be present. The visions in your mind's eye are what you share; however, being private, you may prefer to express indirectly through complexities and abstractions.

INFJs develop an understanding of individuals by evaluating past context with present events. Connecting the dots in people's personalities allows them to construct multifaceted composites. Besides people, they also notice patterns and trends. And when they overlay their understanding of people with the trends that they see, a vision of the future emerges.

An Inspirer's ideas may bubble up through different creative outlets. In spite of his "mad genius" persona, Vincent van Gogh's eight hundred letters reveal a theoretical and intelligent dreamer with a grounded side. Religion played an important part in his life, and he particularly empathized with the poor. INFJs often strive for something beyond material or financial rewards, and Van Gogh was particularly rewarded when he made others happy. After completing a commission for one dealer, he said, "Because my work pleased him from first to last, I consider myself already sufficiently paid."[27]

Van Gogh was methodical and planned his painting with preliminary studies made on location. "I try to grasp what is essential," he explained.[28] Once the bones of a painting were planned, he felt free to work from his Intuition: "My brush stroke has no system at all. I hit the canvas with irregular touches of the brush, which I leave as they are."[29] If you are an INFJ, do his words resonate with you? Try to start projects by roughly planning the essentials and overall theme like Van Gogh did. Then use the strength of your Intuition to follow through.

As Inspirers, INFJs also share their visions through words. "They use an unusual degree of imagery in their language—the kind of imagery found in complex and often aesthetic writing, such as novels, plays, and poems ... They are masters of the metaphor."[30] Metaphors can persuade and enlighten by making intangibles into something physical. Gandhi frequently spoke in metaphors to get his point across: "You must not lose faith in humanity. Humanity is an ocean; if a few drops of the ocean are dirty, the ocean does not become dirty."[31]

Like Gandhi, INFJs contemplate and strategize about interrelationships, and prefer to quietly lead and direct from behind the scenes. By keeping many of their thoughts to themselves, their creativity isn't immediately apparent to others or even to themselves. Isabel Briggs Myers explained, "A masterpiece of insight into human relations may not look original at all. It is so accurate that it looks obvious."[32]

With INFJs not being entirely sure where their thoughts come from, one idea sparks the next in their minds. Yet, in spite of this flurry of ideas, these Inspirers are decisive, and their thoughts are categorized, evaluated for feasibility, and then executed upon. INFJs wish to bring people together and create harmony, and being goal oriented and purposeful, they often achieve this. As people who consider the big picture and are inspired to advance human causes, they are aided by remembering to take the extra step to look beyond themselves and consider other people's values.

Mostly, INFJs aim to create what others experience on an emotional plane. Their stories are planned, multilayered, and interconnected by relationships and complex situations; the words they choose contain multiple meanings. As actors, they use their understanding of people to morph into almost any role, especially if it doesn't require them to divulge too much of their true self. And they are most interested in projects that correspond with their aim to advance their social, religious, or political views.

INFJs aren't bound by traditions; however, what they create often looks orderly—sometimes in an abstract way. Just as they connect large ideas, they also connect large shapes without dwelling on the details. An INFJ creation is usually full of interconnections related to the people they know, though INFJs are also open to trying and adopting new techniques—as long as these ideas don't conflict with their ideals. For example, if an INFJ comes to believe that a poem should follow a certain format, they may feel that a deviation is a betrayal to their craft.

The Inspirers are reminded to share their ideas and show the steps they traveled to reach their conclusion in order gain others support. Also, as they connect the dots about possibilities in people to form patterns, the Inspirers are cautioned to verify the facts before jumping to conclusions.

Overall, as Inspirers, INFJs use their creativity to align people for a mission, to beautify the environment, to teach people to see what can be, or to improve the human condition. They're determined to bring to life what they envision, and they have a high completion rate for the range of creative projects that interest them. Furthermore, INFJs implement visions that are integral with themselves, as Gandhi conveyed: "My life is my message."[33]

The Crafter (ISTP)—Introverted, Sensing, Thinking, Perceiving

Creative solutions don't need to be sentimental, abstract, or planned—and certainly not pretentious. At the scene of an accident, ISTPs keep cool heads, but they also don't follow rules. They disregard plans, they don't waste time, and they cut the red tape of bureaucracy. Instead, they quickly size up the trouble, survey their resources, and take immediate action to stop the bleeding. When others are slowed by regulations and concerned about hurt feelings, ISTPs provide the creative solutions that are vitally needed.

Jackson Pollack said, "It's all a big game of construction—some with a brush, some with a shovel, some choose a pen."[34] If you're an ISTP, you're the Crafter who's quietly building and constantly searching for opportunities to be active. About 9 percent of men and 2 percent of women are represented by this type.[35] ISTPs are all action with little talk, "shooting first" but also uninterested in "asking questions later." At times, Pollack would spend a dinner party in silence, leaving his wife to explain to their guests, "He does not believe in talking; he believes in doing."[36] Since ISTPs don't say much, we must watch what they do to understand them.

As an ISTP, your greatest strength comes through the logic and clarity of your Thinking; but as an Introvert, you keep this to yourself. What you show is Sensing, your second-best strength. ISTPs are realists who see objective details like a camera. In a tight real-estate market, how do you accurately photograph an apartment to maximize its appeal to potential buyers? ISTPs make quick fixes, working with what's available as they size up the space. They use their imagination to reposition the lighting; they rearrange houseplants and pillows; they polish the coffee table and remove the clutter as they shoo the dog outside and sweep the dust under the rug. One click of the shutter later, and they're gone.

Being curious, ISTPs collect vast amounts of information as facts, then treat them as singular experiences that don't need to be further analyzed and classified. Like INTPs (the Idea Mills), they are private and content with the intrinsic satisfaction that comes from the "Aha!" moments that cross their minds, so they don't care to share with others.

What ISTPs make is often seen as impersonal and detached, and is rarely considered warm or emotionally expressive. As Crafters, they are likely to work directly with tools, indirectly with people, and from their imagination. One ISTP marketing specialist explained that she makes her presentations for clients to "get their attention and to get them excited in the first two minutes." She uses her strong visual memory in her work, and when she is creating, she says, "I love to simplify and re-create past experiences."

An ISTP's purpose is frequently the task of creating action, and the act—the process—is more important than the results. ISTPs are always looking for an opportunity to collect facts, turning every doorknob to see if it will open the door to new information or reveal new weaknesses to exploit.

In the creative process, a lot of unexpected events come about. These surprises are important to ISTPs, but they don't waste time predicting or planning for them. When the planets align, they notice the perfect timing and instinctively capitalize on the chance. As Crafters, they are hands on, developing techniques for using tools and machines with the precision of a surgeon or the knack of a mechanic. In fact, they seem to know how to use the right tool with just the right amount of energy to get their desired results without overexertion. ISTPs innovate best to solve immediate problems by working alone, offering practical solutions that use unorthodox techniques and whatever material is currently available.

An ISTP graphic artist explained that he gets his inspiration by just starting to work, and then one idea leads to the next. He finds his process to be long and over-whelming, however, since there are so many different avenues to pursue and the details matter to him. To help him along, he likes to have music on, some toys around, and a window to provide distractions when he needs to defocus. He says the process is what it's all about, as "thinking about art or having art is not the same as making art." Disliking the thought that art needs meaning, he wants his animations and 3-D models to look so textured and authentic that the viewer "can rip away the computer screen and fall right in."

For ISTPs, beauty is skin deep, because it's the surface qualities such as color and texture that matter most as they design and create. Another ISTP artist said that he loves to sketch figures and especially enjoys seeing the different shapes that bodies have, but he limits his interest to their skin's surface. He elaborated, "Models are figures, not people, and I have no interest in what happens under the skin." If you are a Crafter, remember that you can create with more depth and communicate with more reach if you stop to consider people as living and breathing human beings.

Without worrying about regulations, procedures, traditions, or what other people think, ISTPs are independent, original, and free to create as they please, without constraints. This allows them to challenge and disrupt the status quo. And since their least developed function is Feeling, they don't typically feel a need to consider other people's values, which can make their creations seem irreverent. ISTPs enjoy being unpredictable and avoid routines, and their creations can develop in a self-determining way that takes its own zigzag course. If you are an ISTP, take the occasional step back to look at the larger picture by considering how others may react to your solutions. This will help you to avoid traveling down some blind and ultimately unproductive alleyways.

Georgia O'Keeffe, famous for her floral paintings, was practical, unsentimental, and straightforward. As she explained, "I hate flowers—I paint them because they're cheaper than models and they don't move."[37] Although ISTPs reflect on practical matters, they take pleasure in the physical much more than the mental. "My thinking time does not make me feel like I am doing anything," said Andy Warhol. "My thinking time isn't worth anything. I only expect to get paid for my doing time."[38] ISTPs enjoy working alone, get satisfaction from the act of creating, and are more interested in keeping people guessing than in sharing. Warhol, for one, would not give a straight answer to questions.

Rarely does the innovative Crafter show his or her pencil marks, brushstrokes, or first drafts; ISTPs cover their tracks, concealing their process and their techniques. Creativity for the ISTP looks clear and fun, as they juxtapose everything under the sun. Georgia O'Keeffe said, "I really played with the material . . . I did not work unless it was easy."[39] As performers, they improvise; as comedians, they are witty and literal; as cartoonists, they outline; and as authors, they are concise, and use the latest expressions and slang.

If you are an ISTP, you are most creative in patching up immediate problems with quick fixes during emergencies. You can be even more effective by considering how people will react to your solutions and by thinking about how your solutions will fit into the global scheme of things. Recognize that you follow your own path and use your creativity to create actions that aren't directly expressed with words.

The Dreamer (ISFP)—Introverted, Sensing, Feeling, Perceiving

Thinking back to the time when he was a schoolboy, Pablo Picasso recalled that he would purposely get into trouble and provoke his teachers because he enjoyed the isolation of detention. There, nobody could bother him, and he could dream and draw in peace. If you are an ISFP, does this sound like something you would do?

Searching for opportunities to make action and promote harmony, ISFPs are all action with little talk. There are about 8 percent of men and 10 percent of women who represent this type.[40] Although Feeling is their greatest strength, they conceal this and show in public their second best—Sensing.

Although they may be embarrassed to say so, ISFPs often see themselves as creative and are drawn to the arts. "When an especially gifted painter, sculptor, choreographer, film director, song writer, playwright, poet, novelist, chef, decorator, or fashion designer shows up, he or she is likely to be an ISFP."[41] Expressing through their creative pursuits is one of the best avenues for them to show their true self and to engage with their work. However, for ISFPs, inspiration comes via their deep emotions and inner passion—two things that are not very easy for ISFPs to express. Jung said that Feelers "demand a more than ordinary description or artistic ability before the real wealth of this feeling can be even approximately presented or communicated to the world."[42] In order to fully present their ideas, ISFPs must first make the effort to develop a threshold level of artistic skills.

ISFPs are Dreamers who quietly sense the beauty and intricacies of the natural world around them, and they have the "ability to work with the slightest nuance of color, tone, texture, aroma, and flavor."[43] Their reflectiveness—along with being a Feeling decider—positions them to have a great understanding of the people and animals around them. And when this understanding is expressed through their creativity, emotionally deep and nuanced characters are made for the stories ISFPs create.

Another personification of the ISFP type was the very humble Charles Schulz, as well as the Charlie Brown character he created. Schulz observed small distinctions in human nature and was able to simplify them into cartoons that everyone relates to. His advice to prospective cartoonists: "I think what you have to do is draw from your own personality and your own experience,"[44] something he did with the Peanuts gang, who were based on bits of himself as well as his friends and family. Ideas came to him spontaneously—Monday's cartoon led to Tuesday's—which was fortunate, since he dreaded his deadlines and had trouble sitting still for long. "I never go too deep that it's not funny," he said. "I think, if I have a knack, it's a knack [for] kind of skimming the surface of information and making it funny."[45] Even so, Schulz checked his facts with doctor and lawyer friends to ensure his medical and legal jokes were accurate, and his character Schroeder played actual musical notes on his piano.

As idealists who are rooted in reality, ISFPs "contrast between the real and the ideal,"[46] and this gap is explored in what they create. If you're an ISFP, try to create using fictional characters alongside real characters, such as the cartoons in *Who Framed Roger Rabbit*, or try placing a real character in a dreamlike setting, like Dorothy in *The Wizard of Oz*. As Dreamers who are adventurous and curious, and who collect vast amounts of realistic information about people, animals, and nature, ISFPs reflect on all their data by personalizing it with their internal values. They borrow innovations from their contemporaries (just as Picasso borrowed from Braque, Matisse, Degas, and Van Gogh, among others) and make those ideas their own. Whether it's a painting, story, or dance, the ISFPs create by juxtaposition highly personal and emotional expressions of their deepest feelings. And as they strive to promote harmony, all of the colors meld, the cast of characters fit the story, and the musical notes flow flawlessly together.

Consider this example: A Filipino ISFP chef who cooks for hundreds of people at church gatherings was too humble to say she was creative in the kitchen (even though she clearly is creative). In her process, she follows a recipe once to get the idea of how it's done and then never looks at it again, going beyond any procedure to mix and match techniques and do it her way. Driven to avoid wasting ingredients, she looks around to see what must be used that day and substitutes accordingly. She also has such an attuned sense for the weight or quantity of each ingredient that she doesn't have to use a scale or measuring cup. With grace, she slices up the vegetables and rolls out the dough to just the right thickness. The subtle textures of each piece of food matter too; whether it needs to be crispy or tender, she cooks each ingredient to perfection.

After opening up a little more, the chef admitted that her creativity really comes out when decorating boring-looking food, like adding some leftover red peppers to the top of tofu slices to make them look more appealing. Outsiders may assume her extraordinarily creative meals are whipped up, but it's all in a day's work for this and other ISFPs wielding their unique, innovative style of creativity.

Living in the moment and responding to meet immediate needs, ISFPs are most creative in environments where unexpected interpersonal events occur. Not trying to make predictions, they see little value in wasting time planning for what may never happen. They are hands on and tactical, developing excellent techniques for using their various implements. Whatever forms of creativity ISFPs pursue, their creations are spontaneous and heartfelt.

Like other SPs (Sensing Perceivers), ISFPs avoid routine, ignore procedures, and don't typically feel the weight of time pressure. This leaves them free to create without following tradition, but they can be influenced by the people around them. Their lack of urgency and their continual search for additional data results in many unfinished projects. Thinking is their least developed function, and generally, as Feelers, they don't consider any logic that clashes with their personal values.

Although these Dreamers reflect on the concrete elements of life, they value the physical to a greater extent than the mental. ISFPs are independent; they like working alone behind the scenes; and they don't care to persuade or compete, quietly waiting for their talents to be discovered. At times, they aid causes they believe in. However, the main reason they create is for the personal satisfaction of engaging in an activity.

Much like ISTPs (the Crafters), ISFPs keep their process to themselves, concealing all clues that lead to how they achieve their results. This includes eliminating brushstrokes or pencil lines, and keeping preliminary sketches private. Emotionally charged expressions of nature, friends, family, and animals are favorite subjects for ISFPs, and what they create cannot be easily explained with words. They're also encouraging to others but rarely criticize others' work.

If you are an ISFP, are you anything like Charles Schulz or Pablo Picasso? And if so, how can you be connected to two artists who have the same creative type but create products that look so different?

Despite these differences, Schulz and Picasso had things in common. As Feelers, both artists included people they knew as subjects, and their values were shaped by their own society—whether it was a Bohemian life in Spain or hockey, church, and family in Middle America. As Introverts, each preferred to work from his imagination instead of directly from life. They were both action-oriented SPs (Sensing Perceivers), and the figures in their work were outlined and often in two dimensional form. Having the same four-letter preferences is like starting with the same four crayons: with these four crayons, vastly different results can be obtained—especially if you're an ISFP Dreamer. This is a testament to the range in styles that are possible with the same inborn personality type.

We learn from Picasso about how ISFPs create, seeing that they need time alone to contemplate. They absorb ideas and gain inspirations from the values and people who are important to them. This means borrowing exciting ideas from their contemporaries and morphing them into something personal. And following the ISFP lead, we learn that if you are going to borrow ideas, borrow from the best, as Picasso did. We also learn that not everything has to be finished; a work in progress can still hold up as a creation that inspires others to think of the possibilities.

The Idea Mill (INTP)—Introverted, Intuitive, Thinking, Perceiving

Despite what you might think, creativity doesn't have to be touchy-feely, emotionally moving, or collaborative. In fact, INTPs demonstrate that creativity doesn't even have to exist outside of one's own mind.

Albert Einstein said, "I am enough of an artist to draw freely upon my imagination. Imagination is more important than knowledge. Knowledge is limited; imagination encircles the world."[47] Einstein, along with Carl Jung, was among some of the great

INTP theorists. If you're an INTP, your creativity comes from your love of pondering infinite possibilities in the abstract as you make sense of randomness.

If you're an INTP (an Idea Mill), you are theoretical, flexible, and responsive as you adapt to immediate and future needs. You are independent and work best alone, as you have the greatest ability of all the types to concentrate and block outside stimuli. About 5 percent of men and about 2 percent of women are INTPs.[48]

J. M. W. Turner, regarded as one of Britain's greatest painters and the father of modern art, was a shy academic who acted as an INTP. Making his own rules, he once hung blank canvases at a prestigious Royal Academy exhibit. When the show opened, he spontaneously painted his entries as he tried to overshadow his competitors. Like Turner, INTPs accomplish much at the last minute, and although their expressions appear to be wholly spontaneous, what they create often comes from connections made over a significant amount of time in their imagination.

Driven by competition and to develop competency, INTPs' greatest strength comes through logically analyzing and objectively processing data—through Thinking. This isn't the face they show in public, however. To others, they can appear scattered since what they voice is often the haphazard information they gather through Intuition, their auxiliary function.

Drawing upon inspiration from outside-world connections and being especially comfortable with chaos, INTPs see abstract patterns and meaning where others see randomness. They strip away emotional aspects and irrelevant factors to see the logic of underlying principles. As Idea Mills that are constantly churning, INTPs contemplate and transform possibilities like the patterns of colored glass in a turning kaleidoscope. For INTPs, solving problems is similar to building a jigsaw puzzle to which new pieces are continuously being added. In fact, they masterfully make new designs to accommodate these new pieces without disturbing the system, as new information is always welcome. One INTP said that although she doesn't think about people much, in the context of business, she's always trying to introduce people who might help each other, enabling them to complete their own "network" of puzzle pieces.

As INTPs try to express their big ideas, they seek to do so with clarity—but this is a relative term. Using their own symbols, shorthand notations, and assumptions, what they consider to be clear can still be ambiguous to the average viewer, much like Einstein's equations and Jung's writings.

Although you can be productive as an INTP in your chosen field, for you, your thoughts matter more than the end product. Being private and lacking the need to persuade others, INTPs are motivated by their own internal satisfaction. Thinking through an idea is enough, and they rarely have the need to bring their ideas into tangible form for others to see. So, much of their greatness never gets exposed or expressed.

Since much happens in their vivid imaginations, Idea Mills need a call to action with some urgency—a deadline for a proposal, a performance, or even a pointed question—to coax them out of their mind to form a creative expression that can be appreciated by others. Once they trust you, they will let you in to see their world without these external motivations.

With so much in hidden in their minds, what does it look like when INTP creativity takes a tangible form? Einstein, Jung, and Turner were complex and abstract. If you saw Turner's seascapes from a distance, you would recognize them right away as they glow from across the room. Examine them close up, however, and they look like entanglements of colors—free-flowing shapes without firm boundaries that blend into each other, join with the background, and run off the canvas without making a recognizable image. Up close, Turner's paintings make no sense.

Turner had "no systematic process" as he "drove the colors about on the paper until an image emerged that expressed the idea in his mind."[49] Clawing with his fingers, scratching with tools, purposely blurring outlines by making random lines around their edges, he did whatever it took to achieve his vision. And he was never really finished, as he continuously tweaked his work, even after it was hung on the wall.

Back in his day, Turner painted abstractions and spoke in riddles, but today's communication demands clarity. If you're an Idea Mill, ask yourself: *Do my creations make sense to others? Or do others need more clues to understand my work?* The writing of an

INTP novelist tends to be nonlinear, containing assumptions, metaphors, and seemingly unrelated storylines. Yet as the pages turn, most of the threads gradually interconnect. One INTP writer we interviewed had this process: "I say what I had to say and then write the introduction and conclusion. How could you know what you wanted to say until you said it?"

If you're an INTP, remember that it's productive to step out of your head once in a while. An INTP described that she was initially excited by the prospect of going to a teacher's conference to learn more about what was happening in her field. When the day came, however, she felt constrained by the back-to-back schedule of talks and dreaded the thought of spending the day with strangers. Afterward, upon reflection, she was happy to have gone since she learned some new ideas and made some new contacts.

Futuristic, enjoying science fiction, generally comfortable with technology—all these traits, along with a curious nature, compel INTPs to push every button and lose track of time as they endlessly explore possibilities. Creating computer animations, three-dimensional models, or spreadsheets are especially appealing, as the computer's virtual space extends an Idea Mill's inner world. Computers also allow INTPs to create in a theoretical and private way without having to roll up their sleeves or put on an apron, and as Introverts, remote communication is often preferred instead of face-to-face meetings.

Experimental and innovative, INTPs are always running tests and starting new endeavors that, even when left unfinished, are seen as future possibilities. As absent-minded professors, their workspace may have piles of implements, media, supplies, equipment, references, and remains from past projects scattered about. What is in plain sight to others is invisible to an INTP until it's needed. Then, after the item is used and set down, it once again disappears into the sands of their workspace. One INTP we interviewed explained it this way:

> I have aspirations to learn and prove to myself that I can do things, such as learn to play guitar, but have little need to master it. I get a lot accomplished because I hate

deadlines and complete them to get them out of the way—so I don't have to think about them. I am relatively neat but have stacks of papers and books everywhere. When I must clean, like before people come over, I often get distracted and start reading, and never get organized. When I do put [the materials] away, I tend to not go back to them again.

I embrace change and lead change at work by focusing on why the future will be better. I started a new monthly summary report at work. The fun part is gathering information from everywhere and designing a new format. When I ask for help, it's when the design is finished, and it has to be updated each month. Repetition is drudgery.

With time to reflect, INTPs enthusiastically generate alternatives and initiate change as the architects of complex initiatives. Their great contributions come through seeing the big picture and creating theories, systems, spreadsheets, or paintings from what others see as messy, complicated situations. If you are an INTP, you benefit from watching deadlines, sharing your ideas with others, and thinking about how other people will react to your innovations. It's also best to present your ideas in a tangible form, such as blueprints, models, drawings, or even written notes. Additionally, you must remember to make sure your audience understands your ideas before you leap ahead to the next round.

INTPs are endlessly curious, independent thinkers whose designs are more likely to follow the laws of nature than to follow the rules of humans. One Idea Mill says, "Though I can read and follow directions when I must, I find that my mind immediately goes to editing and altering the directions to incorporate experimentation and deviation from any standard way of doing things." Constantly asking "Why?" and needing to understand the context, INTPs are mainly inspired by the quest to understand the dynamics of systems. Once a system is fully understood, however, they often lose interest.

The infinite possibilities, complexities, and directions of an INTP's creative pursuits can keep an him or her engaged for a lifetime. As Einstein wisely instructed, "The important thing is not to stop questioning."[50]

The Muser (INFP)—Introverted, Intuitive, Feeling, Perceiving

If you're an INFP (a Muser), you are most comfortable generating possibilities at the beginning of the creative process. Because of your curiosity, your ideas are endless (especially those related to possibilities in people). You provide leadership by adhering to your own values. If you enjoy spending time in your own world, playing with ideas and patterns associated with people—and if you are frequently misunderstood—you may be an INFP.

INFPs have a vivid imagination, and are autobiographical and poetic. Although making up only about 4 percent of the general population, they are one of the most common types to be writers or to work in the fine arts (theatre, sculpture, music, and so on).[51]

As an INFP, you contemplate before acting, and although it's unseen by others, this is the real strength of your creativity. You sort through endless connections and patterns from present and past experiences, making and breaking links as you synthesize what is whole and new.

Topics of morality, ethics, and the human condition are often a central theme in INFP work, as INFPs approach problems from multiple dimensions by putting themselves in other people's shoes. They wonder about how others would feel, interweaving many sources and time periods into a tapestry of thoughts to create characters that are real and multidimensional. If a Muser writes a story about war, it is about more than planes and tanks; it takes on the personal story of a soldier, his dilemmas about using deadly force, the suffering he experienced as a child, his misunderstandings with his father—and all of this before a backdrop showing the hardships of the economic conditions of the time.

Although Feeling is their strongest function, INFPs keep this to themselves and share their Intuition instead. In comfortable environments and when talking about subjects that interest them, INFPs can be confused for Extraverts, as they freely share the ideas flowing from their endless Intuition. What INFPs say and create may seem spontaneous and random as well, but as Musers, their creations are often drawn from ideas that have been spinning around in their minds for some time.

INFPs have strong opinions based on their personal values and learn to trust their individuality. In what they wear, for example, INFPs may visualize a nontraditional outfit, put the pieces and accessories together, and wear it without regard for others' opinions. They don't impose these preferences, however, and they don't try to control the groups they join. Instead, their presence as part of a group supports the creative culture. An adherence to values, an innate understanding of people, and an encouraging nature—especially when searching for the right solution—make INFPs an inspiration to others.

Although they are fun loving, INFPs aren't superficial in what they express. If they don't like their world, they create their own world, generating abstract symbols with layers of meaning. INFPs are the most likely type to think in abstractions as they make connections and use analogies steeped with personal meanings and future possibilities. "They have a gift for interpreting symbols, as well as creating them, and thus, often write in lyric, poetic fashion."[52] And INFPs have no desire to reveal the key to interpreting their symbols to anyone beyond their trusted circle of friends. Like a partially obscured self-portrait, INFPs abstract as a way to express without revealing their whole self. In fact, everything they create is a kind of self-portrait, as they create to try and better understand themselves. However, they still aren't inclined to share what they uncover.

With so much fantasy in their minds, INFP creativity can look dreamlike, whimsical, mysterious, or romantic—like an enchanted scene with medieval knights on horseback riding through a mist-covered forest. This creative type has a heightened awareness of certain contrasts, and they may create imaginative and fanciful stories where good triumphs over evil, the weak usurp the strong, or the poor outwit the rich. These Musers may see themselves in the role of the hero who slays the dragons or demons that lurk in their imaginations, and their creations may range from whimsical to dark, sometimes at the same time. Although INFPs are most interested in overall themes rather than details, they are so imaginative that instead of using actual facts, at times, they create their own details when necessary. Animals and plants are frequent subjects, for example, and INFPs have a way of empathizing with the feelings of anything—even the inanimate. A flower can have an attitude and a soul.

An INFP's least developed function is Thinking, and in decision making, personal values are considered over cold logic. As creative individuals, this frees INFPs from the laws of physics and rules of nature. In their stories, the mouse can be larger than an elephant, and they both can float in air. In their drawings, the sky can be green and the trees can be purple.

This type, like other NFP combinations, bears a keen insight into human emotion and a gift for producing expressive and emotional language. Furthermore, when INFP insights are united with their imagination, they create images of enormous emotion, like Edvard Munch's *The Scream*. Munch was speaking as an INFP when he described the purpose of art: "We need more than just photographs of nature. Nor should we content ourselves with painting pretty pictures to hang on sitting room walls . . . Let us try . . . to lay the foundation of an art dedicated to mankind. A style that will fire man's imagination, an art that springs from our very heart."[53]

With their internal connections to people, processing inner feelings is the great INFP strength—but this richness isn't easily articulated. It's especially important for INFPs to develop a means for expressing their visions, and participating in various creative activities could be the way. If you're an INFP, you need to develop a technique in something like writing, painting, or dance so you can translate your feelings into a form that others can understand. Some INFPs are driven to become superb craftspeople to better share their emotions and visions. Without developing skills in some medium, however, INFPs can get frustrated.

Of course, every person is different, and we all have different values and make different life choices. But INFPs, in all their varied flavors, most often use their personal values to make decisions. INFPs want to make a difference, so they believe in and become inspired by causes that help other people—causes that promote harmony, serve the betterment of humankind, beautify the world, teach others. But harmony may also be sacrificed on occasion to uphold some value that they hold dear, in order to defend their belief system.

If you're an INFP, you contribute to the creative process by generating new concepts and directions, especially as applied to interpersonal relationships. Although this provides fuel for the train to go, you are less interested in actually laying the track or completing the line all the way to the station. The possibilities are usually more exciting than the actual doing, and INFPs leave projects unstarted and unfinished. So, you must step back and take a moment to consider how your ideas can be put into practice while focusing on deadlines and sharing; this amplifies your strengths. Also, like other Feeling deciders, remember to consider logic and the fact that other people's values may be different from your own. Draw on the richness of your imagination. Since introspection takes time, start early on projects to allow for your many experiences to be reflected upon and sewn together.

The Realist (ESTJ)—Extraverted, Sensing, Thinking, Judging

ESTJs would rather play the game than change the rules; however, they are extremely creative in their own way, developing skills that are transferable to *many* applications. As bakers, they can make any kind of bread or cake. As machinists, they can bend a piece of metal or plastic into any replacement part. As painters, they produce realistic landscapes. ESTJs are ingenious in solving real-world problems in practical, elegant, no-nonsense ways.

As organizers of the world around them, ESTJs are realistic and grounded in their outlook; they see things in "black or white" and are motivated by tangible goals. According to Isabel Briggs Myers, they consider "the abstract idea as unsubstantial and of negligible importance."[54]

ESTJs express their strongest function—Thinking—by projecting a controlled, structured, and clear outer persona. Although they are objective, realistic, and sure of themselves, to make their point, they may, on occasion, "exaggerate for the sake of emphasis,"[55] perhaps by adding bolder colors, making bigger projects, playing louder notes, and selecting more sensational facts to report.

About 11 percent of men and 6 percent of women are represented by this type,[56] and these men and women express their logical ideas in an orderly way. Like other SJs (Sensing Judgers), ESTJs are traditionalists who use their creativity to arrange, classify, and set everything in a proper place and on a proper schedule. They measure twice and cut once to ensure accuracy. One ESTJ who was interviewed for this book joked that he can cut anything from metal pipes to potatoes to within one thousandth of an inch.

If you're an ESTJ, you internalize your second-best strength, Sensing, as you rely on your five senses to perceive information as literal and tangible. You perceive the world as a vast array of sounds, smells, tastes, textures, materials, shapes, and colors. And since you focus on the "here and now," each moment is masterfully organized into a separate experience. You think out loud (rather than internalizing your thoughts), and you organize concrete items in your immediate environment. While an Introvert may visualize the act of moving a vase into the sunlight, as an Extravert, you walk over and slide the flowers toward the window.

How does ESTJ creativity look? An award-winning ESTJ watercolor artist combines Eastern and Western techniques to paint realistic flowers that are sharply in focus from edge to edge of the picture frame. Think of serious paintings where the rules of composition and perspective are obeyed along with natural laws. Similarly, in her work, every flower is identifiable, every leaf is clearly set apart from the others, and every detail is authentic. But instead of relying on her imagination or photographs, she prefers to work from life. Her inspirations come from the immediate surroundings of objects more often than people, and if a particular type of flower isn't in season, it can't be painted.

As Realists, ESTJs express the facts as they see them. They are the most literal type and tend to follow the rules to the letter. A group of ESTJ friends floats around the lake where we both live and points out every new shed or fallen tree. They notice when rules are broken and complain about remodels that don't follow the community guidelines, or docks that extend too far from shore.

One ESTJ has his retirement all figured out. Although he isn't part of the jet-set crowd, he's found ways to spend his winters alternating between skiing in Colorado and enjoying the warmth of Florida. Managing several residences takes creativity, however. He explains: "It's hectic and takes lots of planning to make it all work. Most of the planning is not around the place you are but the places you're not." Unexpected maintenance problems and getting mail forwarded are logistical nightmares, for example. "You need a mental attitude that you're always on vacation and home is wherever you are," he says. "Whether a neighbor calls about a mysterious beeping sound or you find water damage when you open the front door, you can't anticipate everything and have to react." The answer to keeping up is something he learned as a pilot: "Ask 'What if?' questions to develop backup systems for bad weather or if an engine quits. Plan for emergencies by having a system."

In solving problems, ESTJs use stored facts and follow standard procedures for what has worked before, mixing and matching routines to solve reoccurring problems. They make incremental improvements on what already exists by developing new processes to improve the efficiency and precision of systems.

A retired ESTJ German engineer with twenty patents for his inventions has helped friends over the years with arcane problems, such as molding an impossible-to-find replacement visor clip for an antique Mercedes, or forming a stainless steel shield to cover the rungs on a boat's ladder to deter raccoons from boarding at night. He explained, "My apprenticeship in a machine shop helped me to learn about the properties of metals and materials. This allowed me to get more than just theory from my engineering studies, and I became a better designer by using the most appropriate materials."

He continued, "I enjoyed getting involved in the beginning of projects, where there was always something new." He made his career by designing prototypes for high-speed manufacturing machines:

I would take step-and-repeat machines that could handle 50 units per minute and make them continuous processes so they can handle more than 1,000 units per minute, bringing about huge cost savings and increased productivity.

The simplest ideas are the best, and I was always looking to make the machines simpler to build and simpler to use. I would think about the process and ask how I could make life easier. My small suggestions didn't alter the product but improved the handling and packaging.

I'm proud of one my improvements where I took a complex requirement of mixing several flavors of candy in the same package and made a simple modification that saved jobs by allowing a major manufacturer to keep a plant open. The workers gave me a standing ovation.

ESTJs have a sense for what is appropriate in every one of today's circumstances, and are very open and direct about it. They are comfortable giving orders, and when they do, people listen. Artists of this type can be easily imagined as old masters who taught armies of protégés their techniques.

During times of change, people look to ESTJs to lead from their experience of what has worked in the past. But Realists can have difficulties breaking with the tried and true, and with the evaluation of wholly new solutions. Though ESTJs trust the chain of command, they must remember that good ideas can still come from outside the chain, beyond traditional channels. Also, ESTJs are reminded that many worthwhile ideas are theoretical and may not be immediately practical, but that doesn't mean they won't yield results.

Being aware of challenges helps ESTJs to find workarounds. Without question, ESTJs will follow the necessary steps to reach clear goals with a clear direction. But the creative process is often messy and chaotic, so it's important for ESTJs to temporarily suspend judgments by realizing that, at times, proceeding without direction is the only way to find a true bearing. Like a spinning compass needle, the process will eventually settle on a course. And though ESTJs are excellent at focusing their efforts on improving systems, they also have to consider other people's reactions to these improvements.

It's easy to see an ESTJ leading an orchestra. They hear the music, sense what is missing, make objective decisions, and keep all the musicians on time. Being results oriented and efficient, ESTJs have high rates of productivity and completion. You can depend on their creations to be realistic, impersonal, detailed, and traditional as they work to improve processes and solve immediate problems.

The Teacher (ESFJ)—Extraverted, Sensing, Feeling, Judging

"This pocket watch belonged to my grandfather. Feel how smooth the gold has become from years of wear. Have I ever told you that it's the only possession he carried with him from the old country?"

Having family heirlooms they can touch and telling the same stories over and over is how ESFJs keep memories alive. Isabel Briggs Myers says they are "interested in possessions, beautiful homes, and all the tangible adornments of living."[57] ESFJs represent 8 percent of men and 17 percent of women.[58]

Traditional, organized, and people oriented, ESFJs develop a model of what they consider appropriate behavior, and this guides their creative style. This framework of beliefs also provides a structure that steers them to what they feel they should and shouldn't do. They so appropriately follow protocol in how they act and what they wear that they even match the color of their underwear with their clothes. Within the guidelines of their own value system, and with Feeling as their strongest function, ESFJs express their emotions and opinions freely.

How can people this proper be creative? The creative style of ESFJs seems to be the biggest wildcard in the deck when it comes to creativity. As Feeling types, what they create is based on their core values. Females may act traditionally feminine while males may take on traditionally masculine roles. As SJs (Sensing Judgers), they are decisive, focused, and consistent. Since their core values developed from early influences (and since everyone's childhood is different), ESFJs are highly individual and unwavering in their beliefs.

ESFJs are Teachers with three preferences that point toward realism: Extraversion, Sensing, and Judging; but this is balanced by their dominant Feeling, which is abstract and subjective. ESFJ creativity often looks lifelike, neat, precise, representational, rich in detail, and highly personal, as they are expressive in their beliefs and in their service of others. They create by making incremental improvements in systems that are consistent with their values.

The ESFJ sense of appropriateness allows them to be decisive, because an action either fits immediately with their values or it doesn't. Being social and protective of the traditions of institutions, ESFJs often develop their core values from family, mentors, and other groups with which they have an association. Even if the groups they belong to have guiding principles that seem tough to others, ESFJs hold the tenets as law. The fertile grounds where they innovate are within the boundaries of their core beliefs.

Engaging real objects through touching, drawing, or molding is the manner in which ESFJs prefer to create. A textile artist of this type follows in her mother's footsteps to make novel, three-dimensional designs within the tradition of embroidery, but she also innovates, developing new designs and new procedures to reach new markets. As an expat, she is inspired by the fauna and flora she remembers in her home country as well as in the places she travels. She describes her process: "I pick up a bunch of flowers, research the plant, see how others depicted it two hundred years ago, see how the stems are constructed and how the petals are formed."

By mixing techniques and combining the threads and fabrics of various textures, she has found commissions in innovative markets, such as luxury homes, hotels, and restaurants. She always has more work than she can finish, yet still finds time to teach and write, sharing her unique art form by producing patterns and procedures that others can follow. "Creativity is a survival skill that must be accompanied by an underlying sense of responsibility," she says. Always fine tuning her work, and taking into account the different seasons, she can turn an ordinary-looking space into a place that is enjoyable to live in any time of the year.

Interestingly, she started her career as a teacher and says she prefers middle-school-age children: "You don't have to start from scratch—you have something to work with."

ESFJs internalize Sensing, their second strongest function, by using their five senses to gather and store details from their present environment, especially any particulars that pertain to people and relationships. Like wearing a pair of rose-colored glasses, ESFJs filter facts using their personal values: "They will not acknowledge doubts raised by the senses concerning something valued by their feelings."[59] ESFJs focus on details that fit their viewpoint, then express in their creations only those details that are in harmony with their values.

Another ESFJ writes songs and poetry about immediate events related to friends and family. She has an ear for music and sets the poems to songs, and as a Teacher, she makes copies of the words so everyone can sing along. At her day job running an office for ten dentists, she uses her creativity to meet all of their needs, even stocking ten different kinds of coffee and tea. Nothing is beyond her when it comes to organizing, meeting the requirements of others, and carrying out her responsibilities, but people of this type are reminded to set some time aside to meet their own needs too.

Creating and copying from observations in life versus the imagination, ESFJs rely on their strong memory of personal detail. Being nostalgic, the paintings they make or the stories they tell often include nuanced interrelations of people they respect personally and sometimes historically. And the texture of the fabric, the smell of the paint, the roar of the crowd—all are the types of sensory incentives that lead ESFJs to create by being formal, practical, and hands on. As a carpenter, an ESFJ enjoys using hand tools to restore antique furniture, trying to get every detail historically correct. As a performer, they are comfortable with audiences but can get overwhelmed since they cannot get to know everyone personally.

For whatever ESFJs create, their purpose is to meet the needs of others. They make great strides to be on time and on budget, and always with the aim to please. ESFJs also plan out loud, are pragmatic, have a knack for arranging what is around them, and are particularly good at organizing people. Dwight D. Eisenhower said:

> Plans are worthless, but planning is everything. There is a very great distinction, because when you are planning for an emergency, you must start with this one thing: the very definition of "emergency" is that it is unexpected. Therefore, it is not going to happen the way you are planning.[60]

ESFJs trust authority, respect credentials, and are particularly sensitive to both positive and negative remarks by critics. When serving as evaluators, ESFJs have strong opinions; however, they tend to tone down their criticism by avoiding confrontation. As great harmonizers and teachers, they must remember that innovation often comes from challenging convention. And sometimes innovation requires cold logic to provoke short-term disruptions before long-term benefits can be achieved. Within the bounds of their values and beyond, there are enormous opportunities for ESFJ creativity.

If you're an ESFJ, you are most creative when expressing your feelings and when engaging the world, promoting harmony, and making tangible output. You encourage others as a Teacher, whether directing a movie, playing in an orchestra, or serving a meal, and you do it with all the elegance of afternoon tea at Buckingham Palace.

The Commander (ENTJ)—Extraverted, Intuitive, Thinking, Judging

Do you know confident and commanding leaders who have both ideas *and* plans? Someone who envisions the future and also makes the future happen? ENTJs show their creativity by strategically executing their plans to reach their goals, and they become leaders in virtually every field. If they are involved in the arts, ENTJs "maintain a conceptual command over scores of people—audiences, art buyers, potential readers, professional clients, community, and society— while seizing vast spaces figuratively and indirectly."[61]

With so many ideas to consider, ENTJs take project selection seriously, using their own experiences to develop their own set of laws and provide standards by which everything is judged. "Everything that conforms to the rules will be right; everything that violates them will be wrong; and everything not covered by them will be unimportant."[62] These rules provide clear roadmaps that attract followers.

ENTJs trust their imaginations but quickly judge their ideas for merit. Having an aura of control and organization, their strongest function is Thinking, and they express their point of view with clarity. Intuition, their second-best function, is internalized. With this engine under their hood that produces infinite possibilities as they enlist their TJ (Thinking Judger) preferences, they make objective decisions swiftly. This combination keeps them realistic but limits their choices, as they often settle for the first acceptable solutions.

What these Commanders create shows select details, as they are happy to leave the finer—and in their mind, inconsequential—aspects to others. They prepare rough sketches or outlines as they record and plan their visions. Although they enjoy abstract thought, all the complexities and vagueness pass through their Thinking filter, resulting in expressions that are clear and direct.

One ENTJ economist's work involves using theories and data to build models. To solve a problem, he says,

> I first do what I can to understand everything I can—what people are saying and what has been done in the field. Then I put all of this into a mind map, and I use that to relate everything to everything, and ask a lot of "What if?" questions. This helps me define where I need to go. As I become familiar with the data, and look at what fits and what doesn't, I start to look for patterns [to] decide if I need more data where there are holes.

He said that he systematically looks for alternatives, new questions, new interpretations, and solutions to decide where he is and how to efficiently get to where he wants to be: "There are always client-related time constraints for bid proposals, meetings, and court appearances (as an expert witness) that make you have to stop playing around." He calls this "triage," where he prioritizes what is important. Always on the lookout for new software and tools, he finds that "You can have a tool over here and somehow realize you can use it for a problem over there. And perhaps through subconscious or heightened awareness, those 'Aha!' moments come about."

Looking toward the future as they learn about the latest concepts and technologies, ENTJs use broad strokes to make progress toward their goals, and they finish most of what they start. An ENTJ Air Force colonel was the first to bring databases to the US federal government back in the 1960s to keep track of legal cases. He envisioned a better way to retrieve information and explained that he fought resistance from those who thought it would eliminate jobs. His system was successful and expanded throughout the government, and it certainly didn't cost jobs. Like this colonel, ENTJs seek to understand relationships within systems and to identify drivers. Everything is questioned, and any inefficiencies are eliminated. Whatever their vocation, these Commanders develop a high level of competency, have a need for control, and leave little to chance.

Inspired by learning and improvement, an ENTJ neighbor who wanted to plant a vegetable garden bought some books and found a layout for the approximate plot size. "It told me what to plant—'row 1, plant this; row 2, plant that'—and the garden was supposed to grow enough for a family of four," she said. But some plants never grew and some vegetables she didn't like. After learning the techniques, she gave up on the instructions and took charge, planting vegetables like tomatoes and zucchini: "It's not the prettiest or neatest garden, and I call it the weed patch. But I did it my way and share the harvest with the entire neighborhood."

Organizations, authorities, hierarchies, and even gardening books are respected ENTJ resources as long as they are competent. When they don't work or don't support the Commander vision, however, ENTJs challenge the status quo and build new organizations, new authorities, and new hierarchies.

Claude Monet was known for rebelling against the establishment to create paintings that captured fleeting moments in nature. It was revolutionary for Monet and his group of Impressionists to paint "unworthy" subjects like nature and industry, and it was unconventional to bring an easel outside to paint in the open air. But ENTJ creativity boldly blends big ideas, and Monet's paintings reflected the same bold brushstrokes and blurred edges. This can be seen in the way he represents subjects like the House of Parliament, which he blended into the sky and the river to become a big, collective mass. As an ENTJ, Monet created spacious landscapes with shapes made of interconnected colors, yet his themes didn't necessarily include people.

Monet was frustrated by the lack of control he had over his environment and had preconceived ideas of what he wanted to find there. One morning, during a trip to London in search of foggy vistas, he relayed, "When I got up, I was terrified to see that there was no fog, not even the least trace of mist; I was in despair."[63] When things didn't go as planned, he became critical of his paintings, writing to his wife, "I am a complete imbecile—the least little thing throws me right off course."[64] ENTJ rigidity caused Monet to be too self-critical—perhaps even of his works that are now considered his masterpieces. And with this story, ENTJs are reminded not to be self critical about external events they can't always count on.

While in the midst of his series The Poplars, Monet ran into another problem: he learned the trees were going to be cut down. To solve the problem, he went to great lengths to spare the trees until after he finished his paintings. With so much of his environment in flux, Monet eventually planted his own gardens to gain the ultimate control of his subjects. But ENTJs must remember that they can't control everything in their environment and not to worry about what is outside their reach.

Overall vision is more important for ENTJs, and as James A. Michener described, "When it comes to graceful writing, I'm more like a pachyderm than a hummingbird."[65] Michener was the winner of the Pulitzer Prize in Fiction for *Tales of the South Pacific*, one of his many thoroughly researched, epic sagas—sagas that sometimes ran over a thousand pages. He acted as an ENTJ by taking the long view of history, writing about how generations of families were interwoven with the events and geography of a location. With the massive scope of his novels, immense amounts of information had to be organized, filtered, and distilled into sentences.

ENTJs make their decisions quickly and hold fast to their convictions. "In my case, my first incandescent reactions often enlighten the entire experience," said Michener.[66] As an Extravert, to get the full context of the environment, Michener always visited— and often lived in—the places he wrote about, and he always talked with the local people. His secret to telling a good story was to be a good listener. While ENTJs are interested in and skilled at gaining the whole picture, as Commanders, they should be aware that their Sensing followers may be more interested in knowing the "what" than the "why."

When he first started a book, Michener wrote a mission statement, an outline, and character profiles. In the mists and chaos of writing, this gave him a blueprint and reminded him "why" he was doing it. Michener's passion: "The organization of experience . . . the organization of knowledge, and the sharing of this with other people, in the hopes that they will get out of it what I got out of it."[67]

As Commanders, ENTJs are purposeful in what and how they express. Michener wrote his novels in such a way that every word helped to advance the story; Monet made his paintings in such a way that every spot of color on the canvas was valuable real estate that contributed to the overall image. ENTJs also recognize their need for quiet time—and the right conditions—to create. Michener avoided interruptions by writing early in the morning in a quiet space, and he preferred to work on a big surface. He often made his own desk with two file cabinets for support: "I have written all of my good books on the top of a door."[68]

Michener gained inspiration from his surroundings like an Extravert, imagined and predicted like an Intuitive, wrote about the truth with clarity as a Thinking type, and planned his outlines and structure like a Judging type. As an ENTJ, he wrote about big subjects and said, "I decided early on to choose as my subjects the entire earth, all terrains, all people, all animals."[69]

ENTJs are best at innovating as Commanders: they lead change by expressing clear visions that others can follow, and they are extremely good at predicting how systems react to change. But as ENTJs move their pawns across their life's chessboard, they must remember that their pawns are people too.

If you're an ENTJ who's challenged by these "people issues," it helps to think ahead about how people may react, just as it helps to keep an open mind about other, less traditional paths. Even when you're making steady progress on the local train's regular route, there may be an express train to your destination on the next track.

The Persuader (ENFJ)—Extraverted, Intuitive, Feeling, Judging

ENFJs are often charismatic Persuaders who put people first as they carry out their plans. As an ENFJ, Martin Luther King Jr. did more than have a dream; he set actual goals for obtaining freedom and civil rights, and then took the steps to achieve his objectives. King was influenced by Gandhi (an INFJ/Inspirer) and borrowed nonviolent protests; however, while Gandhi internalized his message, King externalized his as a gifted orator. He spoke in metaphors—"we refuse to believe that the bank of justice is bankrupt"—and demanded that black people's "promissory note" be honored.[70]

To achieve his goals, King realized that laws had to be broken, as he explained in his 1963 "Letter from Birmingham Jail": "How does one determine whether a law is just or unjust? A just law is a manmade code that squares with the moral law or the law of God. An unjust law is a code that is out of harmony with the moral law."[71] As an ENFJ innovator, are there any rules that you feel are out of harmony with moral law and need to be bent to carry out your mission?

ENFJ creativity is typically intangible and takes the form of leading missions for causes relating to humanity. Instead of being alone in a library, studio, or lab, ENFJs prefer to be with people, as audiences energize them whether they are acting, reading their poetry, or giving a speech to entertain or to influence. Their greatest strength comes through their expressions as Feeling deciders, so ENFJs are often charismatic, master storytellers; they fill a space with their presence much like Martin Luther King Jr.'s words filled the National Mall in front of the Jefferson Memorial. As natural Persuaders in person and on paper, ENFJs think on their feet and benevolently sell their personal values to others. When they say to a crowd, "I have an idea," they can make everyone in the room feel like they are being personally addressed. Not surprisingly, they are among the rarer types and only make up about 2 percent of the population.[72]

One ENFJ explains that she connects the dots related to people by picking up vibes and clues from such things as how they dress and their handwriting. She relies on her Intuition, saying, "I may be psychic about people." And she finds meaning in the ordinary, always seeking new ways to interpret what she notices.

As an executive coach, this ENFJ also puts people through formal assessments, helping them find the right track for themselves and preventing them from getting derailed. She understands that people can take many possible paths to reach their goals, and she tries to keep them going in the right direction. She asks, "What is going on with you?" while asking herself, "What am I not seeing that is missing in your life?"

What matters most aren't her clients' jobs or income levels but their families and their mental and physical health. She helps others look at problems from all angles—for example, asking a perfectionist, "What is the worst thing that would happen if what you make isn't perfect?" Although she likes to come up with ideas, she prefers to be the Persuader, encouraging people to generate and execute their own ideas. As she says, "I wish I had more authority from the bigger part of the wheel."

One way ENFJs communicate with others is through their creations. This type has an innate sense of what is appropriate to preserve harmony, and they act on this with the right words at the right time. Their strong organizational skills—especially with people—make them ideal for leading large events, like directing an epic movie, producing a Broadway play, or organizing a community group to provide disaster relief for victims in need.

President Ronald Reagan was called the Great Communicator and talked like an ENFJ. Starting his career as an actor who appeared in numerous motion pictures, he used his way with words and his power of persuasion later in life to lead a nation and to inspire on a global stage. Since this type sees the world for what it *can* be and shares this vision in a personal way, Reagan could have been talking of himself in his 1986 Walt Disney Recognition Day speech: "Walt Disney's true drawing table was the imagination:

his themes were virtues like courage and hope, and his audience was composed of young people—in years or at heart."[73] ENFJs project their own aspirations in their endeavors, and Reagan's words on imagination, virtue, and hope, along with his understanding of the audience, are all attributes of this type.

ENFJs transform complex topics that may be unapproachable or boring and make them come alive with a narrative. Reagan cut through the tangle of political issues with the straightforward question, "Are you better off now than you were four years ago?"[74] His stories voiced the hopes and fears of the people behind the concepts when he explained why his own ideals were relevant to American lives and why these stories were essential for Americans to know. Reagan recognized that "the arts and the humanities teach us who we are and what we can be."[75] After all, they taught him to be the Great Communicator. Though ENFJs are teachers and leaders of others, they are also teachers and leaders to themselves. What they create is often a search for their own identity and a view of who they can be in the future.

To see tangible ENFJ creativity, look toward Henri Matisse's paintings. Matisse, a giant in modern art, was known for his bold use of color to create visual satisfaction. He loved the human body and needed direct proximity with his subjects to make the strong connections that inspired him. He advised his students to "assume the pose of the model yourself" in order to better understand their subject.[76] The feelings that he projected to the model were more important to him than their actual shape.

Matisse's process started with a vision, and then he planned a composition. With this framework in place, he was free to listen to his intuitive instincts and his emotions to choose his colors. If you are an ENFJ, for whatever you create, plan your structure but don't lock it in. Let it serve as a guide, and then use the strength of your Feelings and Intuition to lead the way.

ENFJs internalize their second strongest function—Intuition—and often talk of needing brief amounts of time alone to listen to their inner self and tap their imagination for ideas. They notice patterns and make connections (mostly regarding people), and organize their information into visions of the future.

Being Persuaders, ENFJs enjoy collaborating and leading groups. They are open and public with what they create, and they seek accolades, applause, and opportunities to please others. The down side to this exposure is that they are easily hurt by criticism. For ENFJs, people come first, and as Judgers, they organize by placing people in the center. Social media and online gaming are examples of people-centered innovations that relate to technology—and on a global scale. ENFJs are among the innovators who achieve significant accomplishments like this. Focusing on an endpoint, they successfully implement abstract and subjective concepts, and they stay grounded by keeping an eye on their audience.

One of the greatest ENFJ strengths comes through their empathy—especially for the people who carry out their visions. Even as they influence others, they strive to emulate their own role models. They express complex ideals in ways that motivate audiences, and they act best when aligned with causes they believe in, like those that advance humanity. However, because ENFJs go to great lengths to preserve harmony, they must remember that conflict is sometimes necessary to advance ideals. Perhaps the ENFJ reluctance to confront can be softened by following King's lead of nonviolent demonstrations.

ENJFs can be expected to complete many projects and lead change that makes a positive impact on people. True to this type, Henri Matisse wrote, "A work of art is the climax of long work [and] of preparation. The artist takes from his surroundings everything that can nourish his internal vision, either directly . . . or by analogy."[77]

The Adventurer (ESTP)—Extraverted, Sensing, Thinking, Perceiving

Ernest Hemingway is an ideal representation of an ESTP's core personality and creative style. He was a fun-loving, action-oriented adventurer who lived a life peppered with stories of fighting in wars, boxing, bullfighting, mountain climbing, big game hunting, and deep sea fishing. He liked to drink, socialize, travel, gamble on horse races, and generally enjoy life. In order to write, however, he found time without distractions in the mornings. Drawing from his many experiences, his escapades in the real world provided the fuel for his creativity.

Describing the source of inspiration for his novel *The Old Man and the Sea*, Hemingway wrote, "I was thinking about actual sharks when I wrote the book and [it] had nothing to do with theory."[78] He also said, "I knew about a man in that situation with a fish. I knew what happened in a boat, in a sea, fighting a fish. So I took a man I knew for twenty years and imagined him under those circumstances."[79]

Graceful, oblivious to personal risk, and seeking adventure, ESTPs are like Jack (or Jackie) in the classic nursery rhyme: they're nimble, quick, and are quite adept at jumping over many things, not just candlesticks. If you are an ESTP, you carefully sense all the facts in your environment, objectively evaluate the situation, and take action on the spur of the moment, looking as you leap. There are 6 percent of men and 3 percent of women who are represented by this type.[80]

As an ESTP, your strongest function is Sensing, which you willingly show others through your concrete language and expressions. In fact, as a Super Sensor, you ultra-realistically observe specific details using your five senses. Your second-greatest strength is Thinking, but you internalize this, only using it to clarify these collected details when necessary. Curiosity and tremendous objectivity leads you to gather enormous amounts of information, but you treat each fact as a standalone experience that doesn't need to be thoroughly analyzed or classified.

Although ESTPs are often seen as impersonal and detached, they do notice the details of people's features and body language—and they use this to their advantage when sizing up negotiators, running with a football, or determining who is bluffing in poker. ESTPs are Adventurers, as they enjoy working with people and are highly skilled at persuading others through factual debates. On the other hand, being straight shooters who tell it like it is, they sometimes inadvertently offend others.

At a time when writing was often elaborate, Hemingway was awarded the Nobel Prize in Literature for originating a new, simpler style. He wrote about his experiences (via his characters) by using plain words with few adjectives. Simplifying to the bare essence, Hemingway created his own device for evoking emotions in the reader, which he passed along to other writers: "[Remember] back until you see exactly what the action was that gave you the emotion . . . Then make it clear so the reader will see it too and have the same feeling that you had."[81]

ESTPs create to make an impact, and what they make often experiments with physical space (like buildings or cars) where the users can experience a full immersion of senses from lights, aromas, sounds, and textures. Billionaire business magnate Richard Branson is the perfect example how an Adventurer may act. Whether it's an airline, private spacecraft, or music distribution company, he channels the innovation through the products and services he provides. His endeavors are designed to disturb the status quo or address underserved niches while providing a chance to play and gain new experiences in the ways he wants you to.

Without interest in theories, ESTPs don't know if an idea will work until they try it, so that's what they do. Living in the moment, craving action, and dismissing the need for much advanced planning, their creative process is fun filled; what they eventually make is secondary to the excitement of the deed. In the words of Donald Trump, "I don't do it for the money. I've got enough—much more than I'll ever need. I do it to do it. Deals are my art form. Other people paint beautifully on canvas or write beautiful poetry. I like making deals, preferably big deals. That's how I get my kicks."[82]

During the process of creating, things naturally go wrong. And while this causes anxiety for others, problems generate excitement for ESTPs; problems provide an action to jump into. Donald Trump orchestrated comeback after comeback in a true ESTP fashion, demonstrating fortitude in the face of adversity. As Theodore Roosevelt said, "The credit belongs to the man who is actually in the arena; whose face is marred by the dust and sweat and blood; who strives valiantly; who errs and comes short again and again, because there is no effort without error or shortcoming."[83]

Out of sight and out of mind, ESTPs work with who and what is available. A director for a play becomes impatient when the lead actress is late and he starts without her, using a replacement to fill the role. ESTPs solve immediate problems with available resources without considering their own safety; they are wide receivers who take openings to catch the pass regardless of whether or not they'll get clobbered. Since these

Adventurers are risk takers who reach for available opportunities, future consequences can be overlooked in the wake of their creative flow. If you are an ESTP, think about not only the concussions but the repercussions of your actions. Taking into account how others may react will considerably increase your effectiveness in what you create and how you collaborate.

ESTPs are easily bored by routines, and instead find pleasure in what is new and by making original creations with their fresh viewpoints. Without learning the rules, they inadvertently challenge convention, trying what makes sense over what has been done in the past. ESTP creativity looks direct, spontaneous, and may even be bold, shocking, and grotesque. When unexpected events come about in the creative process, they (like other SPs [Sensing Perceivers]) believe these moments to be unpredictable, so planning for them is often considered a waste of time. They are hands on and develop excellent techniques over time, cleverly using machinery and material to meet immediate needs.

Living life as a contact sport, ESTPs make excellent improvisational actors or musicians. As comedians, they have a literal sense of humor and effortlessly handle hecklers with witty responses. As painters, they enjoy working outside and dealing with spontaneously changing conditions. These Adventurers also enjoy action, and what they create describes or provokes it. As police officers, they objectively diffuse heated arguments; as short-order cooks, they keep up with busy lunchtime demands; and as emergency room doctors, they stop the bleeding.

One enthusiastic and inventive ESTP hops from job to job—from bartending to top-secret military operations—and is always coming up with new ideas. She says her "crazy ideas" come from using mechanical and electronic devices, and watching how other people use these things; she's always asking herself, *How could this be better? and How could this make people's lives easier?* Observing her dog has inspired all kinds of pet-related products and toys, for example. Unfortunately, without having the experience to bring all her ideas to the market, most are abandoned when another exciting idea takes their place.

This ESTP makes reference to a person who she believes, unlike herself, is highly creative because he has actually followed through with his ideas. This is a common misperception among ESTPs, who must realize that their creativity is defined differently than other types. She is creative through her observations of immediate problems, her resourcefulness, her spontaneity, her ingenuity, and through recognizing that her final product is often a byproduct of her actions.

If you're an ESTP, the best way to inspire your creativity is to surround yourself with people, resources, and problems to be solved. You innovate best by addressing immediate issues with what is on hand—and without regard for procedures or traditions. Like an all-purpose handyman, you quickly size up a leak, patch the pipe with a strip of duct tape, and move on to the next issue. ESTPs usually have many projects going on simultaneously and tend to focus on the thrills, the emergencies. With lots of pots to stir, some pots find their way to the back burner and can simmer for years without being touched. Though they'll be quick to notice when a pot is boiling over, ESTPs are reminded to keep an eye on the other pots too.

ESTPs are willing storytellers and "can be so wrapped up in the moment that they tell a story, overload it with exciting and colorful details, keep everyone in stitches, and have no point whatsoever."[84] Their creations are full of details, excitement, and interest but often devoid of deeper meaning. And though they are concrete and literal, they still get the attention of their audience. Hemingway actually exaggerated with the purpose of making his stories seem truer. His recommendation: "Have a truth and a reality ten times stronger than the original reality you are drawing on."[85]

The Entertainer (ESFP)—Extraverted, Sensing, Feeling, Perceiving

For the lighthearted ESFPs, it doesn't seem right to use the word "artwork" to describe what they create since "work" isn't how they describe what they love to do. "Artplay" is more appropriate. If you're an ESFP, then your actions, enthusiasm, and empathy help to inspire others.

Psychological type theory doesn't explain every aspect of personality, as there is a large degree of latitude in individual behavior within each of the sixteen types. This is clear when we consider the vast differences between two creative people who share the same creative type. For example, 7 percent of men and 10 percent of women have a preference for ESFP;[86] however, there was only *one* Truman Capote and *one* Salvador Dalí, and each was extremely different. Capote had a pleasant persona, was the life of the party, and was engaged with his friends. Dalí was an anarchist and an occasionally violent man. He advised young artists to "give a very hard kick to the right shin of the society that you love."[87] Obviously, one's individual experiences and values also play a role.

With Sensing as their strongest function and the one they show in public, ESFPs gather facts—especially those relating to the people and objects in their environment. As Super Sensors, they absorb the music, foods, aromas, and attitudes of those around them, and all is poured through a mesh of feelings to make a brew that can only be described as "today's special," the *art du jour*. Then, true to their "Entertainer" ways, ESFPs enlist the effects of colors, scents, sounds, and textures in their creations in an effort to stimulate the senses of others as well as for themselves.

ESFPs are the least likely to be productive when alone in their studio, office, or home. They are inspired by distractions and interactions with people, and they are known to be graceful, hands on, and good with machines and material. ESFP creativity—their process—is literal, concrete, and full of life's details. It is exciting, uncontroversial, and fun. The products of their creativity are usually warm, cheery, full of action, and personal. ESFPs aim to meet the immediacy of today's needs.

Bypassing the dreadful and the unpleasant, ESFPs retain the uplifting components that agree with their values by inspiring hope, and promoting happiness and harmony in what they create. After a devastating fire, they point toward the beautiful white flowers growing from the black ash. To alleviate boredom or to avoid something disturbing, they create fun by making up games, just as the upbeat nursery rhyme "Ring Around the Rosie" was said to help children deal with the horrors of the plague. In the face of tragedies, it's a creative feat to find a reason to be uplifting and make others smile, and this is something these Entertainers manage to accomplish.

As realists who see the world in a detailed, photographic way, ESFPs tap in to their enormously curious nature to collect extensive amounts of relationship-based facts.

Like ESTPs (the Adventurers), they consider these facts to be singular experiences that don't need to be analyzed or classified. They trust what they can see and touch, and notice varied shades of life that others miss.

Two SP (Sensing Perceiver) artists showed creative differences through the preferences they didn't share. For Jackson Pollock, who as a Thinking type, his action was his work (in other words: his act of creating was actually what his creativity was about and not about the final painting that resulted from his work); and as an Introvert, he was promoted by others. In contrast, Salvador Dalí was a Feeling type, and his action was himself. Likewise, as an Extravert, he also promoted his work himself.

Salvador Dalí serves as a fitting caricature of an ESFP. He was a larger-than-life, eccentric showman who clowned around, went to great lengths to seek out publicity, and was most known for his surreal scenes, such as the melting clocks featured in *The Persistence of Memory*. For this painting, he was inspired by an ordinary, real-life happening of Camembert cheese melting on a table. With ESFPs especially, creative inspirations come from reacting in a spontaneous way to current actions. And it is fortunate when these moments are captured, since many of them pass without comment and are lost.

Dalí also strived to re-create the reality of his dreams by bringing them into a tangible form. He did this through a host of mediums, including painting, sculpture, jewelry, and film, and although his work was widely analyzed by others, Dalí didn't attribute meaning to it. As he explained, "It is enough to do the painting, much less trying to understand it."[88] The least developed function for ESFPs is their Intuition, as they have little interest in theory and future possibilities. Instead, they paint, play music, act, and dance for how it makes them feel *right now*.

Another ESFP described her creative process this way:

I don't think that I'm creative, but I enjoy watching television—especially the house-hunting and remodeling shows. What I like best is seeing how people react: sometimes they are surprised and sometimes they are not. I like to include everyone and don't like to see people standing by themselves; I like to get them to join in. I solve my own problems by looking at the small parts since the whole thing can be too overwhelming. I figure them out by trying one thing, and if it doesn't work, I don't get upset. I just try something else and everything falls into place. Where I worked, there were so many rules and boring procedures, we couldn't do anything without asking permission. It was drudgery. I didn't think I would last, but I got to know people. And then I made a game out of my work.

In the middle of the interview, she asked if David knew how to juggle. He said he didn't, and she said she didn't either. Always ready to try something new and to Entertain (an ESFP to the core), she grabbed three oranges from a basket and threw them up in the air.

ESFPs enjoy reacting to the crowd, which makes them great spontaneous actors, improvisational musicians, and comedians. "They are natural performers . . . love the excitement of playing to the audience . . . and try to generate a sense of showtime wherever they are."[89]

Realistic, action oriented, and interested in people, ESFPs may find portrait and sports photography appealing, or take to the unpredictability of making watercolors from life. As painters, they nonchalantly tackle the challenges of working outdoors—the boat drifting on the pond, the changing lighting, the fidgeting model. Living in the present, assessing the current situation, and taking action in the heart of the moment, ESFPs are exceptional at sizing up opponents, whether it's in a business negotiation or out on the playing field.

If you are an ESFP, be aware that your second-strongest function—Feeling—is internalized and relates to how you make decisions: based on trusted values developed over time from the influences around you. Absorbing your surroundings and the persuasions of your friends, you prefer to follow the latest fads and trends, swiftly moving on to whatever is currently hot. Having SFP as the last three letters in your creative type means that your styles are most likely to change because you are continuously seizing the moment.

Being highly practical, ESFPs value what makes sense over what was done in the past. They get pleasure from what is new to their senses and are bored by routines. With little desire to learn the rules, they seem unorthodox as they inadvertently challenge convention. And their fresh viewpoint on things enables them to make things up as they go along without regard for tradition, resulting in original creations.

Living in the moment, craving action, and being unimpressed by advanced planning, you can imagine artists of this type splashing paint purely for the fun of it. What ESFPs eventually make is secondary to the excitement of the deed. In the creative process, when unexpected events or problems come about, the Entertainer's strength shines through as he or she reacts and capitalizes on it. Like other SPs (Sensing Perceivers), they believe these moments cannot be predicted and don't wish to waste time by planning for them.

ESFPs are great observers of the inner aspects of people and their emotions. They project their own feelings into subjects and characters, breathing life into whatever they create. An ESFP hair stylist says, "I can't just do what I want—even if I know it will look good—because I have to go by what the customer wants. Creativity is using my experience to meet the needs of other people."

ESFP Truman Capote was best known for his two books *Breakfast at Tiffany's* and *In Cold Blood*. He was described as gregarious, fun to be around, and was always surrounded by people. Capote got his inspiration for *In Cold Blood* from a newspaper article about the murder of a prominent farm family in Kansas. To get all the facts, he felt compelled to travel to the town and personally interview all the people involved—to accurately record how they were touched by the event. In the process, he developed a strong attachment to one of the murderers and discovered that he couldn't write the end of his story until he knew how the real story ended.

Working with others is something ESFPs like, and they are highly skilled at smoothing over differences. Being team players and being adaptive to change, ESFPs can contribute greatly to innovation through their ability to understand the discomfort some people feel about the changes brought about by new innovations and technological advancements. With so much that never leaves the drawing board or fails to fly beyond the launch, the first few moments after an idea is hatched are critical to gaining acceptance. ESFPs are instrumental in promoting the harmony needed for new ideas to flourish.

If you're an ESFP, you are reminded to increase your impact by having patience for people who plan ahead and by occasionally taking a step back to look at the big picture. Also, you tend to avoid conflict, but it may be helpful to understand that conflict is sometimes necessary to bring new ideas to light. Furthermore, by looking toward the future, being wary of overcommitting, and remembering to consider deadlines, you will cover your bases and boost the impact of your creativity.

People pull ESFPs in many directions, so this type is likely to have many projects going on simultaneously. ESFPs are Entertainers who tend to get distracted by the thrill of a new idea, but they would be wise to keep an eye on all their endeavors, old and new. Though planning ahead is somewhat boring, it does help to avoid unnecessary problems and conserve energy for the fun stuff. As a catalyst in getting people to try new things, a typical ESFP says, "How do you know if you like it if you don't taste it first?"

The Brainstormer (ENTP)—Extraverted, Intuitive, Thinking, Perceiving

While most of us are discouraged by something that can't be done, the word "impossible" is the single most exciting word that inspires ENTPs. They aim to solve the unsolvable, and their orientation toward technology contributes to their inventiveness. Like other NTs (Intuitive Thinkers), they are continuously pursuing knowledge as they seek to prove competency; however, ENTPs set their own bar higher and higher. What they create often breaks new ground in some way, whether it's in size, technology, or complexity. And when a milestone is reached or something else more interesting comes along, they move on accordingly.

Always testing, wondering "what if," challenging assumptions, shaking up the status quo, ENTPs are catalysts looking for a better way. One ENTP physicist explained that although he causes subatomic particles to collide without really knowing what he's looking for, he knows something new is there—even if it's hidden—and he comes up with ways to measure it.

For ENTPs, their greatest strength is their Intuition, and this is how they express themselves. As they innovate by making connections among people, ENTPs also make connections among patterns, concepts, and theories. They are full of ideas, and life is a never-ending brainstorming session in which they bounce hypotheticals off whoever is around. "To dream up and pursue possibilities without any follow-through or account-ability is the ultimate form of relaxation for the ENTP. It is also probably the greatest source of ENTP creativity."[90] This type makes up about 3 percent of the population,[91] and this part of the population is extremely curious and always questioning. They don't accept any answer as final, especially if it comes from a figure of authority.

One ENTP says, "Change is inevitable and always brings opportunities that wouldn't have presented themselves if things stayed the same." He purposely puts him-self in situations where serendipitous moments can occur, as diverse events and new people spark unlikely connections that everyone can learn from; problems can be solved. A universal problem he has championed involves finding humane ways to resolve the conflicts caused by wildlife wandering into populated areas. The purpose of the noninvasive solutions he tests is more than animal protection; it also encourages communities to interact, communicate, and share resources.

ENTPs challenge established beliefs and explore beyond the confines of boundaries to test their assumptions and find new ways to do things. While the INP combination generates and endlessly contemplates ideas, the ENP combination in this type prefers to test ideas in the real world. Nothing is sacred in this testing process; all people, objects, and systems are fair game for experimentation. This leads ENTPs to many enthusiastic starts and far-flung projects, but most of these endeavors lose momentum before they are completed and stall in various stages of progress. One ENTP said, "I see hundreds of opportunities, and I can't finish them all. So, I prioritize and try to complete the important ones that have the leverage to get the biggest results with the least effort."

Inventive and nontraditional, for ENTPs, doing the tried and true is probably the only thing they are reluctant to do. Another ENTP explained, "I don't challenge for the sake of challenge, but if I don't like the current way things are done, I find a new way that I would want to do."

Similar to others with the ENP combination in their type, they plan by making rough sketches and outlines; however, they prefer to think on their feet. In writing, inventing, speaking, or painting, each idea leads to the next, and too much planning disturbs the flow. An ENTP artist noticed a bird sculpture made out of chicken wire, and she was inspired to make a three-dimensional bird out of fabric. She says, "Every moment is creative, whether I'm cooking or arranging lemons in a bowl; I don't do ugly."

Robert Motherwell was an ENTP who was active in painting, printmaking, and collage while also serving as the unofficial spokesman for the Abstract Expressionist movement. He outlined some ideals that, although he didn't always follow, seemed to describe what ENTP creativity looks like: "no nostalgia, no sentimentalism, no propaganda . . . no autobiography . . . no clichés, no predetermined endings, no seduction . . . and no obviousness."[92] Motherwell described his creative process as covering layers of mistakes through enduring trials and errors that are finalized only when the timing and need was satisfied. "What I was looking for flashes into view," he said.[93] He saw his art as a collaboration between himself and his canvas, and what he created were large, black, abstract shapes meant to be metaphors for big ideas, such as contrasts between life and death.

ENTPs are independent people and abstract thinkers. As such, they are often in tune with the latest technology and practices and use them as stepping stones to make the next leap forward. If ENTPs land on new ground and others see the value in what they create, they become the founders of the next big thing. And once they have inspired others to emulate and refine the techniques they created, ENTPs move on to innovate elsewhere.

As Brainstormers with an Intuitive outer persona, others may see this type as having a flurry of wild ideas, like an improvisational actor who jumps from topic to topic. ENTPs embrace change but may prefer to work in a medium like oil paints since they can continually modify a piece by adding and pushing paint around without bringing it to completion. As novelists, their stories may take new directions with each new draft, generating more loose ends that may never be completely tied. Fortunately, their public disarray is balanced by their second biggest strength, internalized Thinking, and this leads them to precision, logic, and objective decision making. Consider an ENTP who has been tasked with selecting a design for a new transportation system to improve the flow of rush-hour traffic. If the choices are among popular options, such as trendy light-rail or nostalgic trams, they tend to ignore the hype and choose a less glamorous but more effective alternative, such as widening the road near bus stops so cars can pass.

If you're an ENTP, you innovate best by connecting ideas, challenging conventions, and driving positive change. Like other Intuitive types, however, ENTPs make abstract leaps without explaining their basic assumptions, leading to miscommunications and confusion. Also, because you continuously generate ideas and express them in real time—without first thinking of the other people involved—some of your thoughts may sound harsh. If you are an ENTP, you swing at wild pitches with no fear of striking out. And along with your many misses, you also hit some home runs no one else thought possible.

The Socializer (ENFP)—Extraverted, Intuitive, Feeling, Perceiving

ENFPs creativity is centered on people and human behavior. "The last time I checked, [the Gettysburg Address] said, 'of the people, by the people, and for the people,'" Bill Clinton said in a campaign speech.[94] For him, it's *people* that matter, and he showed leadership by feeling our pain and understanding our problems. He innovated within government and through philanthropy by creating a culture where positive change could thrive. For this type, creativity and innovation doesn't come by acting as a lone wolf but through understanding people, collaborating, and motivating team members to be their best.

If you are an ENFP, your creativity comes through self-expressions that describe your life. By putting yourself in others' shoes, you consider what life is like for them, asking yourself, *If that were me, how would I feel?* With your empathy for and comprehension of human behavior combined with your passion, you create powerful and moving stories—whether it's in politics or in the movies or whatever medium you choose.

ENFPs have a zest for living, as they generate and express big ideas with limitless passion about their beliefs. They make up about 8 percent of the population and were found in a much-cited study to be the most likely type to be artists.[95]

Successful innovation, especially large-scale creation, requires people's support, and one of the great ENFP contributions comes through anticipating people's varied reactions to change. Flexibility and responsiveness to people's sentiments can make all the difference in launching something new.

As the Socializer, ENFPs talk through issues to find solutions, explain ideas to others (as a way of also teaching themselves), and communicate authentically with people. Through this, they develop strong verbal skills, but even as strong communicators, out of all sixteen types, ENFPs have the most difficulty listening since they are constantly bombarded and distracted by their own ideas. One ENFP said that although he's good with words and apt at persuading people, he sees room for improvement. Interestingly, several of his perceived weaknesses seem to describe his personality type: he believes he doesn't prepare enough (Perceiver) and wishes he listened better (Extravert), but this doesn't stop him from understanding his crowd (Feeler) on some level (Intuitive). Describing a pitfall that faces some Intuitives, he said: "Sometimes I assume the audience knows more than they do, and I start speaking from the middle."

The same ENFP considers himself somewhat creative but not in an artsy way. His creativity comes through his work in real-estate developing. For example, looking at a financial model, he found that he could increase the expected return on a project by adding an extra floor to increase the living space. He also realized that he could optimize the use of the land by repurposing excessive parking areas and allocating the space for extra units.

In true ENFP form, the humorist Will Rogers explained it best: "I never yet met a man that I didn't like. When you meet people, no matter what opinion you might have formed about them beforehand, why, after you meet them and see their angle and their personality, why, you can see a lot of good in all of them."[96] Rogers' jokes were about life, people, and government. Being a generally positive person, he used his humor as a spoonful of sugar to soften negativity and boost his persuasive skills. "Be thankful we're not getting all the government we're paying for," he joked.[97]

If you're an ENFP, your Intuition is your greatest strength, and what you express are grand ideas and future possibilities. Seeing personal meaning in everything, you combine patterns of the past with the present to project a future you would like. An ENFP was likely the creative type who had a hand in the concept for the opening ceremony of the Beijing Olympics. By taking the ancient Chinese invention of paper and linking it on a grand scale at the modern-day Bird's Nest stadium, a symbolic and personal image was created: an enormous paper scroll was unfurled as a stage for modern dancers, whose movements transferred to the paper as they danced with hidden, ink-dipped brushes along its surface. When people's motions are embodied in brush strokes, and when people's lives of the past are linked with the present, this is what ENFP creativity can look like.

As NPs (Intuitive Perceivers), ENFPs readily observe patterns and generate unique ideas with infinite possibilities—without judging them. As Feelers, they make decisions by weighing all of the ideas they gather against their intense personal values and principles. Often, their creative mission is to inspire others to see things in a new light. To do this, they stitch infinite possibilities with personal beliefs to weave our social fabrics in religion, politics, and human rights.

According to Isabel Briggs Myers, both ENTPs and ENFPs "operate by impulsive energy" and "value inspiration above everything else."[98] Honing techniques takes a backseat to expressing ideas, and these types prefer trying out ideas for fun. This leads to many enthusiastic starts and lots of projects in progress, but then ENTPs and ENFPs tend to lose the momentum to finish.

Whether or not they finish what they start, as innovators, ENFPs particularly capitalize on unplanned encounters, as human contact inspires them. As Feelers, they bounce ideas around with others to develop exciting possibilities, and are usually as comfortable with old friends as they are with virtual strangers. Not surprisingly, these Socializers prefer collaboration and lead groups more often than solitary pursuits. If they do practice solitary pursuits such as writing or painting, instead of toiling away alone, they come up with ways to include people.

One ENFP entrepreneur said, "If a society is to grow and not repeat old patterns and become obsolete, we must question. Not in a rebellious way, disregarding knowledge of those who came before, but in an open-minded way." The product of ENFP creativity looks fun, bold, abstract, free flowing, and spontaneous; and it seeks to challenge, influence, and inspire others. ENFPs tell meaningful stories that explore emotions and focus on big themes, often glossing over the details. They don't let pesky facts ruin a good concept. And since Sensing is their least developed function, they are reminded to occasionally glace at their blind spot to consider the details of the present moment.

An ENFP paramedic says his work requires him to go against his normal ways to be highly structured, almost paramilitary:

I use a different part of my brain for this kind of work. If shifts start at 6 AM, you have to be there or bad things happen—people suffer or maybe even die. At a medical emergency, it's a dynamic situation, and I think on the fly. Things are changing on the scene, there is a family dimension, and you have to adjust and develop a connection with the patient. My favorite part of being a paramedic is interacting with the patients.

An ENFP commercial photographer who produces "inspirational, lifestyle, and environmental portraits" says his creative process is quick. He asks himself: *What was done before? How can I make my idea different? What emotion do I want to portray? How can I use lighting and colors to emphasize this?* He is known for spontaneously capturing life and fleeting human emotion. Working on location, he explains, "When I get to the site, it's an unknown place, and it may not be what I had in mind . . . I have to learn the ground, make rapid choices, and develop rapport with models and crew. The part I enjoy isn't the planning or setting up but the actual shooting." Interestingly, he doesn't use the latest technology but has settled into using a camera that has become "an extension of himself."

ENFPs personalize by giving meaning to objects and people alike. Their ideas are a part of them, and the newness of their ideas is a way for them to forge their own identity. These Socializers are natural entertainers and actors who are able to get into many different types of roles. As novelists, they create complex and authentic characters with layers of emotion. When you are an ENFP, your subjects come alive with feelings, gestures, and drama whether they are characters in a story or inanimate products and services.

As an ENFP wanting to help others find their unlimited potential, Bill Clinton very fittingly stated, "It is time to heal America. And so we must say to every American: 'Look beyond the stereotypes that blind us. We need each other.'"[99]

Part III

CULTIVATING COURAGEOUS CREATIVITY

6

USING YOUR CREATIVE TYPE
FOR MAXIMUM EFFECT

Have you ever started talking about something you were excited about and your enthusiasm was met with blank stares? Did you feel like you were interrupting a group of theater buffs to talk about soccer? When you're talking about your creative ideas, if you don't have the right audience, you can fail to make an impact or you might simply be ignored. So, how do you find the groups who will be most receptive to your ideas and your creative style? With the power of "self-selection" and your personality type, you already have all the tools you need to find a group in which you can thrive.

Back in grade school, our path was assigned to us, and we were required to study basic reading, writing, and arithmetic. As we finished our primary education, however, and moved on to secondary education and perhaps college, we were allowed more and more freedom in making these decisions.

Self-selection involves making choices to join certain groups. We choose what sports to play, our hobbies, our profession, and where we live. When we self-choose, we find other likeminded people in the groups we join. Of course, the groups we associate with play a role in influencing our decisions, and they also tend to reinforce our inborn qualities. While we all can act outside our preferences and join groups where we don't exactly fit in, it becomes tiresome, takes extra effort, and makes it more difficult for us to be ourselves and to act creatively.

Different eras seem to produce predominant creative styles that allow certain personalities to succeed over others. The style of business structures has changed over time, for example. SJ (Sensing Judger) leaders like Ford built pyramid-shaped hierarchical organizations that thrived during the post-industrial revolution. Later, NT (Intuitive Thinker) leaders of technology companies like Steve Jobs at Apple established flatter, matrix-type organizations. In recent years, spontaneity and flexibility have been prized among businesses moving at net speed, and SPs (Sensitive Perceivers) have thrived—people acting like Branson and Trump, and SPs in nimble companies like Google, who pounce on new opportunities and seemingly switch directions with the changing of the wind. Today, there are opportunities for different styles to thrive together and different types of firms to coexist as an era of social responsibility is ushered in by NFs (Intuitive Feelers).

Different people are drawn to opportunities at different times. As Steve Jobs explained,

If you study these people a little bit more, what you'll find is that in this particular time, in the '70s and the '80s, the best people in computers would have normally been poets and writers and musicians. Almost all of them were musicians. A lot of them were poets on the side. They went into computers because it was so compelling. It was fresh and new. It was a new medium of expression for their creative talents. The feelings and the passion that people put into it were completely indistinguishable from a poet or a painter.[1]

But this historic predominance of creative styles doesn't only occur in business. Our history of creative achievement is really a history of self-selecting. Would the Abstract Expressionists have participated or survived during the renaissance when realism was valued? Though dominant styles have changed over time, the inborn ways individuals create have not. What changed were the types of groups people were drawn to and the manner in which they thrived. To generalize, Realism was the work of SJs (Sensing Judgers), Pop Art was populated with SPs (Sensing Perceivers), Abstract Expressionists were largely NTs (Intuitive Thinkers), and Romanticism and Expressionism were the work of NFs (Intuitive Feelers).

When speaking about the difficulty some artists face when they do not flow with the mainstream, John F. Kennedy said, "In pursuing his perception of reality, he must often sail against the currents of his time. This is not a popular role."[2] Unlike other times in history, today, there are many channels and opportunities for every style to successfully find a place. Knowing your type gives you a way to match with likeminded supporters to take advantage of these powerful collaborations.

7

COLLABORATION

Imagine an all-star baseball team who meets for the first time, and the coach doesn't bother to learn about the players. Instead, he assigns the star pitcher to right field and puts the best hitter at the end of the lineup. If we don't make the effort to understand and use each other's strengths, how can we effectively work together?

Collaboration in creative pursuits can be tricky. How do we work together for a common goal when creative pursuits often have unclear directions? Everyone has heard of the breakup of famous rock bands and the inability of partners in highflying startups to work together. Sometimes they explain their problems as "creative differences"; however, if they truly understood and embraced their creative differences, they would know how to use their differences as strengths to propel them to new heights in creativity. Successful collaboration starts with trust, and requires give and take. The more we understand who our partners are, the better we can communicate and contribute, and the more our cooperation pays off.

Sometimes achieving greatness requires collaboration between creator and promoter. For example, as an SP (Sensing Perceiver), Jackson Pollack loved the action of dripping and splashing paint, but as an Introvert, he had very few words to describe what he had done. Fortunately, his work was thrust into the limelight by the Extraverted critic Clement Greenberg, who, as an Intuitive, attached meaning to Jackson's paintings. This successful collaboration created the Abstract Expressionism movement. If a lone wolf like Jackson Pollack could found something so monumental through collaboration, other creative people can too.

When we think of creativity, we often think of toiling artists alone in their studios, scientists in their labs, advertising people staying late at the office—all waiting for inspiration to strike. Today, with increased specialization, everything is complicated, and we can't be an expert in all of it. Whether you're making scientific discoveries, launching new products, planning a wedding, or writing books, everyone—including Introverts—can benefit from collaborations.

Do you know people who have plenty of ideas, but they don't follow through? These people need collaborators to help them implement. What about artists who paint masterpieces that nobody sees? They need a collaborator to help them promote. Then there are inventors who need help protecting their ideas; entrepreneurs who need help gaining capital; or composers who need help with lyrics. Working together allows for different points of view and sparks new ideas. It's not enough to be a lone innovator. Good ideas can be made into great ideas when we utilize each other's specialized expertise. In fact, venture capitalists say the most important quality they look for in businesses isn't the ideas but the teams. Look for partners who don't duplicate your skills but complement them.

For years, people have been reading *Type Talk at Work* and using it to build effective teams; here, we take it at step further by showing how to effectively use teamwork for creative pursuits.[1] The more you understand your personality and that of your associates, the better you can build diverse teams, cooperate with your teammates, and leverage your creative strengths. When you know yourself and your type, you know your limitations and when it's best to surrender your ego to ask for help.

Pairing—Two of a Kind

How do you find the right new partners and work better with the ones you already have? Ideas evolve quickly when like-minded people join together. Take two INTJs (the Visionaries), who are among the most independent types, and put them together in a quiet setting. If they trust each other, they will probably find much in common and easily generate concepts for billion-dollar ventures, plans to reduce traffic in cities, and strategies to end wars. However, it is also likely that they will fail to consider how people may react to these ideas, and the majority will remain as concepts that never leave the drawing board.

In contrast, another pair of two highly collaborative and action-seeking ESFPs (the Entertainers) may like each other as people and share a passion for making things happen, but they will probably dare each other into thrills like extreme sports without much thought toward the extreme dangers. "Birds of a feather flock together," and people of the same type amplify their strengths while also widening their blind spots.

So, what happens when we pair opposites? Like magnets, opposite creative types may briefly attract at first, but unlike opposing magnets, they soon start to repel each other. In fact, a collaboration of opposite types often creates stress. Sensors don't want to waste time sitting around debating theories, and Intuitives don't want to jump right in without establishing context. While INTJs (the Visionaries) gravitate toward strategic planning, ESFPs (the Entertainers) tend toward tactics for resolving immediate people issues.

How do good ideas survive committees of opposites? With patience and understanding. Opposites can make strong pairs and become powerful combinations when they work together to cover each other's blind spots. To make it work for you, however, you must first understand—and respect—your differences. And since the people we choose to associate with are more likely to be similar to us, you'll probably have to look outside of your normal circle to find this partner.

One mother-daughter creative pair successfully works together and enjoys each other's company—but that wasn't always the case. Before starting their business, the daughter, a strong SJ (Sensing Judger), used to be a full-time teacher, while her mom, an NP (Intuitive Perceiver), was an artist. Shared preferences usually provide some common ground; however, in their case, the only preference they share is Extraversion. As a result, they talked over each other, with neither listening to the other. This put a strain on their relationship.

After learning about their type differences, this creative pair found that things work best when the NP takes the lead in generating ideas while the SJ finds creative ways to implement them effectively—and they both concentrated more on listening to each other.

Innovation has two parts, the idea and the implementation. While NPs frequently generate pie-in-the-sky ideas, they're grounded by SJs' practicality and decision-making skills. SJs implement within current systems and take the pie out of the sky to serve the slices. Today, the SJ mother and NP daughter celebrate a successful collaboration. When team members are aware of each other's types, misunderstandings can be avoided, efficiencies gained, and work can become more enjoyable.

How We Help Each Other

Technology allows us to be in constant contact with each other. If you're unsure of which dimmer switch to buy as you stroll down the aisle of a hardware store, you can get the clerk, call your handy neighbor or your electrician, or use your phone to check the internet. Today, there are few circumstances where you are on your own without available help. Never before have we had more tools for collaborating remotely; our interconnected world allows us to work together without geographic limits. That also means that, as an entrepreneur, you don't have to do it all. Whatever you need to do, finding a collaborator will help. With a world full of choices, you have a lot of ways to combine creative types. Extraverts still get to work in groups of people, while Introverts can participate from afar, allowing them to contribute at their own comfort level.

Introverts usually prefer to create alone and behind the scenes; however, there is great benefit in their teaming up with Extraverts. Like Greenberg did for Pollack, Extraverts route thoughts into the open that would otherwise go unsaid. Pairings between Introverts and Extraverts often work well since neither type competes for the limelight. In comparison, pairs of Extraverts must make an effort to listen to each other, and pairs of Introverts must share in order to work effectively.

By the way, without people around, Extraverts may find themselves interacting with and sometimes even talking to the material around them—as if their sketch book and pencils were silent partners. Indeed, as Robert Motherwell said, "A picture is a collaboration between artist and canvas."[2]

Consider the way opposites approach new problems. Posed with a challenge, EFs (Extraverted Feelers) race to gather the troops to bounce ideas around while ITs (Intuitive Thinkers) head off to start researching and contemplating alone, sharing their findings later. Both approaches add value to the effort.

People with other opposing pairs of preferences help each other see around corners. Feelers help Thinkers consider people and relationships while Thinkers help make tough but necessary decisions based on logic. The N-S (Intuitive-Sensor) team benefits from considering the big picture and the details, as well as the present and the future. The J-P (Judger-Perceiver) difference creates the most friction, since Judgers like to have set decisions and Perceivers prefer to use new information to change decisions. Regardless, having the best of both worlds allows for the benefit of planning and the flexibility of reacting in real time. It helps that roles aren't fixed, so everyone can contribute as they see fit.

Collaborative Roles of the Four Main Temperaments

NF (Intuitive Feelers): Putting people first and fostering relationships among members, NFs are the glue that holds teams together, as they determine the needs of both the team and the clients. They see possibilities in people but hold back from sharing to avoid controversy or offending others. They also have difficulty collaborating with people who have opposing values.

NT (Intuitive Thinkers): Generating visions and long-term strategies are NTs' strength, as are considering systems and keeping an eye on the mission. NTs are blocked, however, when they are unsure of their competence, and they tend to overcomplicate issues. They also have to remember to consider other people and their opinions.

SJ (Sensing Judgers): Following through by taking ideas, putting them into practice, and keeping an eye on the schedule is all in a day's work for SJs. They're also adept at following procedures and complying with policies, but they hold back from contributing when talk becomes too theoretical.

SP (Sensing Perceivers): Testing the practicality of ideas, SPs are in sync with current needs and coordinate these resources while adding fun to the process. Though they are resourceful and adept at handling unpredictable events, they tend not to participate when tasks become routine or when they become distracted.

When collaborating, representation from each temperament helps to fill in the gaps and shore up weaknesses. If your project is a screenplay for a science fiction movie, a well-rounded collaboration helps to ensure that a wide swatch of the audience will have an interesting thread to follow. Simple division of labor can do the trick—as long as it allows each type to play to their strengths. The SPs will write the snappy dialog and battle scenes between the starships; the NTs will add a scientific basis for time travel and apply the special effects; the NFs will provide the emotional tension between the characters and their romantic threads; and the SJs will keep the group on point, paying homage to the traditions in the genre, and making sure the story remains consistent and believable. Even if your team doesn't have representatives from each preference, being aware of your blind spots helps you to prompt the right questions to strengthen your creative potential.

8

HOW TO INTERPRET WHAT CRITICS SAY

How do we know when criticism is worth listening to? Have you ever created something in an hour, a day, or over your lifetime and shared it with someone who took a quick glance and instantly found fault? Hearing criticism can be difficult and is sometimes enough for people to lose their eagerness to share, or worse, their desire to create anything new. It seems much easier (and more fun to some) to stomp on sandcastles than to build one. Even so, there's often an opportunity to find valuable grains of constructive criticism among the ruins.

First, you need to qualify the commentator. A good question to ask: "Did the critic spend an hour, a day, or a lifetime acquiring the knowledge to make their judgments?" If they are knowledgeable in the field, you may be in luck, but even with a lifetime of experience, a critic has the ability to cause more harm than help.

How we receive criticism has a component related to type. Suppose you create a frozen banana-strawberry smoothie. You pour it from a blender and set the glass down for others to taste. Whether they say that they like it or not, it's just information to a Thinker, who keeps an arm's length from what they made. A Feeler, on the other hand, is more attached to what they make. For them, it's more like passing a piece of themselves around for others to sip. They are more prone to identify with what they created and may see criticism as a personal attack. In order to gain the benefit from constructive criticism, we suggest that you momentarily set your glass down and detach yourself from your work.

Next, consider whether the advice is useful or points you in the wrong direction. Can you use it to improve this project, or your next? Are those anonymous social media likes or dislikes representative of your true audience? Is it specific or accurate? Is the criticism too late to be useful or too early? Does it discourage you before your idea is fully formed?

"I want the most severe criticism," explained ENTJ James A. Michener who sought out experts in various fields to read his drafts. "But I sure don't want it while I'm in the process of writing."[1]

Not all criticism is on the mark, and knowing when to dismiss, delete, and erase it from your mind is an important skill. Much advice is a matter of opinion, where critics unknowingly state their personal values. If their values and objectives happen to coincide with yours, their words could be useful. If not, then confidently dismiss the criticism.

Have you ever needed a recommendation for a plumber and asked your neighbors for suggestions? One says, "Call Frank, I've known him for years. And he tells the funniest jokes." Another says, "Call Sam. He is dependable and the cheapest guy in town." Meanwhile, someone else says, "I've done several luxury remodels with Neil. He uses high-tech equipment and does a first-rate job—but it'll cost you." And yet another neighbor says, "If he answers his phone, Pete is the best for emergencies." Since type involves the process of gathering information and making decisions, all critics have biases, and an understanding of their predisposition allows you to filter the signal from the noise. So, if you know your critic, you can wade through their own type biases to make the choice that is right for you.

Critical Bias

Is the criticism really about your work? "The things they write sound so strange and far removed from what I feel of myself," noted Georgia O'Keeffe, an ISTP.[2] She went on to say that critics were writing their "own autobiography," and it "really was not about me at all," as she was a realist, and her paintings aimed to portray the truth at face value.[3]

Perhaps there is no greater extent of critical bias than in creative fields where many people have definite opinions even though the product is highly subjective. Sensors say of Intuitives, "too sloppy and vague." Intuitives respond to Sensors with, "where's the concept, and what is your meaning?" Judgers say that Perceivers' work looks haphazard and unfinished, while Perceivers say the Judgers' work is too regimented and constrained. Can you see how this kind of type bias is infused into practically every piece of advice you are given?

SJ (Sensing Judger) critics value technique and adherence to tradition; NT (Intuitive Thinker) critics value concept and the overall effect. NFs (Intuitive Feelers) prefer personally moving works that coincide with their feelings toward subjects, and SPs (Sensing Perceivers) just want what is new and entertaining, without being boring.

When the Critic Is An . . .

Extravert: They share, but beware: an Extravert may just be talking through their immediate thoughts about what they see. This gives you valuable information on how they reach their conclusions, and allows you to learn and react. They sometimes wish that others were as expressive and open as they are.

Introvert: Prone to providing written comments, an Introvert shares their criticism with a trusted few; however, if you aren't in their inner circle, they may not say what they are really thinking. Without knowing their objections, you can't dispel misconceptions. The worst kinds of criticisms are the ones you aren't told about—criticisms you can't correct or defend. So, the best way to learn what an Introvert is thinking is to establish trust with them.

Sensor: They're first to criticize and dismiss ideas that seem impractical or abstract. The value of their advice comes from showing what is specific and workable as they comment on the details. However, they may miss your deeper meaning or your overall theme unless you state it up front. They aren't impressed by vague promises and they particularly appreciate technique. Their criticism is grounding as they call for details to be refined, facts to be checked, and omissions to be filled. These critics praise the immediate and appreciate the intricacies of what they sense.

Intuitive: Don't expect them to acknowledge the fine details you labored over. Instead, Intuitives are best at providing an overarching impression of the intangible qualities of your work and may criticize your overall premise. However, their general advice is often devoid of specific suggestions, leaving you without clear steps to proceed. What they praise is content, new concepts, and meaningfulness. They appreciate being challenged to think and being taught. Beyond what you actually show them, these critics are most excited to see possibilities and their criticisms can guide you to increase your scope and define your purpose.

Thinker: As a critic, a Thinker is objective, treating everything and everyone equally by comparing performance with a standard. Helen Hayes described the Thinker mentality well: "My mother drew a distinction between achievement and success. She said that achievement is the knowledge that you have studied and worked hard, and done the best that is in you. Success is being praised by others—and that's nice too—but [it's] not as important or satisfying. Always aim for achievement and forget about the success."[4]

Feeler: A Feeler praises what concides with their beliefs and what they can personally relate to. Although they frequently wish to preserve harmony by avoiding confrontation, they do provide criticism for our own good, or to defend and promote their beliefs.

Judger: As a critic, a Judger is often initially closed to anything new. When they speak, they tend to sound critical as they express their views. They push for conformity and completeness, and are impressed by the order of the execution of plans.

Perceiver: The Perceiver critic is usually open to new and changing ideas, praising spontaneity in others and prizing it in themselves. They are critical of what they feel is constrained and leave little room for revision.

Be Your Own Critic

Critics have always been gatekeepers; and though the gates still remain entry points for a select few, the fence is a relic of the past—full of holes that can be easily stepped through. Right now, there are unprecedented opportunities to kick-start a project, raise funds, and create and distribute your work—whether you are designing a new product, offering a service, exhibiting your paintings on the web, recording your own song, producing your own videos, compiling an app, sharing your cooking, or publishing your writing. We can easily make small batches of custom products to reach niche audiences. Now, more than ever, you don't have to depend on another's permission to do what you are passionate about, but it does mean becoming your own critic.

Give yourself permission to create and then critique yourself. This is something that creative people have always had to do. "The one man who could write a pamphlet about criticism is me," said Salvador Dalí.[5] And Vincent van Gogh noted, "I could say things against it myself by way of criticism that would probably escape most critics."[6] Be your own critic—without being *too* critical. If your criticisms are inspiring you to continue and try again, then you're on track; but if they're discouraging you from what you enjoy and keeping you from exploring new opportunities, then dial it down. Self-manage by seeking out qualified criticism and pass it through a type filter before taking any of it too seriously.

The only one who can determine if your work is a success is you. Van Gogh also said, "How preposterous it is to make oneself dependent on the opinions of others in what one does."[7] You must be your own critic to maintain your confidence and fulfillment. The following are some typical questions you can ask yourself to determine if your work is a success to you.

Extravert: *Do I need to add something that will give it some flair? Does it grab people and draw them in?*

Introvert: *Does it show what I set out to accomplish? There is no impression without expression—did I share enough of my idea? Does the work stand on its own and need no further explanation?*

Sensor: *Are the details gripping me? Is it real? Can I touch it?*

Intuitive: *Will the symbols and meanings make people think? Will anyone else be able to understand this?*

Thinker: *How do I measure up to my criteria? Are all the important elements included?*

Feeler: *Are the things that I value most included? Does it represent who I am?*

Judger: *Is it on time, within budget, according to plan, and finished?*

Perceiver: *Was I able to capitalize on new information? Will the picture ever be finished? Does being unfinished add to the project's excitement and possibilities?*

Advice flows like water but is often mixed with biases. So, it's important to know what is happening upstream before you drink. Some biases are unintentional or inherent at the source. Once you know the predisposition of others, you know how to filter their advice. Trust yourself to pick and choose which advice is relevant and right for you.

9

ART IN YOURSELF: MORE CREATIVE OUTLETS

Whatever the activities that engage you, there are so many ways to be creative. Whether you're a painter with an easel, an actor behind a mask, a dancer filling tap shoes, a gardener with a trowel, a chef wielding a spoon, or a parent under pressure, this section provides a starting point for thinking about how your personality is related to the ways that you are most creative. In the end, you'll have a unique perspective on how to personally gain your inspiration to act creatively, how to make decisions about what you create, how to interact with your innovation, and how to restore your creative energy after you're done.

Painting

Do you enjoy painting, looking at paintings, or maybe just wish you could better comprehend them? Understanding your creative style gives you insight into your own creative ways, as well as the process and inspirations behind what other artists have created. It also gives you more creative confidence, decision-making ability (on what you like and don't like), and context than any art class or visit to a museum. Here are some questions to ask yourself to determine what your creative style may look like on a canvas:

- *Do you prefer working from life or from your imagination?* Extraverts like Monet are inspired from the world around them while Introverts like Picasso rely on their imagination.
- *Do you prefer paintings with factual details using actual colors in a realistic style, or do you tie together abstract concepts in a painterly way?* Some Sensing artists like Hopper notice rich detail and have a realistic style. Alternately, Intuitives tend to look at the big picture and make abstract connections, like Van Gogh.
- *Do you prefer portraits or landscapes?* Like Matisse, some Feeling types are passionate about people; and like Cézanne, some Thinking types are devoted to landscapes.
- *Do you plan your compositions with the aim to finish them, or do you work spontaneously, leaving your options open to make changes?* Judgers are usually careful planners like Rockwell, while Perceivers like Dalí prefer to work spontaneously.

We all can be creative in our own way, and the above principles can be extended beyond painting to virtually every creative pursuit—as you'll see in the coming sections.

Sculpting

Many of us remember the joy of molding clay as children; as adults, however, our problem with sculpture is that, while it's often designed to be touched, it's usually displayed behind glass or in a roped-off area that prohibits direct contact. This is especially troubling for Sensors, who make up 70 percent of the population and prefer to gather information by touching.[1]

Intuitives have less of a need to actually touch things. For them, sculpture is appreciated differently, as they enjoy looking at three dimensions from various angles. Matisse, an Intuitive, said of his bumpy and rough sculptures, "You don't need to touch the surface to understand the texture, and they certainly don't invite caressing the way a smooth bronze or marble does."[2]

It seems, however, that sculpting—whether molding clay, welding old bike parts into candle holders, or shaping wedding cakes—is especially appealing to those with the preferences E (Extraversion), S (Sensing), and F (Feeling). First, in a both a mental and a physical sense, sculptures fill creative space, and Extraverted Sensors (ESs) love to create by filling spaces. Secondly, as mentioned above, Sensors can't keep their hands off things! Sculpting fulfills this need nicely. Finally, sculpting is an ideal medium for Feelers, who like to embody their subjects in order to better understand themselves, and sculptures are often devoted to the human form. Extraverts use space, Sensors take pleasure in touch, and Feelers personify objects—perfect creative leanings for manipulating the reality around these three preferences.

Of course, people of any creative type can find pleasure and success as a sculptor. The famous abstract sculptor Henry Moore talked like an INFJ (an Inspirer) when he said, "We must strive continually to think of and use form in its spatial completeness [Judging] . . . inside his head, he thinks of it [Introversion] . . . he mentally visualizes a complex form from all round itself [Intuition] . . . he identifies himself with its center of gravity [Feeling]."[3] Just as the Extravert uses physical space, the Introvert uses his or her inner space. As the Sensor reaches out to touch, the Intuitive does so with his or her mind. As the Feeler emotes about the creation before him or her, the Thinker keeps an arm's length from the innovation.

Acting

Whether you consider yourself an actor or not, at times, everyone plays roles to entertain or persuade in life. Beyond the role we are playing, our personality influences our acting style.

Acting is different than other creative pursuits in many ways. When inspiration strikes, the author writes, the painter paints, the sculptor sculpts; however, actors can't often control which part they play, but acting still involves creating a character. When the curtain is raised, the actor doesn't have the luxury of waiting for inspiration. The show must go on, and the ways an actor is inspired varies by type.

For Extraverts, "All the world's a stage, and all the men and women merely players."[4] They are inspired by their surroundings. They are energized by the warm glow of the limelight, and are brought to life by the audience and ensemble. Fortunately, there is always a story to tell and an audience to entertain. Acting is more collaborative than most other forms of art, and 63 percent of actors were found to be Extraverts.[5]

On the other side of the coin, the remaining 37 percent were found to be Introverts.[6] "I want to be alone" was a powerful line spoken by actress Greta Garbo in the movie *Grand Hotel*,[7] but it was also characteristic of her personality and how she derived her inspiration. This method is especially fitting for Introverted Intuitives (INs), who use their imagination to internalize their subject's hopes, dreams, and fears.

There is one major difference in the ways actors gather information for an upcoming role: 80 percent of them are Intuitives and 20 percent are Sensors, which is nearly the opposite of the makeup of the general population.[8] Intuitives study to understand the meaning and motives of the subject they are portraying; meanwhile, the Sensors are apt at observing the details of their subject's actions, which they then mimic.

What draws an actor to a script? For Feelers, and especially those with an NF (Intuitive Feeler) temperament, they project themselves into a role as they aim to identify with the character, often preferring roles where they agree with the character's personal values. NTs (Intuitive Thinkers) take roles for the challenge while SJs may be drawn to the American Realistic Theater, in which each actor is cast close to their own age and physical characteristics. Then there are SPs (Sensing Perceivers), who are attracted to something else entirely. SPs are drawn to do their own stunts in action roles that go beyond the expected behavior of a character, giving them a chance to surprise the audience.

While Extraverted Feelers (EFs) can be natural entertainers who want to see—or even know—their audience, Introverted Thinkers (ITs) have their own strengths. ITs act without depending on audience reactions, allowing their performance to be consistent whether the seats are filled or empty, or the audience is receptive or cold. Thinking actors have to work harder to access their emotions. However, they easily step outside of themselves to create characters.

Reacting to the audience and responding to other actors, Perceivers spontaneously create great impromptu moments. Their flexibility helps them to naturally fill undefined roles, but they are challenged to follow scripted parts and see little value in rehearsals. One the other hand, Judging actors tend to follow their scripts, and they depend on rehearsals.

Who could be better at interpreting a role than a "type-alike" actor? All acting aside, when there is a close match between an actor's personality and the part, award-winning performances are produced. Even outside the theater, as we "play" all the different roles in our life, we have the confidence to act—to be—ourselves when we know ourselves, and this is better for everyone.

Language

What did you say last night to your friends? How was your tone received in your email? Which anecdote did you use to toast the bride and groom? The words we choose, the way we construct sentences, and the examples we share all say something about our personality. Understanding how your personality relates to your language helps you avoid miscommunications and improve the way you reach your audience. Also, as readers learn to identify the personality of the author, they gain greater context and insight into what is written.

Much advice about word usage is biased by type. In *The Elements of Style*, William Strunk and E. B. White wrote the rules on word usage. "Prefer the specific to the general, the definite to the vague, the concrete to the abstract," advises rule sixteen.[9] Strunk and White favor the specific sentence—"It rained every day for a week"—over the general—"A period of unfavorable weather set in." However, the advice to use specifics is a Sensor's bias. Whether writing or speaking, Sensing writers express "what is" in a straightforward way, reducing the possibility of misinterpretation with the help of laden facts, details, and lists—and often, by making comparisons using similes. This is different from Intuitives, who write about "what could be" by using analogies and generalizations that infuse their prose with multiple layers of meaning between the lines.

In terms of the creative process, Intuitive writers typically compose by first making rough drafts with themes, and then going back to refine points and fill in the details. "Typing out the first draft of a manuscript is fierce work and often frustrating, for composition goes neither swiftly nor accurately, and disappointments are many," described Michener.[10] In contrast, Sensors prefer to initially write with more detail, paying attention to grammar by editing as they go. Hemingway, for example, would edit each morning. Sensor writers can often benefit from assistance in "sorting the irrelevant facts from the relevant," and Intuitives can "be blocked in search for originality."[11]

Extraverts, on the other hand, often write in their speaking voice and are natural storytellers. During the initial stages of writing, they are more likely to find it useful to talk through their idea with others, and they benefit from putting their words on paper as a way to see their thoughts. But writing is a solitary process, and the lack of companionship can be a challenge for Extraverts. Some resort to locking themselves away to increase their productivity; however, long periods of time alone drain an Extravert's energy.

The opposite of Extraverts, Introverts are energized by being alone. And with the time to reflect, they find inspiration in their inner world, writing about imagined experiences as if they were real. With the ability to escape into their mind, Introverts can be "alone" to write—even in a crowded coffeehouse. Introverts also create characters that are introspective and speak from an inner monologue. J. D. Salinger, the very private author of *The Catcher in the Rye*, used this technique for expressing the thoughts of the main character, Holden Caulfield. With the benefit of time to compose, Introverts often write better than they speak. "I think like a genius, I write like a distinguished author, I speak like a child," said Vladimir Nabokov.[12]

Thinking type writers "are more likely to organize their writing into clear categories, and focus on clarity to the point that they forget to interest the audience," while Feeling type writers "at times, in a search to capture the reader's interest, overstate their points for emphasis."[13]

Strunk and White urged the writer: "Place yourself in the background," and "Write in a way that draws the reader's attention to the sense and substance of the writing, rather than to the mood and temper of the author."[14] This is unnecessary advice for Thinking authors, since they already remove themselves and strip away their own emotion. In contrast, following this advice would deprive Feeling authors of their strength; their power comes from expressing what is personal—sometimes in an outpouring of emotion. Feelers prefer to use the personal pronouns, "I," "me," and "myself," in their descriptions. "I Taste a Liquor Never Brewed," "My Life Closed Twice Before Its Close," "Because I Could Not Stop for Death"—all of these are poems by Emily Dickinson, and all are personal. Feelers frequently use phrases like "If you are anything like me," "I feel that," and "In my experience." They personify with their words, putting themselves into their subjects. For Feeling authors, the story is their story.

Imagine a love letter devoid of emotion or an annual report expressing love, joy, or grief. Both describe writing that isn't generally appropriate. We all have Thinking and Feeling capacities for making decisions, and a good balance is healthy. Writing a personal note is a time when the Thinkers need to remind themselves to think of the feelings of their audience. For business correspondences, the Feelers find greater success when they remember to omit their personal feelings. Knowing when to use your preferred style and when to use your balance is the key.

As with the other pairs of preferences, Judging and Perceiving create their own unique balance too. Perceiving authors prefer to express the information they gather, such as "It's a clear and sunny today," while Judgers express their judgments: "It's the nicest day of the year! You should go outside." Of course, Judging writers prefer to form outlines, follow paths, write in concise sentences, and tie up loose ends before coming to a strong conclusion to meet deadlines. They are masters at developing plot and structure, but often, once they reach a conclusion, their books are closed. Since beautiful and effective prose rarely flows from the mind to the page, Judgers are reminded to consider improving and revising their first drafts.

Meanwhile, Perceiving authors are continuously collecting new information to modify and recast in their writing. As Hemingway described in *Death in the Afternoon*, by waiting too long to start, you do "not want to write about it but, rather, to keep on learning about it."[15] So, Perceivers may have difficulty starting at times because they're too engrossed with collecting. Once Perceivers do begin writing, however, they will often jump right into new projects with little advanced planning, preferring to write in meandering sentences with nonlinear storylines, letting the activities of their characters lead the plot. "I start to make it up and have happen what would have to happen as it goes along," said Hemingway.[16] And with little need for closure, Perceivers are comfortable leaving unanswered questions—an effective device as long as the story is clear and fully developed.

Writing Temperaments

Writers of different temperaments tend to gravitate toward different genres and styles. From the SJ (Sensing Judger) point of view, authors are descriptive, methodical, and complete in what they report, so it's not surprising that they are often inspired to write historical novels and stories with classic plots. An SJ author would be thrilled by the comprehensiveness of the official government weather website in Hong Kong. On a day with heavy clouds and an approaching typhoon, the weather website lists the UV index, relative humidity, temperature, and mean wind speed, along with static satellite images, radar, pressure charts, and the unlikely possibility of earthquakes. SJ writers are equally precise, including every facet that is part of the complete system of standard reporting—much like journalism and police reporting.

In contrast, writers with an SP (Sensing Perceiver) temperament have a more immediate style, expressing what they sense in the present tense, like the breaking news report that interrupts your regularly scheduled program to alert you of the approaching typhoon. Leading with urgency and action, the onsite reporters make their report while bravely standing in harm's way at the edge of the storm, hair blowing in the wind and dripping from the downpour. Likewise, SPs create excitement by using words to show the waves crashing over wharfs, bridges flooding, and clouds swirling on radar images. If they're also Extraverted, they usually write in the way that people naturally talk, including pop culture references and the latest slang. Thrillers, mysteries, screenplays—page-turners are the preferred work of SPs.

On the Intuitive side, those with the NT (Intuitive Thinker) temperament strive for the improvement that comes from revision. "Sometimes, working on that second draft, I get the feeling of real power that I never do with the first draft," described James A. Michener.[17] NTs writing of the approaching storm describe the latest Doppler radar and weather satellites. They report the meaning of the storm and its future implication—they predict the rain will reduce next year's price of rice. With meaning, complexity, and metaphor, NTs write in an objective way as they try to teach you why. Authors with this temperament often use technical jargon and write college textbooks, nonfiction, and science fiction.

NF (Intuitive Feeling) writers, like the NTs, also write with metaphor and analogy, but they tend to do so in the first person, for their prospective reader. "Who am I?" they ask, then answer, using their strong command of language and writing embedded with personal meaning. To describe an approaching typhoon, they would examine the human element and report on how the storm is affecting people. Instead of expressing the immediacy of an emotion as an SF may, the NFs *explain* their emotion. Their tensions are transferred to the audience, as they empathize and infuse their own feelings onto the victims. With heart-wrenching drama, they raise the question: "What if this happened to me?" Intuitive authors with a Feeling preference are inspired to write when they have a story they need to tell, usually in the poetry, self-help, and love story genres.

If you're still not sure about how you should proceed in your given writing temperament, here's a quick list of tips:

NF (Intuitive Feeler): Write about how you feel to a person you care about.

NT (Intuitive Thinker): Write about something you want to learn about.

SJ (Sensing Judger): Write about what you know or about what happened.

SP (Sensing Perceiver): Write about what's happening now.

A Word on Poetry

Poetry plays on meaning, sound, rhythm, and visual aesthetics. And those with an NF (Intuitive Feeling) temperament stretch the literal meaning of words by making metaphors that come from the heart and are infused with their personal values. Expressing poetic observations at a bakery, for example, an Intuitive poet may compare a rising soufflé to the growth of a delicate flower, while a Sensing poet might focus on a baker kneading powdery dough and the wafting aroma of baking bread.

Movements in poetry have evolved over time, and the personality types that were attracted to poetry seemed to change too. Early poems were largely passed as oral record in rhymes, and this was perhaps more attractive to Extraverts and Sensing types. Forms that require precise grammatical rule and structure are more likely practiced by SJs (Sensing Judgers), with the looser, free verses used by Perceivers. Lyric poetry expresses our personal feelings along with Romanticism, which stressed the expression of strong emotions and was probably favored by the Feelers, who felt displaced by the Age of Enlightenment's order and reason—a movement that was probably dominated by Thinkers.

A Word on Public Speaking

When it comes to language, there are times when an audience seeks us to speak. Whether requests to share come informally from a friend or more formally, like when we're invited to make a wedding toast or a keynote address, it becomes evident that each type has their own speaking style (which is essentially a combination of our writing style and our performance style). When preparing to speak, for example, Introverts and Judgers tend to practice and memorize every word and gesture, and even plan in advance where to make their pause. On the other hand, Extraverts and Perceivers prefer speaking off the cuff, reacting to their audience.

A Final Word on Language

Although we all can't be Emily Dickinson or Ernest Hemingway, good communication skills are vital, whatever the medium for expressing your words. Look at the categories on a first grader's report card—and also the criteria on the performance reviews for top executives—and you will see that they are both graded on how well they communicate their ideas. Every day, at work and at play, in our routine life and in our artistic life, the words we choose to write and say facilitate how we interact, collaborate, and share our expressions. It's your own responsibility for getting your message across, and knowing your own style allows you to reach your audience more effectively.

Music

Whether we play an instrument or play the radio, music is a part of all of us. It's the universal language understood across cultures by everyone, from infancy to old age. This has a lot to do with music's many facets, which allow a musician to take part as a performer, composer, conductor, recording and audio engineer, and instrument maker. And there are different genres within music (classical, rock, chamber, large ensemble, solo, and so on) for exploring every one of these creative directions. For performers, the uniqueness of music comes less from the page and more from the way artists interpret and express the notes through their energy, intensity, and touch. The way we express music, as with every art form, is influenced by our personalities. For the Introvert, a private studio recording may be more preferable than the live concert performances of the Extravert. Perceivers may be prone to improvisation while the Judger is more comfortable when keeping time with the score.

Some types gravitate toward certain instruments; however, every type can have their own individual reasons for the choices they make. As her drumsticks fly to drive the beat of the band on her drums, an Extraverted Sensor (ES) enjoys playing loud because she loves to be surrounded by sound. One the other hand, an Introverted Intuitive (IN) may be an oboe player who's happier in the back of the orchestra, imagining the music and meanings in his head, beyond what he actually hears. Whether it's the seriousness of music composed by a Thinking Judger (TJ) like Richard Wagner or the light, foot-tapping melodies by a Sensing Perceiver (SP) like Johann Strauss, we can hear their personalities in the notes they play. An instrument serves as an extension of personality and voice, presenting all kinds of options to the diverse creative types who are drawn to them.

Many people say they can't sing or play an instrument; but any level of musical ability improves with practice, and different temperaments have their own motivations. The NFs (Intuitive Feelers) practice their lessons to please teachers, parents, or a mentor while NTs (Intuitive Thinkers) study to improve their skill for future performances. SP (Sensing Perceiver) musicians are motivated by excitement, sound, and vibrations while SJs (Sensing Judgers) are driven to practice in order to follow the notes with precision.

Regardless of whether you enjoy playing music or listening to music, understanding type can help you to appreciate others for their own style as you continue to play to the tune of your own fiddle.

Dance

If your thing is swaying to the music at a wedding or dancing as a form of exercise, or if you undertake the enormous effort in training to become a professional dancer, your personality influences your actions. Dance is a form of nonverbal communication, and its movements are purely in the moment. With its immediacy, physical nature, and athleticism, dance is especially engaging to Sensors. The use of the body as a medium is often natural for Sensing Feelers (SFs) who are most aware of their physical selves. One dancer we interviewed said, "Dancing . . . makes you part of the music or at one with the music, which is really a neat sensation." But dancing isn't just for SFs; each type can participate in their own ways.

As you're moving your body to disco, folk, or tango, you are externalizing what is in your mind. How much stays in your mind, how much is translated through your body, and how much of yourself you are sharing in the physical space is part of our Introversion or our Extraversion. Introverts may prefer to be mentally engaged by complicated routines, and they enjoy anonymously dancing alone or intimately with a partner. Though Extraverts may like dancing this way too, they tend to prefer socializing through group circle dances or line dances. Meanwhile, Sensors prefer to imitate their experiences of reality through dance; and Intuitives lean toward abstracting their reality, attributing meaning and symbols to their movements through styles like modern dance.

Dance is part of our common heritage. For geishas and Polynesian dancers, dance is a way to preserve their cultures, follow traditions, or tell stories—and this gives SJs (Sensing Judgers) active involvement in protecting these rituals. Thinking Judgers (TJs), on the other hand, rehearse techniques to achieve precision in their moves, a sentiment echoed by Fred Astaire when he said, "I have never used [dance] as an outlet or a means of expressing myself."[18] Feeling Perceivers (FPs) are different too, as they use dancing as a means to express themselves. They may prefer uneven rhythms or improvisational dance, and are inspired to bring joy to others. For Perceivers, pleasure is found in fluid movements and playful dancing, while Judgers prefer seriousness, timing, and structure. Though we all cater to either function at times, we find that the Perceiver is the child in us while the Judger is the adult.

No matter what your creative inclinations, it's important to keep in mind that we all must dance through the ballroom of life, sometimes swaying alone and sometimes partnered up. Knowing your strengths and preferences will keep you flexible and light on your feet.

Cooking

Whether you work as a gourmet chef, provide quick meals on the go, or frequently burn the toast, personality plays a role in how we prepare food. With a little effort, anyone who wants to cook can do it! "Food + fire = meal," and sometimes you don't even need the fire. What's standing in your way?

For Sensors, you're in luck, since cooking involves engaging all five of your senses. If you're an Intuitive, your key to success in the kitchen is remembering to actually smell and taste the ingredients. One bad egg spoils the omelet no matter how many wild mushrooms you add. We often hear Judgers say, "I can't cook because I don't improvise," while Perceivers say, "I can't follow a recipe even if my life depends upon it." The good news is that neither is necessary. So, rest assured, Judgers; it's okay to follow the recipe. And to the Perceivers: substitutions and deviations are always allowed.

The scene from two Italian restaurants differs. The first serves antipasto and spaghetti with meatballs as the main course. The other offers beef carpaccio as the starter and risotto and veal with penne in a wine reduction as the entrée. When we compare the traditional and modern menus, what can we glean about the personality of the chefs or the patrons? If Italian restaurants had a personality type, they would have a Feeling preference, since the maître d' is usually warm and welcoming, and the waiters are friendly and attentive. Contrast this with the impersonal and abrupt service often found in New York delis, and you see what a Thinking establishment is like.

For NF (Intuitive Feeling) chefs, food is love and has meaning. One NF caterer said, "Food is a concept, and I cook to please." Caring about the health and happiness of their guests, NFs may also pity the big animal hanging in the market and are more likely to be vegetarian. Some are attracted to cooking through encouragement from a close relative, because NFs often look to family role models and want to please them. And their cookbooks have titles that include words such as *joy, celebrate,* or *entertain,* or may have been written by a chef they admire.

For NT (Intuitive Thinking) chefs, food is about ideas. They surround themselves with complex cookbooks for inspiration, and the titles may feature classics that they can use as springboards, containing words like *secrets revealed, all about, fusion,* and *professional.* Their kitchen is a laboratory where they experiment and invent by blending together different cuisines.

Food is a basic necessity for SJ (Sensing Judger) chefs. They relish time-honored recipes and procedures passed down for generations, which they make as authentically as possible. Their cookbooks have titles with words such as *classic, proven, old world,* or *home.* They cook in a step-by-step manner, following and refining procedures with precision as they innovate by adapting past methods to modern kitchens.

SJs prepare appropriate foods for breakfast, lunch, and dinner, and aim to serve the "right" vegetable with the "right" main course. Their kitchens are orderly and clean, and their knives are sharp and ready. To eliminate stress and gain inspiration, SJs do well to remember that it's usually OK to omit certain ingredients they don't have on hand. Pizza comes out fine with substitutions—as long as you're not missing the dough.

SP (Sensing Perceiver) chefs seem to operate in one of two extremes: they're either masters of shortcuts, simplifying to the bare essentials; or they're masters of the craft, sparing no time and expense to cross the world to find the most exotic, difficult-to-use-and-pronounce ingredients, and then produce elaborate, one-of-a-kind dishes. It's hot dogs on the grill versus famous, wagyu beef flown fresh from Japan for making *shabu-shabu.* If SPs have any cookbooks at all, they have words in the titles like *pure and simple, real world, craft, quick and flavorful,* or *on the run.*

If the chef happens to be an Introvert combined with being an NP (Intuitive Perceiver), he or she gets distracted and is reminded to set a timer. Cooking is a very hands-on activity, and a meal has to actually be made, not just imagined.

Whatever you're cooking up, the more spoonfuls of your personality that you can heap into the meals you create, the more others will be sure to appreciate it.

Humor

Have you ever started laughing and then realized that what you found funny wasn't funny to someone else? Extraverts like to tell funny stories and laugh out loud at others, while Introverts tell one-liners and laugh on the inside, or at themselves. Literal and physical humor is favored by Sensors: "A man walks into a bar—*Ow!*—and hits his head." Figurative and absurd humor is favored by Intuitives: "A building catches fire while a couple is in their apartment on the thirteenth floor. They go out on the balcony to escape, and the woman says to her husband. 'We have to jump!' He says, 'We can't jump—we're on the thirteenth floor!' To which she replies, 'What are you, superstitious?'" Intuitives are also the joke tellers who leave out details needed for the punchline to be funny.

As for the other four preferences, Thinking types depersonalize humor and laugh at the harshness of life through good-news/bad-news jokes, while Feeling types laugh at what is sentimental. As a Feeler, Charles Schulz found humor through his own life and the people he knew. Judgers want closure in their jokes, while Perceivers laugh at flakiness and open-ended jokes. A Judger may say to a Perceiver, "You answer every question with a question," to which The Perceiver replies, "Is that bad?" Sometimes, Perceivers' jokes can go on and on, and they forget where they are going.

The four temperaments also have unique humor preferences. Their capacity to laugh helps NFs (Intuitive Feelers) to defuse charged situations and allows them to heal. They also laugh to rescue the teller from a bad joke. NTs (Intuitive Thinkers), on the other hand, like riddles, puns, and plays on words, and SPs (Sensing Perceivers) are attracted to practical jokes and jokes that make light of what is presently happening. Meanwhile, SJs (Sensing Judgers) tend to have a dry wit.

Laughter is universal; however, what people find funny says something about their personality and creative types, as well as their individuality.

Gardening

It's time for the annual spring cleanup, and four neighbors are talking across the back fence where their properties meet. Much needs to be done, and for Extraverts, talking about it is part of doing.

The NF (Intuitive Feeler) neighbor says she is going to plant some environmentally friendly native plants that prevent runoff and attract local wildlife—and "While we are all together, will you sign my petition for banning pesticides?" She is a part of her garden, and happy flowers brighten her life and that of her family.

The SJ (Sensing Judger) admires the apple tree that she cares for, which was planted by her grandfather. Today, she says she needs to thatch, seed, and fertilize—just like her family has done for generations to maintain the perfect lawn on this property. Plus, the hedges need trimming, and the evergreen needs pruning to keep its shape. Owning a complete set of tools; being comfortable with the routines of the growing cycle; having determination, austerity, and a desire for tangible results all contribute to SJs' success as gardeners and farmers. Gardens are more than neat rows of perennials planted for ornamentation; gardens are tomatoes that provide food, hedges that serve as a wind barrier, and evergreens that provide shade. SJs are also conservationists who save heirloom varieties of vegetables from extinction.

The SP (Sensing Perceiver) gardener climbs down from a tree with a chainsaw in her hand. She is already muddy, as she enjoys getting her hands into the dirt. To ensure blooms in every season, she buys flowering annuals at the nursery and rotates the plants in her garden beds regularly. But she doesn't keep track of what she plants since the surprises are exciting. She asks, "Does anyone have a shovel and a rake I can borrow?"

The NT (Intuitive Thinker) replies, "Check your shed; I loaned them to you last year."

The NT gardener uses his soil as a medium for testing experimental concepts of colors and contrasts. He says, "I'm putting herbs in three locations. By the end of the season, I'll know the best location for next year. Some day, I'm going to add a retaining wall and get new stones for my path. I also planted some saplings, and by the time I have grandchildren, we could build a tree house. Does anyone know where I can find some *Bellis perennis*?"

The neighborhood's walled-in Japanese garden provides a quiet place for Introverts to cultivate the soil as well as their thoughts. The bright flowers at the front gate are an Extravert's way to attract the attention of bees and passersby alike. And the Judgers' gardens look orderly and well groomed alongside the wilder, more haphazard gardens of the Perceivers.

These gardening examples—in addition to the other creative pursuits in this section—provide a simple template for the many ways type can be applied to our creativity in virtually all of our favorite activities. Whether it's growing sweet corn, building model airplanes, restoring antiques, scuba diving, or scrapbooking, they all have components related to personality type.

Overcoming Blocks

Perhaps you have a paper due tomorrow, or you have a presentation scheduled and don't know where to start. Blocks don't only stop writers; they inhibit people pursuing all kinds of creative activities. Sitting on the piano bench, holding a pristine notebook, staring at a blank canvas, walking across an empty stage—scenarios like these can evoke anxiety and lead to people feeling blocked. Although there are many reasons for getting stuck, understanding your personality provides one of the keys to unlocking your mind and unblocking your creativity. Just as a fire won't start without the right mix of air to fuel, our own combustion of ideas must have the right mix of information to make decisions.

The first way to overcome a block is to relax and not let it get the better of you. (People find they are more creative when they're relaxed.) We can't always be inspired to create, however, so creativity takes both relaxation and inspiration.

When your creative sparks aren't flying, there are still many pre- and post-production tasks that you can accomplish. So, the second way you can address your block is by taking care of these other day-to-day distractions, like paying bills; gathering material, learning new techniques and equipment; and editing, organizing, and marketing. By clearing these tasks away, you make the most of your downtime, and when inspiration strikes, nothing stands in your way.

The ways we get unstuck can be demonstrated by an example of how a couple living in a big city goes about choosing a place for dinner. The husband, who is a Judger, asks his wife what kind of food she wants. She says Mexican, and he immediately gets stuck. Of the three places he knows, one has made them sick, one is too loud, and the other won't have a table without a reservation; he's painted himself into a corner. To help him get unblocked, his Perceiver wife opens up the possibilities by suggesting Cuban or Southwest cuisine, and another group of restaurants becomes available.

Now the Perceiver wife gets stuck by the overwhelming number of possibilities. Fortunately, her husband steps in to narrow the choices by asking some questions: "What kind of food, traditional or experimental? Outdoor seating? Formal or casual?" Eventually, they decide on the little Cuban place down the street, and they both feel better. Together, they show two different ways Judgers and Perceivers get stuck, and how they can help each other to get free.

Judgers often see new information as a distraction and quickly make decisions to filter out the unwanted noise. However, by closing off the flow of information too soon, they get blocked—just like the husband in the example. Like briefly opening a window to let in fresh air, Judgers unclog their creative impulses by temporarily backing off their convictions and opening up to new information. If you're a Judger and you're stuck, try doing something out of order, not according to plan, off topic, and seemingly pointless. Browsing books at the library, walking through the park, taking a new way home, conversing with an old friend, taking a short vacation, trying a new medium, listening to a concert—any new or unplanned experience will help.

Judger's creativity is reawakened by temporarily letting down their guard. Picking a magazine to read that is clearly irrelevant, going to a meeting that you know is going to be a waste of time, talking to someone you have nothing in common with; all may open up new and unexpected possibilities. Sometimes, taking a step backward provides an unexpected vantage to solve problems ahead. If you are playing Scrabble and can't come up with a word, try to drop your self-imposed restrictions and look beyond your letters to take note of what just changed on the board.

On the flip side, the remedies that help Judgers get unblocked are the wrong medicine for Perceivers, since more information drives them further off course and perpetuates procrastination. They get blocked by too many choices, and then they can't decide where to start. For example, if they form an awesome word in Scrabble, they may become stuck by searching endlessly for the perfect spot to put it on the board.

Perceivers gain focus by constricting the flow of new information and making some decisions. While they usually don't like being locked in, a few tentative decisions can help them prioritize and get back on track. Ranking ideas, choosing a subject, going through the exercise of developing a "tentative" outline, and taking steps to reduce distractions are all helpful. For Perceivers, one idea leads to the next. Hemingway had his own method for keeping the ideas flowing: "I always stop at a point where I know precisely what's going to happen next—so I don't have to crank up every day."[19]

For Intuitives, the phrase, "In theory, it will not work" is what sabotages them. Lots of great innovations occur well outside the bounds of theory. By remembering that theory is not fact and rephrasing the sentence to, "In theory, it may not work in all cases," Intuitives can get moving again.

Conversely, Sensors can become blocked if concepts don't have a practical application, or if they don't have access to the experiences they wish to create. A novel set in Bali challenges Sensing writers when they don't have access to the island. By using a nearby, accessible location instead, Sensors get the first-hand experiences they need for inspiration.

If you're an Extravert and you become stuck, see what other people are doing; if you're an Introvert, take extra time to reflect and let your subconscious work. In addition, writing down ideas unclutters the Introverts' mind and helps Extraverts to see their options.

For Thinking and Feeling writers, you can experience added stress when you write for prolonged periods outside of your own character. The Thinker author who is expressing emotional and interpersonal relationships, such as dialogue for a soap opera, is acting outside of their strongest suit. The Feeling author writing technical manuals is another example. Eliminate blocks like these by choosing a project that fits better with your natural inclinations. Whether you're a Perceiver or a Judger, sometimes, you just have to start doing and inspiration will come.

Everyone gets blocked sometimes, for their own unique reasons. But the more you understand your creative type, the more you know which medicine to reach for. Are you writing a book? Looking for a place to eat? Playing Scrabble? Dreaming up the next big invention? The right remedy will help you to get unstuck, no matter what you're applying your unique creativity to.

10

USING YOUR CREATIVE TYPE
TO SUCCEED IN WORK

Some people fall into an occupation where they love to get up and go to work each day, but many of us aren't this lucky and are still searching. Would you like to find more enjoyment in your work?

We spend so much of our lives on the job, and when we are doing what we love, it doesn't seem like work at all; time flies by. If you work as an artist, then you probably already know what this is like. However, well beyond the arts, there are tremendous opportunities to use your creativity at every kind of work—and creativity is in demand more than ever before. Knowing your creative style allows you to use your strengths to become more engaged and get more out of your work.

Although it might not be widely recognized, creativity is a valuable currency in the marketplace, both local and global. Freedom of expression is what keeps us engaged and makes our offerings unique. We interviewed a flower shop owner who loves creating displays and working with his customers. He had this to say about creative expression in his business: "I do a good job, but I'm not concerned if the flowers aren't arranged perfectly. At most flower shops, you can order from a book of standard designs—say 'Give me a number twenty-one,' and it can be designed there, or anywhere, to exact specifications." He explained that his customers want something original, and want to pick a color scheme or flower that is meaningful to them. Because he designs from his heart, it's his unique style that keep his customers coming back. And it's his freedom to create in his own way that keeps him engaged.

Creativity isn't only needed for arranging flowers. Today, some of the fastest-growing high-tech firms are looking to develop apps, web pages, and products with more than function. Their look, the messages they convey, and the ways "real people" use them are all considerations. Computer programmers with a sense for design are now in high demand. In fact, it's part of *everyone's* job description to think creatively, like a designer.

Using creativity at work and becoming more engaged are both required for us to thrive and for our businesses to survive. So many of us are underemployed and have a tremendous capability to do more—a capacity that can be tapped by learning to use our strengths and by following our passions.

We're all experiencing rapid and unprecedented changes as globalization redefines our jobs. People are trying to get ahead, the cost of school has skyrocketed, and the job world seems to be a completely different game than it used to be, even ten years ago. We can no longer depend upon our educational institutions to fully prepare us, or expect our companies to provide continuous employment. While changes are leaving many behind, how can you stay competitive, adapt, and find new opportunities to survive and do what you enjoy most? Fortunately, you can count on yourself to find happiness and success at work by matching your job requirements with the strengths of your personality type.

What are you passionate about creating? Do you, for example, want to create a multi-billion dollar empire? Well, if you do, the first step is to figure out if you are more like Donald Trump or Bill Gates. Clearly, one is an Extravert and the other is an Introvert. One is a Sensor and the other is an Intuitive. However, despite these differences, successful people do have one thing in common: they know who they are and have learned how to masterfully use their self awareness to their advantage. Trump constructs luxury buildings that grace our skylines, and Gates builds intangible bits of software code that do wonders concealed from view. Both men are creative and both are engaged in their work, and neither guy is going to be outsourced anytime soon.

You must know your own creative style to professionally succeed. Perhaps you are more like Bill Gates, but when you go to create, you habitually try to do it like Donald Trump—and it just doesn't work for you. The good news is that this is a problem with an easy solution. Once you determine your particular creative style, you will know how to begin creating in a way that is completely natural to your personality type. Whatever your passion, you will start to enjoy breakthrough success, gaining the respect of your peers and enjoying what you do.

Fits Like a Glove

Like slipping your fingers into a well-made glove, when you are engaged at work, the special skills and talents of your personality type fit snugly into the right opportunities to use them. This includes your relationships with coworkers, clients, and supervisors; everything can begin to improve with the understanding of personality type, and automatically make your work more enjoyable.

Certain personalities are drawn to certain professions, and they all have the potential to fit like a glove. For example, SJs (Sensing Judgers) tend to join accounting departments because of their preference for exactness. SPs (Sensing Perceivers) tend to join fire departments because they seek action-filled professions. If you are already running with your herd, use your strengths to not only match your job requirements but surpass them.

Success and fulfillment come from following your passion, and there is room to find fulfillment in practically any field—regardless of your type. Every accountant, teacher, and police officer may share a job title with others in their profession, but that doesn't mean they all have the same job description. Nobody should ever be discouraged from entering a profession based on their type.

Until you find the right fit, expect to find yourself going against the grain at some point. If your personality type doesn't match the norm for your field, be aware that you're swimming upstream. Your differences can be used to your advantage, however, and you can learn to "fit in by not fitting in." Otto tells of an ENFJ woman (a Persuader) in payroll at Fort Knox. While her type is atypical for accounting, she loved her work, and through her friendliness, she improved the operation and received high performance ratings. You can succeed at any profession by simply being yourself.

The creative ark has room for all kinds. If you're passionate about financial markets, there are opportunities for using your strengths, whatever your temperament. An SP (Sensing Perceiver) stockbroker on the trading floor doesn't worry about history or the future in his work. This person makes instant buying or selling decisions based on what is happening at this very moment, in real time. In contrast, an SJ (Sensing Judger) portfolio manager studies past performances to make her decisions. Other temperaments may approach their work differently, such as an NT (Intuitive Thinker) who looks at analytics to predict trends, or an NF (Intuitive Feeler) who predicts market moves by how people will react.

Extraverted Feelers make fine salespeople who empathize with their customers, but so do Introverted Thinkers, who carefully listen to their customers without projecting their own needs. If you are one of the few Extraverted librarians, then perhaps your standout strength is in leading tours. As the rare, Feeling financial planner, you may have a special way with helping families calm their fear of investing for retirement. Or perhaps you, the Thinking human resources manager, can step in and show leadership when tough decisions need to be made. Whatever you do, seek out ways to contribute—and stand out—using your unique strengths.

Uniqueness comes from going against the norm. Since many preschool teachers have the SFJ combination in their type, an NTP combination could bring a broader, more open-ended perspective to the children. Most college professors are Intuitives; therefore, Sensors could add value for their students by bringing current and concrete examples to the classroom. Many attorneys happen to follow the cold logic of the law, so a Feeling attorney could find a niche in family law, nonprofits, or human rights issues—just as an NF (Intuitive Feeler) engineer may go into green construction or ergonomics. Similarly, while most accountants are SJs (Sensing Judgers) who maintain control and close the books each month, an NP (Intuitive Perceiver) accountant can excel at sorting through the chaos of startups, or leading change and growth. SPs (Sensing Perceivers) aren't often found among the top corporate ranks, but those who seem to be like Trump and Branson certainly are nimble in exploiting our changing environment. Those few Feeling generals can easily win the love of their troops. If you find yourself as a minority in a field, this is a great opportunity to be yourself. Uniqueness is exactly what's needed today.

Know your strengths through your type, become aware of what is required for your work, then use your strengths to follow your passion. If you are graceful in the arts but have a passion for healthcare, you may enjoy becoming a plastic surgeon. If you have an analytical mind and a passion for law, you may enjoy becoming a patent attorney. If you abide by procedures and love to travel, you may enjoy becoming a pilot. Whatever you do, engage with your work by seeking out ways to maximize your strengths.

Your Creative Style at Work

Extraverts: Every organization and product needs a great story, and Extraverts are great storytellers. Collaboration is engaging and exciting for Extraverts, and they often lead groups through discussions. Although they think out loud, not every new idea should be expressed before it's fully developed. If you're an Extravert, find a group of colleagues with whom you can bounce around ideas before sharing in public or up the chain. Hone your listening skills, and be aware that more of what you say is being literally recorded and can be shared easily and widely over the internet. Know when to self-censor.

Introverts: The creative act of pondering and generating ideas is engaging and exciting for Introverts. However, they need alone time. If you're an Introvert, don't depend on others to read your mind or notice your ideas. Increase your visibility by seizing opportunities to communicate. It's not enough to think of ideas; you need to say them.

Unlike Extraverts, Introverts often naturally stop and think before acting. This hesitation can help stabilize organizations by avoiding impulsive changes in direction. Waiting to act provides time to make improvements and smooth out the rough edges—to fit missions and strategies better. The world is getting more transparent and collaborative, so you must share more and form trusting partnerships.

Sensors: Just as a shopping mall is a collection of many separate stores added together, Sensors take related ideas and put them together. Sensors are in touch with current realities, gathering hard data and then scanning the surrounding environment for immediate opportunities. They are hands-on, mechanically oriented people who are always needed for maintenance and repair. In fact, maintenance is the strength of the SJ (Sensing Judger), and repair is the strength of the SP (Sensing Perceiver). Whether it's replacing watch batteries, repairing washer machines belts, or ensuring the safety and operations of a nuclear power plant, a Sensor is the person for the job. If you're a Sensor, when sharing your ideas with an Intuitive, make sure to explain how it fits with the overall mission of the firm, and point out the future benefits.

Intuitives: Like a general store that conveniently carries everything under one roof, Intuitives take ideas and efficiently integrate them. It takes time to bring new products to the market, and Intuitives look toward the future to predict market opportunities. Taking a holistic approach, they look at problems from new angles, seeking patterns and ways to join dissimilar ideas. When evaluating a problem, Intuitives seek root causes to understand why.

If you are an Intuitive, you are reminded to look past what you expect in order to examine the facts. Then, to gain acceptance of your ideas, package them with details and immediacy, and demonstrate their practical applications. Intuitives are also reminded to have patience if you must fill out forms in triplicate when applying for a job. Though it may seem like an inefficient process to you, there could be a reason. And if you learn that reason, you could improve the process once you're hired.

Thinkers: The greatest strength of Thinkers is their ability to keep a cool head and cut through emotions to reach the core issues, making tough decisions with answers that others sometimes consider unthinkable. If you're a Thinker, your challenge is to consider how your decisions affect people, and you are advised not to attach your comfort level to being always being right. Businesses are embracing the expression of emotion through stories, and Thinking types need to prompt empathy. Be aware that sometimes the core of problems can be a people issue.

Feelers: For Feeling deciders, all business is personal. They create by asking "What do I want?" and think about how people experience their products. If you're a Feeler, use your interpersonal skills while keeping your personal feelings in check. Ask yourself: *Do my employer's values coincide with my values?* While business has long been based on cold calculations to maximize profits, the value of social responsibilities is gaining importance. An increased awareness of the need for interpersonal relationships—with employees, clients, and vendors alike—is creating more opportunities for Feeling deciders. Emotions sell and relationships matter. By using the right emotion in the right context, Feeling types provide authenticity and engage audiences. Feelers also do well with crafting marketing campaigns and inspiring teams.

While Feelers may believe in their ideas, they must challenge themselves by asking, "Will it work?" If you are a Feeler, remember it's a slippery slope to identify yourself solely with your occupation. Instead, try defining yourself through your creative accomplishments, and put more emphasis on who you are as a person.

Judgers: The perseverance of Judgers is a towering strength that allows them to overcome obstacles of all sizes. If you're a Judger, you're decisive in selecting projects, and you keep them on schedule. Just remember that innovation is often messy and unpredictable, so don't wait for your plan to be perfect before starting. Recognize unexpected successes when they occur and plan for flexibility, as changes from supervisors or clients are to be expected.

The size of the pie isn't always fixed, and by expanding the pie, everyone can have a larger piece. Judgers often become fixated on the first viable solution, so as an exercise, they should try to continue their search for three possible answers before deciding which one is best. As a Judger, be aware that criticism breeds a culture where ideas aren't shared.

Withhold your judgment when listening to a new idea, and then be grateful, gracious, positive, and constructive in your feedback in order to support a creative culture.

Perceivers: Innovation is often unpredictable, but Perceiving types thrive without defined goals. If you are a Perceiver, you are curious, and you create by trying something new and reacting to the information it provides. Although your flexibility and responsiveness are your strengths, keep an eye on your deadlines, be alert to when neatness and timeliness matter, and help others to see possibilities.

NF (Intuitive Feelers): Creative in ways that promote a better way of life, NFs see people patterns in politics and social causes. They also think innovatively by putting themselves in other people's shoes, asking, "How would Donald Trump, Oprah Winfrey, or my uncle deal with this?" NFs are most creative when they feel personally involved. However, they must take care to not take rejection too personally. They are also advised to keep an eye on the bottom line since this affects people's lives too.

NT (Intuitive Thinkers): When it comes to examining the possibilities and getting down to the nitty-gritty, nothing is sacred with NTs. They disrupt and innovate by questioning and challenging the status quo. They are very comfortable with technology and use it to positively impact their work. Their love of learning also helps them to stay current. If you are an NT, you thrive on complications but need to simplify things to reach your audience. Also, with increased specialization, you need to reconcile that you can't be an expert in everything. Become enlightened by thinking about people. Be more like Steve Jobs, who designed products by considering how people would actually use them: "The most important thing is a person—a person who incites your curiosity and feeds your curiosity. And machines cannot do that in the same way that people can. The elements of discovery are all around you. You don't need a computer."[1]

SJ (Sensing Judgers): Curators of lessons learned and guardians of systems—these are the SJs. Recognizing that every business is different, SJs know how to make ideas work within existing systems without disrupting what is currently working. They find new ways to organize and measure what they already have and learn how things work. If you're an SJ, it's important to realize that being a guardian requires learning from new experiences and changing—so systems can grow. You must balance your efforts between keeping things running and using resources to improve outmoded processes.

Innovations only create temporary monopolies, and to survive, we must continue to improve. SJs are advised to build some allowance into their plans, because every idea won't succeed—but many will. As an exercise, write down the rules and then imagine they don't exist. How would you redesign without rules and what new rules would you write? When at their best, SJs keep tradition alive by saving what's useful and relevant while allowing systems to evolve.

SP (Sensing Perceivers): Thriving on today's trends, SPs reinvent by taking the pulse of what is needed and creating accordingly. Not wanting to be trapped in a meeting or behind a desk for too long where it's no fun, SPs would rather be out in the field solving problems. Agility and responsiveness are two of their unique strengths, allowing them to transform today's crises into today's opportunities. If you're an SP, your ideas and actions have impact. For inspiration, just remember to look outside your walls and see what others are doing— how they're also innovating with their unique strengths. SPs are the first to cut corners, and though we all benefit from their shortcuts, they can have an even greater impact by pausing to think, following through, and considering future implications of their actions.

Your Personal Brand

If you were a packaged product on the shelf of a supermarket, what would your packaging say about you? Brands aren't only for soft drinks and chips; in our super-connected world, we all need a personal brand. And everything you do—whether you are riding an elevator, walking through a lobby, or writing an email—contributes or detracts from your brand's image.

Define your brand by writing words that describe your personality preferences and resonate with you. Construct your brand around your personal objectives, values, or company mission, and ask: *How am I different from everyone else?* Judgers, for instance, are particularly aware of presenting an image of order and control, while the brand

Perceivers' project includes their responsiveness to changing circumstances. What does your brand look like, and who wants to use your product?

Increase Your Competitiveness Using Your Creative Style

With so many distractions demanding our attention and creating noise, you maybe didn't hear the starter pistol; however, the race has already begun. Perhaps you thought you were here to watch, but your team needs everyone to participate. So, climb out of the bleachers and put on your tracksuit. It's time to use creativity to increase competitiveness through innovation—not as a country or a company, but as an individual. What steps can you take to become more competitive personally?

Throughout this book, you've been discovering your unique strengths and your creative style. Now it's time to use them to save your job. Although globalization has fans and opponents, it's been around since the Phoenicians sailed the Mediterranean and merchants caravanned along the Silk Road. More than ever before, efficiencies in communications and shipping are causing standardized work to migrate to the least-cost providers. For us, this means the work we do that is the most unique—and adds value—is the most secure.

Not too long ago, we competed with rivals in the next cubical for promotions and we competed with companies across town for clients; now we compete with everyone on earth. Educated people have become commodities, with hundreds of millions of people having advanced degrees and fast internet connections. Thriving requires you to differentiate yourself among them by adding value, improving processes, inventing, and bringing useful ideas to market in novel ways.

It's more important than ever to use your natural resources, and it's your personality and unique experiences that make you different. While our schooling makes us the same, our differences make us great. Anything standardized can be copied and automated, but our uniqueness makes us competitive.

When dismissing an idea, people typically say phrases like "I've never seen anything like it," "It's not what I expected," and "This isn't how we've done it before." However, these are exactly the times when an idea deserves a second look. Innovating means acting within your uniqueness to make something that looks, feels, and sounds different than what has been done in the past.

With so many people centered in narrow niches, there are boundless creative opportunities if you can think broadly across disciplines. Write down a number of your interests, activities, skills, and unique experiences, then ask yourself: *Where do the items on my list intersect?* How can these combinations add value by filling gaps in the marketplace? For example, our (David's and Otto's) interest in psychology, art, and creativity combined with skills in research and writing were used together to bring about this book project. Like a combination lock, the more numbers (interests and skills) we added, the stronger our code (our book) became. Likewise, by increasing the number of activities and skills on your list, you increase the possibilities. Do what you love to find happiness, and combine the things you love to compete.

Opportunities in the Business Cycle

At times of loss, it's natural to feel sad. Yet, how many times have you heard, "Losing _____ was the best thing that ever happened"? Loss produces necessity and gives us the freedom we need to make positive changes. Fortunes fall and rise, and our lives don't follow a linear path—neither does the business cycle. Awareness of this fluctuation is the umbrella that keeps us dry until the storms have passed. Judgers in particular must remember that you can't control external occurrences; you can only control your reactions to them. You must also recognize that it's your rigidity that gets you into trouble, and even when you can't see your way out, it doesn't mean you're doomed. A Judger's strength comes from the ability to stay the course, while others turn to you for strength and stability. Try to view change as an opportunity.

During bad times, seek assistance from people who have preferences that are opposite your own. Judgers need Perceivers in their lives to point out open paths when they get stuck. Likewise, Perceivers need Judgers to help them focus and make choices when they get overwhelmed by too many paths. If all your friends have peanut butter, look for someone who has jelly.

Balancing future possibilities with actual opportunities is where Intuitives and Sensors can help each other. Playing pool, Intuitives may line up three or four shots ahead yet miss the obvious shots in front of them. Sensors, on the other hand, may shoot the ball in front of the pocket but fail to set up the next shot.

Like minds will almost always attract—to the point that many of our friends have preferences very similar to our own. However, going outside your circle to talk with people who have different outlooks can open your eyes to bigger and better opportunities, not only in business but in life in general.

In good times, when we have excesses, there are plenty of opportunities, but downturns bring their own opportunities. By making things faster, cheaper, stronger, lighter, *better*, we can add value and thrive, even in declining conditions. How can you identify and increase the value you add?

The Value of Your Strengths

For many people, especially SJs (Sensing Judgers), you show up on time, work hard, and play by the rules, yet the game is changing around you. So, it's essential to identify which parts of your job are routines and which parts require your unique touch. The more our routines become commodities and risk disappearing through automation or outsourcing, the more we have to focus on the one-of-a-kind ways we add value.

With fierce internet competition for products, how can a local shopkeeper survive? An ST (Sensing Thinker) shoe-store owner, someone who prefers to verify facts by touching explains, "Not every size 9 sneaker is the same, and neither are our feet. Our customers go through the trouble of coming to the shop and paying a little more because they want to first feel the leather and then make sure their shoes fit." The value he's providing is more than just shoes, and it is unique to us by type: his NF (Intuitive Feeler) customers like him as a person and appreciate his personalized service; the NTs (Intuitive Thinkers) respect his knowledge and want to be educated about their purchase; the SJs (Sensing Judgers) want their foot measured and enjoy the tradition of buying shoes from him; and the SP (Sensing Perceiver) customers were just walking by when they were attracted by the window display.

The executives at Eastman Kodak failed to understand the value they were offering, so they didn't adjust their product accordingly. While they thought they were in the film business, their value came not from film but through the preservation and sharing of memories. Whatever your business, know who your customers are and ask them why they buy from you. Ask yourself, *Who is my real customer and what is my real product?* One SP told us that he really doesn't do much at work at all: "The only reason they keep me around is because I walk around and keep everyone else entertained." This may be true if you're an employee or an owner. Surprisingly, the value you may be adding could be from the entertainment and enjoyment you give your customers.

Even when things are well run, there are plenty of inefficiencies. Every time you or one of your clients is frustrated by a product or service, you're identifying market opportunities. To estimate the opportunity's value, ask how many people share the same frustration and calculate what its relief is worth. As Henry Ford noted in *My Life and Work*, "Save ten steps a day for each of twelve thousand employees, and you will have saved fifty miles of wasted motion."[2]

You don't have to depend on others to offer you the work that you want. Use your creativity to design your own work. Chart your own course as an entrepreneur or within your firm simply by saving people time or money by improving practices. There are enormous possibilities for finding new solutions to unsatisfied needs, and it's something everyone can do. But few of us can expect to be successful the first time. Limit your risk by starting with local problems you understand. Then use the results of your test to scale up what's working. From there, the sky's the limit.

Managing for Change

How would you feel if you were suddenly given a new boss, health plan, travel policy, office mate, project, or client? What if the software on your computer automatically updated itself and rearranged all of your icons, taskbars, and dropdown menus in the process? All changes have the potential to provoke panic; yet, all changes also have the potential to bring opportunity. Changes in laws, consumer preferences, economics, geography, technology, demography all bring new opportunities to drive innovation.

While the unknowns from change can scare anyone, those with one or more of the three preferences Introversion, Sensing, and Judging resist change the most. If you share any of these preferences, try reframing change by taking ownership of the experience.

Judgers are particularly challenged by changes, but they are reminded to save their resources by not fighting the inevitable. If you're a Judger, consider change as a product that you can take ownership of—an item you can put on your list and check off when it's delivered. A friend of ours has a dog named Flip-Flop. Acting like an SP (Sensing Perceiver), our friend embraces change, takes her dog along wherever she goes, chooses the paths that are most exciting, eats the most interesting foods, travels, spends, and lives for today. Contrary to what some believe, there is strength in changing your mind as it allows for chasing better opportunities. Digging in your heels and failing to adapt can cause you to miss opportunities. Flip-Flop is certainly getting the most out of life.

For Sensors, the future is unknown—but it's not real. Making the future tangible through mockups can make it less scary. For example, before landing in the chaotic New Delhi airport, passengers are directed to watch a video that simulates a realistic, three-dimensional walk through the immigration line and baggage claim areas. For Sensing passengers particularly, this gave a clear picture of what to expect and helped them to adjust. This simulation also helped the Introverts, but for a different reason. Introverts react better to change if they're given advance notice and have some time to think about what is going to happen.

Introverts need time to ponder new information and Judgers don't often like surprises. Everyone can help these types make smoother transitions simply by providing enough time and advance notice. Innovation disrupts the status quo and prompts resistance from those who benefit from the current system. For change to be embraced within an organization, it needs to demonstrate that it is clearly better than what worked—or didn't work—previously. Don't be surprised if Introverts, Sensors, and Judgers are among the initial skeptics, but give them credit for their creative strengths and feedback. Change happens with or without us. And a cooperative effort provides far more opportunities than a resistant one.

Idea Incubation

It only takes one acorn to grow a towering oak; one idea can grow to change the world. While some Intuitives endlessly generate ideas, Sensors generally have them less frequently—yet both types of people are creative. Don't compare yourself to others who seem prolific; an oak can drop thousands of acorns, but the forest floor can only accommodate a few saplings. Ideas take time and effort to develop. The key is to recognize good ideas when we see them and then take the steps to implement them.

It's not easy to share new ideas. Sometimes people laugh, and there are plenty of forces in our society that maintain the status quo. But we all can learn something from one ENTP (a Brainstormer) who generates lots of ideas and has plenty of practice airing them in public. He says, "Most of the time, I don't expect my ideas to be adopted; the 'worst thing that could happen' is usually not too bad."

People also get concerned that their ideas will be stolen. Use your instincts to determine who you can trust, but remember that it takes a lot of effort to implement ideas (the stealing is the easy part). This provides some protection since most people won't follow through.

Some people seem to think that all the good ideas have already been thought of, and this just isn't true. To find innovative ideas, simply consider what can be done when existing products don't meet your needs. You could think about ways to reduce costs in energy, labor, and material, or about ways to improve quality or expand products into new markets. There are tremendous opportunities to innovate in health care, renewable energy, sustainable sources of food and water, improved customer service, infrastructure, transportation, and education. Innovations come from making *anything* easier to use, from helping people filter information to making governments more efficient. Whether you want to build market share, increase productivity, develop new products, or better connect with your customers, ideas are needed. Ideas are the new economy's raw material, and those who generate the most valuable ideas lead. How can you maximize your own natural resources to mine the golden ideas from your mind?

Maximizing their strengths is what most business people are taught to do; type theory, on the other hand, warns that by maximizing those strengths, they become liabilities. For example, a maximized Extravert doesn't listen, and a maximized Introvert doesn't communicate. More is not always better, and maximizing is not always optimizing. An extreme Intuitive only sees what they want to see, missing important information. The extreme Sensor may see all the intricacies of a situation but fail to understand how they all fit together. Balancing opposing preferences allows a Sensor to take a brief vacation in the Intuitive realm to generate ideas. And an enlightened Intuitive can benefit from briefly leaning toward Sensing to gather the details needed to develop their theories.

Inventions come from looking at problems you understand well, using your experience, and borrowing from other fields to find solutions. One NF (Intuitive Feeler) receptionist spent her bonus and vacation in a luxury resort in Hawaii. "I know how I like to be treated," she said, "and it's fun to check out what the professionals are getting right about service." Then, when she returned to work, she implemented the resort's ideas, like memorizing visitor's names to make them feel like welcome guests.

As we define our problems to solve, we examine them from different angles. Sensors look at the particulars of today's troubles, while Intuitives tend to consider trouble ahead. To solve current problems, SPs (Sensing Perceivers) grab the latest technologies and quickly sum up available resources. The SP bus driver can leave his route to avoid a traffic jam and still make all his stops, saving his passengers time. However, when SPs need some excitement, they have even been known to create problems to solve, like firemen who set fires. Conversely, NT (Intuitive Thinker) highway patrolmen remove fallen rocks from a mountain road to preemptively nip problems before anyone notices a sign of trouble (and they often get little credit for their efforts).

Brainstorming groups provide the stimuli to spark ideas, where one idea elevates thinking to the next, yet ideas originate in a single mind. Is brainstorming the best practice for everyone? Getting a diverse group of people together to express wild ideas and explore endless possibilities that may never be implemented is exciting and the home turf for ENP combinations—and intimidating foreign soil for ISJ combinations. Extraverts are comfortable shouting out incomplete thoughts and developing them as they speak, while Introverts blossom with alone time to ponder, sometimes brainstorming by themselves. To improve the productivity of brainstorming by Introverts, try making topics available in advance, and provide opportunities to contribute afterward. Also, go around the room to ask the Introverts what they think—so they can get a word in.

One ENTJ (a Commander) explained that the aim of the brainstorming season he led for a homeowners group wasn't about finding a solution, since he had already decided on the best course of action: "Its purpose was . . . getting our neighbors aware of and involved with an issue, and winning their support for my solution." True to his type, he suggested, "When new ideas are really needed, open debate is a better approach."

While brainstorming gathers people to make suggestions without judging, in this ENTJ's experience, judging is good. Speaking like an NT (Intuitive Thinker), he added, "Better ideas come through debate because competition and consequences for bad ideas gets people thinking harder." Debate is also a forum that allows the best ideas to win and gain support from the participants. All the while, Introverted Feelers (IFs) may be uninspired to contribute to this combative format. A mix of brainstorming, alone time, and debate are some of the alternative techniques that can allow people of different types to shine.

Solicit ideas from all levels. In the past, leaders guarded knowledge and spooned it out as needed to workers. Today, the further you go down the chain, the greater the workers' knowledge; more than ever, ideas bubble from the bottom up. Those standing closest to the fire know what's hot—and are the first to notice what's cooling.

Recognizing Greatness when Making Decisions

In a wet market in Singapore, David asked a local how to pick the best dragonfruit, and she said, "The best one is the biggest—they are all the same price." Choosing good ideas isn't so easy. Ideas are everywhere, and our suggestion box is bursting. We talk about ideas all the time, but we know it would be impossible to follow up on all of them. So, how do you sort and select the ones that are worth implementing?

Innovation is often defined as putting creative ideas to use, and this starts with selection. Whether you're a Thinking or a Feeling decider, selection is the home turf for Judgers. Consider how much value is added, whether competitive advantage can be gained, and what the entry barriers are. If you are a Perceiver and get overwhelmed, find Judgers to help you establish criteria to narrow your options. Meanwhile, Sensors consider the facts, and Intuitives trust their gut.

If choices don't feel right, they may not be—but don't confuse this feeling with the healthy butterflies that come from trying something new. While Judgers' strength lies in being decisive, remember to withhold judgment and constructive criticism until you hear about the idea in its entirety and consider its possibilities.

Questions to Ask When Decision Making

NF (Intuitive Feelers): *Do I want this product and does it fit with who I am? Can I leverage my relationships? Does the idea align with my mission, or should I expand my mission? How will my customers feel? How can this benefit humankind?* As an NF, you are highly focused on your relationships, and this is one of your strengths. It's advantageous for you to use your interpersonal skills in business through your formal and informal networks. However, keep an open mind by suspending your values and considering the logic. Beware of falling in love with your own idea and becoming blind to its flaws.

NT (Intuitive Thinkers): *Why am I doing it this way? Is it within my competencies, or is it worth acquiring the necessary capacity? What is the upside versus the downside? How will this affect my future? How long is the shelf life? How large can the market grow? Why is this better than our current plan?* If you're an NT, as you ask yourself these questions, remember to keep an open mind by looking past the credentials of the messenger.

SJ (Sensing Judgers): *What does it cost? Has it been done before? Will it work? Can I integrate it within my system? What equipment will we need? Is the process efficient? How long will it take to develop? What will the transition be like? What is the timeline? Can we get the parts? Can it be contained? Will it make us more secure?* If you're an SJ, keep an open mind by not asking for the proof first.

SP (Sensing Perceiver): *Will this be fun to try? Is it exciting and useful to the market today? What are our competitors doing? Will it allow for flexibility? Will it produce a tangible output? How important are the deadlines? Can we start now? What benefit can we see today?* As an SP, it helps to keep an open mind, even if the idea seems boring at first. Maybe it has exciting elements that will reveal themselves later.

Playing Outside the Sandbox

Children are natural at play—it's how they learn. Yet many adults seem to forget this important activity. Take an instance in which a teacher invited parents to spend an evening in their children's preschool classroom to get an idea of where their kids spent a good portion of the day and experience their world. As you may expect, even with teacher's encouragement, the parents didn't have any inclination to pick up a single block or put on a silly wig. As we become adults, many of us lose our playfulness and learn not to embarrass ourselves among new acquaintances, but this playful tendency is something worth revisiting if you feel your creative zeal has waned over the years.

Play relaxes us and opens our mind to possibilities. Some of the most creative companies have cultures of play at work, and this helps to attract talent and breed ideas. We all learn by doing, and play allows us to try out prototypes and act out services in the real world—to really gauge the experience of the users.

As we discuss in the chapter on encouraging children (chapter 11), people have varying definitions of play. One INTP (an Idea Mill) was astonished when coworkers asked why she looked so sad, and she replied, "Are you telling me there is not a smile on my face?" She was deep in fantasy, excitement, and play, yet her face and body language gave no hint she was having fun. Conversely, it's obvious when ESTPs (Adventurers) are playing, whether with toy cars or sports cars, as they overtly enjoy and physically engage their environment.

Not surprisingly, play looks different to the different temperaments:

NF (Intuitive Feelers): Cooperative role-playing and trust building (socially)
NT (Intuitive Thinkers): Competitive and challenging, in order to learn
SJ (Sensing Judgers): Serious and purposeful
SP (Sensing Perceivers): Relaxed, just for fun

For Henry Ford, "My toys were all tools." He advised, "I always had a pocket full of trinkets—nuts, washers, and odds and ends of machinery."[3] Judging types in general—and SJs in particular—love to play, play hard, and play to win. However, they don't play to fool around. Without a goal or end product, play seems pointless and a waste of resources. Play can be more accepted when we understand that it yields innovation, achieves team building, and fosters trust. Since creativity is messy and inefficient, we must budget for some inevitable waste and cleanup.

A Perceiving advertising executive explained that sometimes we need to forget about making commercial value. Instead, we should spend time like this: "No expectations, just creative play, really. I rediscovered why I got into this business—it was fun to play. Creativity needs to have certain playfulness about it. When we make it so serious—so much business—we often exclude some of the wonderful possibilities due to the client's mandated needs; something is lost." He explained that when he gets back to the "serious" work, he often brings with him ideas he learned through play.

Van Gogh, The Businessman

What can we learn from Vincent van Gogh about business? He barely achieved commercial success in his lifetime, but he created a body of work worth fortunes today. Not every great idea makes it in the marketplace, and he was lucky his paintings survived at all. How do you recognize and promote greatness, and how do you compete? "If I get by, perhaps I'll do it precisely by working more cheaply than others," described Van Gogh, trying ineffectively to compete on price.[4] If you were Vincent and had world-class products that weren't reaching a market, what would you do?

As Feelers often make choices for social reasons, Van Gogh trusted the marketing of his unique product to his brother Theo. Of course, there are benefits to working within your circle, and Theo was an art dealer who was very supportive of Vincent. When deciding where to get help, ask yourself: *Are my personal relationships world-class partners?* Posthumously, for the brothers, Theo's widow popularized Vincent's paintings. But Vincent had already missed the opportunity for success in his lifetime.

Creative Destruction

Leading management coaches freely share their latest ideas—even though it's their most valuable intellectual property. Beyond the Extraverted nature to speak their mind, this forces them to invent new material. Industrialist Andrew Carnegie used creative destruction to retain his lead in steel production. When his factories were state of the art and fully productive, he would order them destroyed, and replace them with plants having greater innovations and improved productivity—an extreme but effective measure to prevent his competitors from leapfrogging him.

If disaster struck and your factory burned down, your computer's memory was lost, or your key employees left, what would you do? You probably couldn't replace all the old machines, find the same version of software, or be able to recruit an identical staff. If you had to start over and redesign your job from scratch, what would it look like?

Instead of replicating what you had, try to discard past assumptions. Access your resources, current needs, and market conditions as an exercise in reinventing your position. Sensors, for example, are gifted at examining their job descriptions and making refinements. The exercise frees them from the unnecessary legacies (or baggage). Intuitives, on the other hand, tend to design wholly new operations and may redefine their occupation entirely. Either way, creative destruction is a powerful tool for staying ahead of the competition.

An Environment for Creativity

We expect to find creativity in R&D, advertising, and the graphics department; today, however, creativity is also needed in sales, customer service, logistics, shipping—in every business function. It's everyone's responsibility to contribute, and the easiest way is to support a culture where creativity can thrive.

A culture of trust is essential for people to feel comfortable to be themselves, take risks, and share creative possibilities. Often, new teams of high-level executives jump-start their team-building by taking the Myers-Briggs assessment to better understand their coworkers. Through this process, it becomes evident that different organizations have different prevalent types. For creativity to thrive, there isn't *one* best culture; the best creative culture is the one that supports the personalities of the people in your organization.

The ideal creative atmosphere is different for all of us, and we can't always control our work environment. Having the awareness of what is best for us helps us seek out the best creative conditions. While Extraverts are stimulated by people and may thrive with an open-floor plan, this can be draining for Introverts. An Introverted and gifted computer programmer said he needs stretches of time alone to be productive. After barricading his office door failed to discourage visitors, he resorted to working at night, when nobody was around to bother him. His employer supported his need to be alone and his achievements earned him an employee of the year award. Get the most from Introverts by allowing space for them to be alone and providing confidential communication channels for them to share ideas.

At times, the very ideas that some organizations put in place to allow innovation to flourish may be holding them back. For example, in an effort to promote an open culture, some organizations flatten their hierarchies and assemble leaderless teams; however, this chaotic lack of structure creates stress for Judgers, who prefer clear lines of command. Innovation is messy enough without knowing who is in charge. Collaborations and cooperation across business functions foster creativity too, but this requires time and unavoidable meetings, resulting in tight, chopped up schedules, which is stressful for Perceivers, who work best with unbounded time. Also, focusing attention on the immediate seems to be in vogue. However, Innovation needs a long time horizon and requires the support of a culture that looks beyond immediate and measurable results often favored by Sensing leaders. Long-term commitment and long-term paybacks must be allowed among managers and employees alike for innovation to succeed.

Whatever is new undermines order, and while this is especially disruptive for SJs, there are other forces acting against innovation too. New ideas take resources away from established processes, so alternative channels for presenting ideas are necessary. Though these innovations could be good for the overall firm, they may not be part of an immediate supervisor's agenda.

You don't want a culture where a manager says, "That's a great idea. Why don't you come in on your own time during the weekend to work on it." We can't stop the line to run an experiment, and for colleagues to share resources, they must have incentives. Top innovative firms like 3M and Google encourage employees to spend a portion of their time on side projects. This allows time for their employees to follow what they are passionate about without interfering with their day job.

Part III: Cultivating Courageous Creativity

Innovation is stifled when success means more work and failure means blame. A creative culture must reward good ideas without punishing calculated risk. Keep in mind that different kinds of rewards motivate different personalities. Judging types are rewarded by closure, while Perceivers are rewarded by flexibility. Extraverts may enjoy public praise, but this isn't the case for all Introverts. As an Introvert, Edward Hopper's success brought unwanted public attention. According to a 1956 *Time* magazine article, when he was offered a gold medal by the National Institute of Arts and Letters, "Hopper fled to Mexico. He came back and accepted it only after being assured that he would not have to say anything except thanks."[5]

A creative culture embraces differences. Groups solely comprised of similar types, whether they are Intuitives, attorneys, or soccer players, will have blind spots. Diversity of backgrounds brings diversity of ideas. And cultures that encourage creative pursuits unrelated to work foster more innovations at work. Albert Einstein said, "If I was not a physicist, I would probably be a musician. I often think in music. I live my daydreams in music. I see my life in terms of music."[6]

When the activities of Nobel Prize winners were examined, it was found that more than one third of the laureates in literature were involved in at least one other artistic area, such as visual arts, drama, or dance.[7] But you don't need to be Nobel Prize worthy to benefit from the arts. Participation in the arts helps develop a workforce with diverse knowledge and skills that encourage broad thinking and practical problem solving. All of our life experiences go into everything we create, and the more varied the experiences we have, the more cards you have to play.

Whether or not you manage people today, you will someday. Whether or not you're a business owner, you need to take ownership. We all can contribute to a supportive culture that encourages calculated risk and accepts a degree of inevitable failures. And we all can understand that different personalities create best in different conditions; further, they all deserve our support.

11

JUNG AT ART: ENCOURAGING CHILDREN TO STAY CREATIVE

What kind of childhood did you have? What kind of childhood do you wish you'd had? For better or for worse, most of our parents and teachers prepared us for life in the best way they knew how, using the resources—and information—available to them. Over the past generation, however, raising children has become much more than avoiding peanuts, arranging play dates, and drinking organic juice. With increased access to both relevant and plentiful data, children have the potential to be safer and healthier. The world is changing too, and the roads we traveled have either changed dramatically or are no longer open. We need to prepare our children to find their own roads by teaching them how to be continuously creative and adaptable for a future world we cannot predict.

You couldn't choose your parents, and your children can rarely choose their teachers. Our grade-school art teachers and our college professors alike—each had their own way of expressing their ideas and their own "creativity types." Naturally, and without realizing it, they tried to teach us to create their way. You probably had some teachers that you connected with and who helped you excel, and with other teachers, you became frustrated and gave up. Though you probably didn't know it at the time, it is a powerful opportunity to discover this disconnect that occurs when we're taught by someone of a different creative type. As adults, we can pursue our interests by continuing our education, often having the option to try several classes—even majors—as we gravitate toward the subjects and teachers we click with. In our massive public school systems, however, children are often assigned to classes, and there are few choices. So, it's up to parents and teachers to become aware of learning-style differences and provide the lessons that provide opportunities for *all* types to excel.

Our children may look like us and talk like us, but the single most important thing for parents to know is this: your children's natural strengths aren't necessarily the same as yours. In fact, with sixteen different creative types—and without having a known link to heredity—the odds are far against you having the same personality type as your children. Your child isn't likely to have the same strengths as their siblings either, despite being brought up in the same house. Of course, every child is unique; even children of the same personality type are different from each other. Once we recognize this, we can identify their strengths and passions to guide them on their own right path. We can also see which of our strengths we have in common with our children and then develop a greater understanding of our differences.

The skills needed to find the right path come through encouraging our children to explore their natural curiosity and exercise their natural creativity. Listen to any successful person talk about their passion and you will probably hear them talk about what they loved to do in their childhood. Many times, they'll say it was a single individual who provided the encouragement they needed to continue; but more often, they'll tell of their challenges to keep their budding creativity, curiosity, and passion from being squashed by their parents, teachers, and peers. Somehow, these few managed to endure, yet many more were discouraged from their passions. Environment certainly does play a role in shaping our development. Even now, as parents ourselves, we are likely to say or do something and catch ourselves feeling like we have momentarily become our parents or teachers.

Fortunately, parents and teachers can provide more support than they had in their own childhoods by encouraging the creativity, curiosity, and passions of children today—first, with the awareness that children have naturally different creative styles. To learn more about this, there's a personality type assessment specially designed for children (age seven to eighteen) called the Murphy-Meisgeier Type Indicator for Children (MMTIC) that's given by trained professionals. Very similar to the MBTI instrument, the Murphy-Meisgeier uses the same scales but has fewer questions. And the questions are written to be understood by young people.

The second way to encourage children is to expose them to an art education. Why the arts? Those engaged in the arts are actively creative: observing the arts provides fertile ground for personal growth, and participation allows children to acquire lifelong lessons unavailable from any other source.

Unlike other disciplines studied in school, we see through the arts that problems have more than one solution, and in most cases no "right" or "wrong" answers. The arts teach that solutions can be fluid, especially in a fast-changing environment. Through the arts, we see there are times when it's best to collaborate and other times to work alone. Complicated concepts are simplified and shown in a different light.

Participating in the arts gives us opportunities to explore the properties of various materials, and allows us to experience combining and constructing items. The arts give us a voice that spreads our innovative ideas to a wider audience, impacting impressions and perceptions, and provoking action. The arts allow us to express and share the thoughts and feelings that aren't always possible to express with standard language. The arts provide a laboratory to test the risks and consequences of our actions. And the arts provide an avenue for exploring curiosity, generating ideas, and implementing and sharing those ideas—a model that all forms of creativity can follow.

Consider this question: Who wants their children to spend their efforts training in fields with a low probability of financial success? Did an arts profession come to mind when you read it? Well, we've got good news: an art education doesn't mean your children are destined to be starving artists. The creativity developed through an art education can be integrated with other disciplines, opening a whole world of opportunity—literally.

Now, let's reframe the question: Who wants their children to develop their creativity for solving problems to thrive in the global economy as musicians, designers, doctors, lawyers, business people? Today, we succeed by being an artist in whatever profession we choose.

A man interviewed for this book studied music in school, became a composer, and collaborated with some of the biggest names in entertainment before making a mid-career lifestyle change. Now he's a real estate agent representing top-of-the-line luxury properties in Manhattan. His music background attracts rock star clients, but it's the creativity in crafting unique deals that makes him successful—his ability to unlock value and help clients develop strategies. He says he is self-motivated to always be improving, and he learns by emulating agents who are better than him. Still, it's his background as a performer that helps in selling, and his experience in music allows him to see opportunities creatively.

Art is the lever that opens doors to other subjects. A child's love of music can be used to introduce math; love of painting can lead to chemistry or history; and sculpture explains engineering principles. Participation in the dramatic arts can develop public speaking and sales skills. Gymnastics demonstrates physics in action. Resource allocation, supply, and demand in the art room can build an understanding of economics. Of course, experience in the arts provides examples, similes, and metaphors to inspire and clarify realistic or abstract thinking.

Many people believe our education needs reform to include more math and science; however, this doesn't have to come at the expense of cutting the arts. Inefficiencies in the classroom can be unlocked and more can be done with our current resources—before we slice the pie, we can add more filling. Instead of choosing between science or art, we could have science *with* art. There is plenty of room for both. In fact, science and math could be integrated with the arts in ways that make all of the subjects more relevant.

The Ugly Duckling

In this well-known children's story, the "ugly" duckling was teased for being different from the other baby birds, but when he matured, it became clear that he was not a duck at all; he was a beautiful swan. How could this wise old tale apply to creative differences?

Children are no strangers to creativity. They invent musical instruments and make up their own songs. They dance, paint, scribble, and tell stories—sometimes all at once. When they're younger, their parents, grandparents, and teachers marvelously praise their accomplishments. Little by little, however, the critics march in. Worse, children are criticized for the very acts of creativity they find most exciting: "Quiet down and stop singing," or "Those flowers should be yellow—what nonsense," or "That's not how you wear a scarf." Hemingway relayed a similar story: "In high school, I once wrote an essay entirely in dialogue and I got an F, not because the dialogue was inferior, but because no one had ever written an essay like that before."[1]

When "yours doesn't look like mine" and when "you aren't acting like everyone else," children's behavior and action becomes the subject of ridicule by adults and peers. Many times, this ridicule simply comes from people with a different personality type, but off-the-cuff criticism can discourage fledgling children from developing into swans. Those most susceptible to mindless criticism are the authority-respecting SJs (Sensing Judgers) and the role-model-following NFs (Intuitive Feelers). Those most likely to keep their creativity intact as they grow up are the NTs (Intuitive Thinkers), who challenge authority, and the SPs (Sensing Perceivers), who resist conformity.

Though well-meaning parents and education systems strive to teach us how to be, act, and know the same as everyone else, our natural creativity suffers from this overall move toward conformity. A more worthy goal would be to allow children to get through their education still believing in the free expression of their own ideas and having the confidence to create without fear of ridicule.

Encouraging Your Children to Retain Their Creativity

A college professor commented that many of her students turn in papers that are grammatically correct but lack ideas. She wondered, *How do you teach original thinking?* but was concerned it might be too late.

How can you encourage your children to remain creative as they learn to function within the rules of society? Just as the best time to plant a tree was twenty years ago and the second best time is today, it's not too late to encourage creativity. Remember: the starting point is to understand that there are different ways of being creative; children of different personality types simply have different needs and preferred means of expression. The following suggestions apply to all children; however, they are especially relevant to children with the following temperaments.

NF (Intuitive Feeler) children: Looking for meaning and taking things personally, NF children are most likely to be discouraged from creativity by a critical remark. Parents must especially stand up for their children through gestures of faith and trust. Feelers in general and NFs in particular are people oriented. As one mom said, "Creative time is family time spent together." Since children copy everything we do, set a good example by showing them how you are creative. One Feeling mother likes to gather her daughters to make homemade Valentine's Day cards for all their classmates.

Even if you don't participate in the arts, show your children how you garden, cook, or organize events. If they're interested in the piano and you can't play a note, introduce them to a teacher who could also serve as a mentor. NF children thrive on approval from their parents, teachers, and role models, so remember to provide praise when appropriate (particularly if you're an IT [Introverted Thinker] parent, as you may not think to mention your approval). Look toward causes you believe in and show the creative ways these causes spread their message. For NF children, using creativity helps them to find their own identity.

NT (Intuitive Thinker) children: Provide NT children with chances to prove their competence by allowing them to see they're good enough and by insulating them from critics.

Give them opportunities to learn through books or classes, and acknowledge their achievements, as their milestones help them to believe in their abilities. One parent said, "Don't shelter them, engage them." The objective NTs like to compete; however, their creative pursuits are often judged by subjective criteria, and this causes problems.

Another father encouraged his children to have confidence in their own ideas by providing them with a healthy *disrespect* for authority, saying there are many times that authority hasn't been earned and is undeserved. For example, when his son was learning about geometry in first grade, his teacher called a parent conference to complain that instead of drawing a straight line, his son drew a clothesline with pins and hanging clothing. The father stood up for his child, and with this same support and guidance, his child continued to be a free thinker into adulthood. The son is now a successful animator who develops characters for hit motion pictures and television shows.

SJ (Sensing Judger) children: Being the most likely to conform, SJ children need the most assistance in believing in their own originality. Show them the value that can be created through making small improvements to existing systems. Provide variation, not by changing the whole meal but perhaps by adding new side dishes to keep them open to new experiences. One parent said, "My daughter loves routines like most kids, and we have a lot of structure in her day. She prefers to get to school early, and every day, we leave enough time to take a different combination of streets to walk across town. We see there is more than one way to get to school on time."

SJ children naturally conform and follow tradition, and this provides the way in. Show them the traditions of innovation. Introduce them to the inventiveness of Henry Ford, the art of Edward Hopper and Norman Rockwell, and the leadership of George Washington. If you live in the United States, point out that innovation is part of our heritage, and it's our duty to continue inventing. If you are of Chinese descent, point to the invention of paper and the printing press, along with the traditions of poetry and painting. Every culture has innovations of which an SJ child can be proud and share ownership.

One father said he "saw everything as an opportunity to teach." And he answered his children's questions with real, adult answers, not make-believe or silliness. He taught them how to use tools and materials to repair household items, and explained every step of the way. He also showed them that creativity is full of risk, which helps SJ children to see that making mistakes is a normal part of the process. Another important message he taught—for SJ children and everyone—is that skill comes through practice.

SP (Sensing Perceiver) children: Moving, moving, moving—that's what SP children would rather be doing, so allow for action, keep it fun, and let them make everything into a game. Keeping them entertained can be all consuming, however, so be aware that it's also fine to let SP children become bored; boredom drives their creativity, and they will make their own fun. Take a moment to also look at the byproduct of their fun to see if something worthwhile was made—and if so, point it out. Parents of all children should remember that fun is good, and innovation comes through play and observation.

Open to new experiences, SP children can avoid trouble by being steered toward safe activities such as sports or the arts, where there is plenty of room for risk and excitement without sacrificing safety. One art teacher encourages children to remain creative by showing them famous artwork and inviting them to incorporate the ideas they see into their own artwork. Try to make SP children aware of other SPs they can emulate, like Warhol, Dalí, and perhaps Richard Branson or Donald Trump. Provide plenty of content to borrow from, and plenty of scraps and bits of material to play with, while understanding their greatest challenge may be to make it on time for dinner. A talented SP artist said, "My parents always supported me through school and a career that was NOT practical—and really, I was not overly good at—and the only thing they ever did wrong was to act surprised when I made a really great piece, like they were shocked!"

Suggestions for Adults

Even if you aren't a parent, we are all teachers, and our words have the power to escalate or discourage the aspirations of children at critical stages of their personal development. With an awareness of our personal biases, guardians are empowered to identify and encourage their children's unique gifts. Fortunately, by matching type with learning styles, we have a blueprint for becoming a more effective teacher as we nurture our children to be creative.

Recalling his own childhood, the Russian actor Constantin Stanislavski remembered going to the ballet and the circus, but his impressions of the music from the ballet are what really stayed with him. He explained that a child "needs impressions of good performances, art, concerts, museums, voyages, and pictures of all tendencies, from the most academic to the most futuristic, for no one knows what will move his soul and open the treasure house of his creative gifts."[2] We don't know which experiences will resonate and remain with our children, so kissing a lot of frogs is necessary to find a prince or princess.

Children benefit from balanced and varied experiences, and too much of a good thing can upset the balance. Most creative pursuits require commitment through the regular attendance of team practices, rehearsal times, music lessons, or art classes, so it's important to distinguish between your passions and your child's. The Feeling types define their identity as "I'm a dancer or I'm a violin player," while SJs (Sensing Judgers) associate with like-minded institutions and are "part of the orchestra." In other words, let the children follow their passion for their own reasons.

For children, pressure comes from all different directions; however, one source of pressure can be easily reduced—and that's you, the parent. For parents, especially Feeling types, you must separate your identity from your child's. You must remain proud and supportive without feeling every success and failure as your own. What's best for you is not always what's best for your child. Another example: Thinking-type parents tend to want to treat every child equally, but every child has different learning styles and motivations. Try to give each child equal attention in ways that are most suited for them.

As for the other parents and personality types, SJ (Sensing Judger) parents are often goal-oriented perfectionists who become impatient with children that don't follow the rules. For them, it's important to recognize that progress in creative activities is nonlinear and chaotic, so they need to give their children a time and place to be messy without demanding results.

Parents with NT (Intuitive Thinker) temperaments are out for improvement and achievement, and in pushing their children to learn, can sound critical. These parents continuously raise their own level of what they consider competent, and just as their children are about to cross a finish line, they extend the endpoint beyond reach. It's frustrating enough when NT parents do this to themselves (and it's difficult for other types to deal with), but it is debilitating to children. When a child reaches a milestone, NT parents would be wise to pause, take note, and allow for celebration of the accomplishment. Wait for the euphoria of success to fade before raising the standards. Since NT parents are naturally competitive, they are reminded to keep a level playing field by not competing with their children. Don't prove to yourself that you can draw a better circle or jump higher than most children.

For children, everything is new, and they use their curiosity to understand the world. For Judging children and parents, however, there comes a point where they'll say, "Okay, I have enough information. I know how things work and no longer need to keep exploring." If you're a Judging parent, although you may have made your conclusions decades ago, you still need to let your children (of any type) make their own discoveries. On the other hand, if you are a Perceiving parent, you are advised to add some structure to the discovery process—a goal, a deadline, or a theme—to provide some stability, boundaries, and avoid too many surprises. This is especially important for Judging children, who like to follow through with plans and thrive within limits.

As an adult, the most important thing for you to remember is that your personality type may not match that of your child. If you have similar preferences, then you have the advantage of greater understanding of their learning styles and motivation. Meanwhile, awareness of your differences helps you do what's best for them, even if it wouldn't have been best for you. Understanding our similarities and differences allows you to be the surest guide, greatest cheerleader, and strongest advocate in supporting our children's pursuit of their passion.

Many Flavors of Play

So often, when we think about our own creativity, we think back to carefree times from our childhood. Children develop cognitive and social skills through playing, and they find lifelong passions. They gain confidence with their creativity as well, whether it's building with blocks or negotiating to take a turn on the swings. Yet today, with the jam-packed schedules of activities we plan for our children, free play is getting squeezed out.

Although we want to give our children everything, it's especially important for Judging parents to remember not to pass their hectic schedules on to their children. Children need uninterrupted, undirected time to play. If children are Perceivers, they will appreciate the freedom; if they are Judgers, they will enjoy the control of setting their own constraints.

Through free play, many flavors of play develop. Watch children go down a slide. Are they wedging their shoe into the side rail to control their descent, like Judging children? Or do they tend to pick up their feet for the fastest possible ride, like Perceiving children? Both are having fun in their own way.

A women who was a talented flute player as a child said, "There was no easy way to practice without bothering people," so she gave up playing. To provide support, all we need to give children is some time, space, and resources in order to play. For children, an afternoon seems endless, a box of yarn and popsicle sticks are a pirate's treasure, and the crawlspace under the staircase is a secret cave. Children don't need much, but they do need unstructured time.

To generalize some of the flavors of play, NFs (Intuitive Feelers) may wish to act out interpersonal relationships by playing house or through role-playing. NTs (Intuitive Thinkers) may use blocks to construct complex engineering feats that test the laws of physics. SJs (Sensing Judgers) see play as their job and may line up all of their cars or stuffed animals in rows. And SPs (Sensing Perceivers) may enjoy the process of building tall towers, only to revel in the fun of knocking them down.

How we engage with our surroundings is related to type too. Do your children run out the front door and gather a group of kids to play outside, or do they prefer to play alone in their rooms? Extraverts usually love attention, playing in groups, and doing physical games like freeze tag. On the other hand, Introverts avoid attention, play alone or with a few close friends, and prefer imagination—a sheet of paper can become a magic carpet for a teddy bear. An Introvert may love playing music but dread performing in public recitals, for example. And for older Introverted children, sending them to their prom is more of a punishment than sending them to their room.

Like everything else, balance is important. Just as a diet of only chicken nuggets isn't healthy, extremes in play aren't healthy either. All children learn through play, so Introverted children must, at times, go against their preferences to learn how to interact with others. Likewise, Extraverted children could benefit from going against their grain with some alone time, when they can learn to explore their imagination.

Techniques Take Practice

Parents often say, "My children aren't creative; they show no interest in coloring or playing music." When asked what their children do enjoy, these parents say something along the lines of "They like to build sandcastles and tree houses, and love to climb rocks." One parent said her son likes to look at the side of a hill and determine just the right path to reach the top. But if you've made it this far in the book, you should know by now that creativity extends well beyond the arts, and making sandcastles, building tree houses, and navigating hillsides are all forms of creative problem solving.

Few of us are taught to dance or sing (among many other creative endeavors), and we assume that if it doesn't come automatically, then it's not our gift. What's rarely explained is that techniques need to be taught and practiced. We all have natural creativity, but to make something extraordinary, our natural talents need exercise and polish. Mozart cautioned, "It is a mistake to think that the practice of my art has become easy to me. I assure you, dear friend, no one has given so much care to the study of composition as I. There is scarcely a famous master in music whose works I have not frequently and diligently studied."[3] Helen Hayes started her long career as a child actor. "All children, I believe, are good actors," she said. "They're born with a sense of make-believe." She also believed that they often fail as adult actors because "they don't do anything really about developing themselves as performers." As for herself, "I went out and studied. I studied everything and anything that I could find."[4] Her efforts were acknowledged with an Emmy, an Oscar, a Tony, and a Grammy.

Many children can get discouraged before they start, thinking, *I can't draw or play the piano now, so I'm not creative.* While drawing and music are skills anyone can learn, it's difficult for a child to understand that developing these skills takes time, effort, and motivation. In the meantime, try introducing your child to more accessible mediums. Give them colored ink pads and stamps to make collages, or give them an assignment to take some photos. Judging children especially need coaxing to try new techniques to see if it's something they will like.

Some children show a natural aptitude for art, sport, or another creative activity. If they have a passion, then they need encouragement and practice to excel at it. Natural aptitude will only get them so far, as they need passion to persist with the necessary practice to develop skills. With practice, however, those with a natural aptitude could reach the top of their field; it's a steeper climb for those with passion and little aptitude. But any person with a combination of passion and skills can still have fun, create value, entertain others, and develop proficiency and personal satisfaction. Sometimes the tortoise beats the hare.

Gold Stars

Do you think that everyone deserves a trophy or only the winners should be recognized? Is it the effort that matters or only the end result? Receiving acknowledgement is a key factor that motivates us to continue with our successes—our strengths—and discontinue those directions that are less productive. Many times, when clients, spouses, and friends are satisfied with something unique we did, they provide no positive feedback and miss the opportunity to do their part to encourage innovation. Fortunately, this is easy to remedy—you don't need an expensive trophy or plaque to be supportive. Best of all, praise is free.

Whenever I created anything, my mom said it was beautiful, and to her, it was. I heard and believed her praise so much that when a neighbor, teacher, or classmate said what I made was ugly, I never heard them. All I heard was my mom saying that it was beautiful, and I became insulated from the critics. Since art and play are subjective, who's to say what is great and what is not? Deserved and honest praise can improve children's self-esteem and give them the courage to try new things. Creativity involves plenty of trials and plenty of failures, and failures are often learning opportunities and not cause for blame.

Although creativity and innovation involve producing something new, it's risky and often met with resistance. As adults, we hear "That's not how we did it last year" or "Our competitor doesn't do it that way." Children are told, "Everyone else in the class made their sky blue; why is your sky orange?" To encourage trying something new, we must preemptively praise originality at every turn—before others criticize, correct, and push what's normal. Of course, not everything new is better, but as parents, we can see when our children are veering off into the weeds. As one father gently says in those cases, "That was a try, but let's try this too."

Children don't always have to draw within the lines. Who determined what the correct color of the sky is anyway? If a child is making some wide strokes by holding a crayon the "wrong" way, with the flat side down instead of the point, perhaps offer a remark like, "Wow, what a good way to color in big shapes!" If a child is making some unusual arm movements to the beat of a song, you could say, "What a neat new way to dance!" When you see a child shaking a box of paper clips, you could acknowledge that it sounds like a new musical instrument. Or when they tell an imaginative story, you could say, "I've never heard that cats could fly up high in the sky to see if the moon is made of blueberry pie."

You should also remember to give children credit for their age and the material they are using. Crayons are safe and easy for little hands to hold, and watercolors are nontoxic and easy to clean up; however, these mediums are challenging—even for a professional artist. How many children get frustrated with their crayons and watercolors because they cannot use them to create the picture that they had in mind? No wonder kids think they can't draw! Likewise, how well could an accomplished musician play using a plastic piano or a kazoo? One art teacher explained that, even though drawing is a skill everyone can learn with the right instruction and practice, many children don't want to try art because they think they can't draw. As an EJ (Extraverted Judger) herself, she recommends starting with pre-cut shapes of materials so the students can arrange the pieces into collages. This can work for older people too and is exactly what Matisse did in his later years.

As extra encouragement, give out gold stars—literally and figuratively—with some gentle and occasional guidance when appropriate. (Not surprisingly, this is particularly effective with NF [Intuitive Feeler] children, who are driven to please their mentors, teachers, and parents.) There are always good parts to praise, and specific compliments are more sincere: "I never thought of putting a square next to a rectangle like that," "That's an imaginative way to stir the cookie batter," "What a nice orange and blue combination," "I like the part of the song where you added your own words," and "I noticed you sang and drummed at the same time."

Only you (the parent) can gauge when praise is overdone. For Introverted Thinking (IT) parents, what's good seems obvious and often goes unsaid. Even though it may sound unnatural for them to give praise at first, it gets easier with practice. For an Introverted Thinking child, too many compliments begin to sound insincere. SJs (Sensing Judgers) may wonder, "Why should I be complimented for doing what I'm supposed to be doing?" However, if they begin to see their job/chores as being creative, then you are on the right path.

When a child is passionate and does something unique, he or she is taking a risk. There is nothing more encouraging than having the very thing they are excited about being recognized and praised by parents or teachers. It gives them the "can do" attitude that insulates them from the critics and gives them confidence to believe in themselves.

Learning Preferences

Does your child's learning style match the teaching style they experience at home or in the classroom? Have you ever had an art teacher tell you to do more planning or say that you should be spontaneous? Did your English teacher care more about your spelling and grammar or about the ideas in your essay? Did your math teacher ask you to show your work or was she happy with the right answer? Did your Spanish teacher grade you on written exams or how well you participated in class? Did your gym teacher have you run around the track or play team sports? Does the history teacher go step by step through an outline, or does she skip around? Teachers all have their own personality preferences and biases; however, curriculums can be made to reach each type of student.

"I had enormous respect for those artists I did not follow, but I did not want them as my teachers," explained James A. Michener, who read all the best authors and decided later who to emulate.[5] *Watercolor* magazine featured an article in their twentieth-anniversary issue that highlighted the practices of the best art teachers. However, the teachers held strikingly different opinions along two fronts: they either stressed the importance of careful planning, or they promoted the free, spontaneous, and random actions of the media. There is clearly a bias—even among top teachers—along the line of Judging and Perceiving that runs through our education system.

We all have a tremendous capacity to learn under a host of different conditions. Some conditions just suit us better than others.

How We Learn in School

Extraverts: Learn by talking through ideas, class participation, and telling a story to the entire class.

Introverts: Learn by listening, reflecting on ideas, and private communication with the teacher or classmates.

Sensors: Follow specific directions step by step but need extra help in tying together overall concepts. Want facts and firsthand experiences of what is concrete, real, and practical, asking "In what way?" or "How is it useful?"

Intuitives: Want overall context, general ideas, and to skip steps when possible. Want to know the reason "Why?" Need extra help in learning to gather details, and prefer abstractions and theorizing about possibilities.

Thinkers: Want teachers to provide equal treatment to all and use logical, objective information. Prefer to learn through cause and effect.

Feelers: Want the teacher to care about them as a person. Want to know the answer to "Who?" and to learn about what they believe in.

Judgers: Like things organized and well planned, with clear goals and deadlines.

Perceivers: Like the freedom to explore topics as they come up.

For the SJ (Sensing Judger) child, teach the techniques and the rules; for SP (Sensing Perceiver) children, make it practical and fun. For NT (Intuitive Thinker) children, lay out the context by explaining why; for NF (Intuitive Feeler) children, provide appropriate praise.

The more we understand our children, the better we can communicate with them, guide them, and allow them to feel comfortable with who they are. Elizabeth Murphy, a psychologist who has studied and written about type development in children, observed a different manner in which Sensing and Intuitive children go about creating. "The Sensing children work from the specific to the general . . . beginning with the parts and building up to a theme." She poses an example where a child begins a drawing by adding a fish followed by a treasure chest, a boat, a shark, and so on to create an ocean theme. In contrast, "the Intuitive children work from the general to the specific, beginning with a theme" and then adding the details.[6] There is a higher percentage of Sensing teachers in the younger grades teaching practical lessons and more Intuitive professors in the universities teaching theory. In fact, elementary teachers are 63 percent Sensing and 37 percent Intuitive. As the children progress through school, they are exposed to an increasingly higher percentage of Intuitive teachers. By the time they get to college, they find nearly the opposite makeup of elementary school, having 64 percent Intuitive and 36 percent Sensing professors.[7]

Not every subject is interesting to every child, so find a way to bring his or her natural learning style into the process. Without the proper amount of context, learning can be tough for Intuitives, for instance. And if there is too much skipping around, Sensors find it difficult. On the other hand, as learners, we have to be adaptive since we don't always have a choice in how information is presented. But being aware of the differences—even as children—helps us get through rough patches.

If you're an Intuitive, have you ever been asked, "How could you possibly know this?" Children who are Intuitives don't need to know they make up only 30 percent of the population to realize they're unusual.[8] They dream up wild, unsubstantiated ideas, seeing things differently than their Sensing peers and guardians. According to Elizabeth Murphy, Intuitive children have not yet had enough life experience to learn to trust their Intuition. When Sensing teachers ask them to back up their ideas with facts, the teachers are sending a message to "abandon Intuition and use sensing skills," and this undermines the development of their Intuitive strengths. She suggests it's better to ask the child for information that proves their idea is the "best possible conclusion," since it first validates the ideas and then looks for supporting details.[9]

Who is the first to answer when a teacher asks a question? Without even raising their hands, Extraverted Perceivers (EPs) begin talking whether they know what they are going to say or not. Sometimes they talk through the question to reach an answer, and sometimes they just talk. On the other hand, Introverted Judging (IJ) children first want time to formulate a complete response in their minds before they raise their hands. (Of course, for both children and adults, the real world often requires urgent responses, which puts IJs at a disadvantage, and we all lose by missing their well-thought-out conclusions.) Teachers can give everyone a chance by pausing a few moments after asking a question to allow all the students to formulate an answer.

Awareness and flexibility are the keys to maintaining a balanced classroom—and life—for Introverted and Extraverted students. Introverted children can be like turtles hiding in their shell, but they don't need to be drawn out. Daydreaming provides a pathway to their creativity, and some time alone at recess may be better for them than being released into the schoolyard. Teachers and parents just need to be patient and provide a trusting environment for Introverted children to allow others into their world. In contrast, Extraverted children are completely comfortable outside of their shells, as they are inspired by engaging their surroundings.

With so much pressure to conform, children with special talents often neglect their abilities and suppress their interests. Until our society rewards uniqueness, it's up to parents and teachers to encourage children's talents and reward their differences.

Motivations

Extraverts: Want recognition through attention

Introverts: Want recognition without attention

NF (Intuitive Feelers): Want to help others and change the world

NT (Intuitive Thinkers): Improve systems and solve puzzles

SJ (Sensing Judgers): Want to uphold tradition and fulfill their duty

SP (Sensing Perceivers): Avoid boredom and seek action

In conclusion, the most important thing to remember is that it's very likely we have a different personality type than our children, and the way we learn is not the same as the way they learn. Let children do it their way, as long as it's safe.

Do keep in mind that it's difficult to determine type in very young children, and it would be wrong to label them prematurely. For example, you may think your daughter is an Introvert, but her environment hasn't provided enough opportunities for her to socialize yet. Or you may call your son an Extravert, but his environment hasn't allowed him enough private time. We all need both opportunities, but it takes time to understand what your children actually need and prefer.

Not every child will grow up to be a painter, dancer, or sculptor, but encouragement in an art education provides tools to be creative in other endeavors. Many good jobs of the future won't go to the strongest or the smartest but to those who are the most creative. The best engineers will be aided by their ability to paint, the best lawyers will be aided by their ability to dance, and the best accountants will be aided by their ability to sculpt. Skills in the arts open our minds, and the companies and nations that attract the most creative people will have the advantage in creating the greatest economic value and the highest standard of living.

12

ACCOUNTING FOR AUDIENCE TASTE
AND YOUR APPRECIATION

Whether you're trying to reach a mass audience by launching a blog, kicking off a political campaign, or releasing a feature motion picture, or whether you're trying to influence a specific group of individuals by pitching a new invention to investors, making a speech, doing a job interview, or asking your boss for time to work on your new ideas, it's best to first know your audience and understand what they like. Typically, we gauge our audience's taste and segment its members using factors such as age, gender, income, and education. Some marketers are beginning to look at our behavior characteristics, like how we surf the web, yet this research doesn't give a complete picture. An often-overlooked component that accounts for our taste is our type preferences. A look into what we enjoy not only tells us something about who we are but begins to predict our behavior as well.

As we transform ideas into viable products, we want to direct promotions toward specific groups of people. To reach the audience you want to influence, you can use your understanding of personality styles to position what you create. For example, the Feeling types, which are 70 percent women, are more influenced by interpersonal factors and personal values, while the Thinking types, who are mostly males, make their decisions by stepping outside their personal values using firm logic.[1]

We know that 70 percent of the population are Sensors, and they respond to immediate sensory details.[2] Sensors want to touch, smell, and taste the merchandise—they want to open drawers on a desk and smell the wood before they make a purchase. On the other hand, Intuitives are more comfortable buying into intangible concepts. If your audience was limited to college professors, who are disproportionally Intuitives, then you could adjust the offering by highlighting theoretical and future possibilities of what they could accomplish and discover at this desk.

Art is in the eye of the beholder, and no two people have the same appreciation; however, people having similar types have similar appreciations. We also have a far broader appreciation for other creative styles. At times, we like what doesn't come easily to us. As an Intuitive, for example, many appreciate the attention to detail and craftsmanship produced by a Sensor. By knowing your audience, you can serve them what they like. However, to please everyone at the table, knowing their type allows you to serve each a slice of their favorite kind of pie.

Influencers

Remember those old Coca-Cola commercials where they wanted to "teach the world to sing in perfect harmony," or those "Kodak moment" commercials that pulled at our heartstrings? Now compare them to Fuji's ads that talked about film speed and technical aspects. Intentional or not, Coca-Cola and Kodak's approach appealed to Feelers, while Fuji targeted a Thinking audience. In your own creations, you, too, can appeal to a certain type of audience by understanding what they each like.

Another marketing approach is to have something for everyone. Take, for example, luxury automobile commercials where the narrator tells us about a car that makes sense. He asks, "How do you feel the moment you sit behind the wheel? Do you feel a sense of your accomplishment? Does the accelerator pedal become a part of you when you feel the surge of the engine's power? Do you appreciate the reliability and safety it provides for your family? Do you marvel at the craftsmanship, our history, the famous people who have owned these cars, and the technical advancements of the engine?" Whatever type you are, at least one of these questions has been designed to appeal to you. Whatever you put out there, it's always advantageous to consider the types you want to influence with your message, product, invention, letter, book, or new computer app.

Appreciating Audience Needs

A candy bar, piece of art, ticket to a movie—what people buy is a good indicator of what they appreciate. And people of different types enjoy a product or service for different reasons. Extraverted Sensors (ESs), for example, enjoy physical objects, while Introverted Intuitives (INs) enjoy what they can process in their minds. Sensors want what pacifies their needs now, while Intuitives tend to look toward satisfying anticipated needs.

For NFs (Intuitive Feelers), enjoyment and appreciation come as a source of self-expression. They wish to relate and reaffirm their personal values and beliefs, wondering, *Do the opinions of the creator coincide with my personal values?* Having an affinity for items that allow them to learn and look deeper at themselves, they connect with what touches their soul and engages their spirit. And NFs make personal and emotional connections to people and objects alike—especially if the person or object reminds them of a valued feeling, person, or family event. One NF found it meaningful to commission a friend to paint a landscape of his house. NFs also focus on promoting harmony, considering how a new product fits with what else they own, who else will see it, how others will react, and how it mirrors their identity.

For NTs (Intuitive Thinkers) on the other hand, it's often disharmony and disparity that speaks to them. Pitting rough against smooth, bright against dull, old against new, they are attracted to contrasts or conflicts. Liking what is thought-provoking and making their own interpretations, they enjoy making links, analogies, and symbolic connections. Their process of appreciation is one of discovery and education as they read playbills, purchase guidebooks, and research online—all to enhance their experience. An NT who purchased an abstract painting of Buddha said, "I associated it with my first visit to Asia." As they wade deeper into the waters, NT appreciation is often a taste acquired from years of learning.

SJs (Sensing Judgers) appreciate order, guarantees, safety, belonging, and what has been proven to bring results while also having an eye for technique, craftsmanship, and perfection. They are the most practical and value what fulfills a need, whether they are providing entertainment on a Saturday night or decorating a wall of their office. In addition, SJs admire items that are part of collections and have recognized value, such as china sets that complement the overall organization of their homes. They find comfort and entertainment in nostalgia, gravitating toward classics like *The Nutcracker* (which one SJ told us he enjoys seeing every Christmas) as well as facts and history. SJs tend to join organizations with which they share cultural, ethnic, national, and religious affiliations.

SPs (Sensing Perceivers) appreciate what is at the peak of freshness right now and don't buy any green bananas that need time for ripening. They want to be entertained and enthralled with the thrill of the hunt, as they are spurred by actions and things that bring pleasure. They are drawn to novelty, excitement, and what is bold, audacious, and easy. One SP said she enjoys the "see and be seen" aspect of art openings and the excitement of auctions. Whether searching for antiques or the latest fad, for SPs, the pleasure of purchasing helps make life worth living, and what they select is part of their own creativity. Drawn to immediate gratification and pleasure in this manner, SPs must be wary of addictions, especially since they often believe it won't happen to them.

Looking at Our Homes

Sometimes we are invited to a friend's home and are surprised at what we find: the place doesn't match the personality. However, more often than not, their home is close to what we expected. When you look at the way homes are decorated, certain generalities can be observed based on temperament.[3] For NFs (Intuitive Feelers), homes are cozy, and everything has a meaning or connection relating to memories or people, especially family and friends. The homes of NTs (Intuitive Thinkers) are full of books—and possibly computers—since their personal space is a center for learning. As Thomas Jefferson wrote, "I cannot live without books."[4] Items in their home often serve as personal reminders or are strategically placed to start provocative and thought-provoking conversation. Meanwhile, SJs' (Sensing Judgers') houses are neat, orderly, and "everything has a place." They tend to design by matching and using symmetry, and with items of perceived value. And SPs (Sensing Perceivers) surround themselves with what they are currently using, such as found objects, and use them for decorating as a visual cue to the process of their lives. Their homes are a work in progress, containing tools, building materials, and projects in various stages of completion that change over time.

Your Appreciation

As a final note, let's discuss *your* appreciation. Have you ever looked at a piece of art and wondered, *What is that?* If you were interested enough to read the description on the little plaque or listen to the audio guide, did you find that it suddenly made even less sense? Many people, especially those who are NTs (Intuitive Thinkers), make art out to be complicated rather than just interpreting it. They especially complicate (intentionally or not) when they explain it to others. But we're here to assure you: it's really not!

Whether you're a passionate art connoisseur or you avoid museums at all costs, knowing about personality type can give you more perspective and appreciation than any art history class or museum visit. Art production and appreciation is influenced by our personality type. All artists develop their unique styles by gathering ideas and making decisions—the same two mechanisms we use to understand our personality types. If you can look beyond the masterpiece and behind the scenes to discover the personality of the artist (who may be very much like yourself), you can increase every aspect of your creation and enjoyment of the arts.

Through the lenses of type, we gain greater appreciation—for the double meanings in an NF's poetry; the complex beauty of an NT's scientific discoveries; the precision with which an SJ plays the piano; or the agility, grace, and sheer joy of an SP dancer. We catch a glimpse of the artist's soul, and gain new reasons and confidence to fully appreciate what we do.

13

THE CREATIVE SPIRIT

What do you find yourself doing when you freely generate ideas? For many, ideas flow while relaxing, exercising, showering, mediating, or praying. Some artists believe their ideas and talents are gifts from God, and consider their spiritual self and creative self to be one. Like the poet and painter William Blake said, "I myself do nothing; the Holy Spirit accomplishes all through me."[1] And Henri Matisse wrote, "Do I believe in God? Yes, when I am working. When I am submissive and modest, I feel myself to be greatly helped by someone who causes me to do things that exceed my capabilities."[2]

One of history's greatest speeches, Abraham Lincoln's Gettysburg Address, summarized the status of the American Civil War, America's future prospects, and set the tone for the republic for the next hundred years. Humbly written on the back of an envelope, it was so inspiring, clear, concise, and powerful, some believe that Lincoln was possessed by ability and eloquence well beyond the capacity of mere mortals—that the former president was willingly receptive and this incredible speech was divinely inspired.

We often associate creativity with an "other," whether it be God or a muse. We use words like *blessed, gifted, inspired, transported, transformed,* and *awed* to describe people who are creative, as well as the things creative people produce. When we are truly proud of a particular creation, we say that we put our self into it. Consequently, exploring our self and our universe has produced some of the greatest works of art.

Whether through religion, connections with nature, or a personal philosophy, being spiritually centered has different meanings to everyone and inspires our creativity to varying degrees as we define spirituality for ourselves. While some access their spiritually creative moments through organized religion, like helping out at the church play or researching ancient iconography, some access it through hiking in nature or practicing yoga. For others, it comes in the form of a calling, a duty, a mode of fun, or an intellectual stimulant. Whatever your belief, you can better embrace your spiritually inspired moments and develop your own strategies for accessing them through understanding your personality type.

The Creative Spirit in Preferences and Temperaments

Understanding how to kindle your creative spirit involves awareness of your inner self. Being aware and trusting your spiritual connections can be the path toward true inspiration. Naturally introspective and preferring quiet time, Introverts have easier access to their inner spirit and tend toward meditation, silent prayer, and private moments with small, trusted groups. Meditation isn't as appealing to Extraverts, on the other hand, whose spiritual moments are often sparked by group experiences. Meanwhile, Sensors respond to the scents of incense and the sound of chants, and Intuitives are drawn to the symbolic and intangible aspects of spirituality.

Intuitive Thinkers (NTs), however, are often skeptical and don't "get" spiritual moments—possibly because they tend to analyze instead of experience them. And though it may seem contradictory, these people can use their Intuitive strength as a way of seeing possibilities while still defining spirituality on their own terms. A walk through an ancient forest can often evoke a sense of awe in NTs, who revere nature and love to contemplate the interdependencies of the universe. "Everyone who is seriously involved in the pursuit of science becomes convinced that a spirit is manifest in the laws of the universe—a spirit vastly superior to that of man," said Albert Einstein.[3] If you see the mind as the only reality, then you are reminded to look to realities beyond your mind. Try seeking a frame of reference for spiritual experiences by opening your eyes to notice the people and places in front of you right now.

In contrast, Feeling types in general and NFs (Intuitive Feelers) specifically make great creative spiritualists. A study of clergy across a wide range of denominations found that 44 percent of clergy were Intuitive Feelers.[4] Creating from their soul, NFs are more in touch with themselves than other temperaments. While the other temperaments think about the meaning of life occasionally, like skipping a stone across the surface of a deep pond, NFs are up to their neck in search of life's purpose. They see meaning between experiences, philosophies, and their own life, and this leads them on a path of self-discovery. Consequently, because they're so involved with thinking about life's meaning, life frequently passes them by. If you are an NF, your spirit is your life, and this is what you express through your artwork. Furthermore, much of spirituality comes through looking beyond yourself. Your interpersonal awareness provides balance by drawing you away from your own needs as you extend compassion to others.

Spirituality isn't a "holy"-owned subsidiary belonging to NFs, however. SPs (Sensing Perceivers) also reach for spirituality, when needed. Although awed by the workmanship of the gargoyles and height of the steeples, they're usually drawn away from tradition to the latest trends and new age practices—in search of excitement. They seek stimulation and answers through pursuits like rock climbing, skydiving, and white water rafting, but they get blocked if things get dull. Often, their own impatience prevents them from appreciating spiritual moments. However, by accepting that not every spiritual moment will be a burning bush, a holistic state can still be reached. Furthermore, an acceptance that rules offer boundaries and security provides creative opportunities is also helpful.

Searching for sharks, stingrays, and turtles, novice scuba divers will go deep and swim quickly, scanning for what's big and exciting. With experience, they learn to hover and notice the small and subtle happenings on the shallow reefs. Similarly, by slowing down, SPs experience spirituality.

Routine is where SPs and SJs (Sensing Judgers) differ. For example, some artists are inspired by the routine of setting up their equipment. One watercolorist goes through the steps of stapling her paper to a board and wetting the paper with even brushstrokes. What seems like a chore is part of her spiritual process, clearing her mind for art. For SJs, spirituality has a time, a place, and a process, and SJs can find comfort from God's authority and direction. The high ceilings, stained glass, history, rituals, traditions, sense of belonging—all of these religious elements confirm their belief and provide comfort, reducing their defenses and enhancing the mood. By letting go and shifting away from rules, however, SJs can achieve a higher level of spirituality and creativity. SJs strive to control the moment, and they notice when something is missing—externally and in their own lives. They are helped along an enlightened path by letting go of some of the rules.

Balancing Act

When it all comes down to it, creative differences between preferences, temperaments, and types can cause stress, but when confronted with strife, think of bamboo. This perennial evergreen of the grass family is made of strong material, yet it bends under stress and remains a balanced whole. Achieving a centered life means acclimating to outside or inside forces by being aware of and balancing your type preferences. Balancing doesn't mean equal amounts or maximizing any one preference; instead, we add the right amount of what's missing to become whole.

When the Judgers are too rigid or the Perceivers are too flexible, they are off balance. Try stabilizing your information-gathering with your decision-making, or modulating your attention between details and the larger picture. Intuitives balance by going beyond their minds and getting in touch with their bodies, while Sensors balance by going beyond their own flesh and blood. Thinkers could try considering their personal values, and Feelers could consider the framework of logic. Adding small quantities of our least preferred functions usually provides the missing ingredients.

Like adding a pinch of cayenne pepper to a pot of chili, it doesn't take much to provide balance. Your spirit is a part of you, and so is your art. Through living a centered life, you'll find inspiration and creativity at every turn. Find your creative spirit by:

NF (Intuitive Feelers): Look beyond yourself.

NT (Intuitive Thinkers): Don't over-analyze your spiritual moments.

SJ (Sensing Judgers): Let go of some rules.

SP (Sensing Perceivers): Slow down to experience spiritual moments.

The Scrappy Ladies and the Spirit of Collaboration

Another way to heighten your creative spirit is through collaboration, which multiplies the creative power of one into many. There can be something truly inspiring and magical about it, especially when you help others by lending your natural gifts.

We have a mutual friend, an ENFJ (a Persuader), who coordinates a group called the Scrappy Ladies. They meet each week to turn donated and recycled scraps of paper into positive, all-occasion cards and gifts for healing and deployed soldiers. They call it Project Boomerang. Originally inspired by an Air Force chaplain at her church, the Scrappy Ladies and their projects represent the true spirit of what collaboration can do for oneself and others.

Our friend at Scrappy Ladies describes the group's purpose as a way to connect with people, and spread the message of love and peace. Like most NFs (Intuitive Feelers) who are inspired by causes larger than themselves—missions that touch people's lives— she knows that she's doing something positive with her creativity. And as an EJ (Extraverted Judger), it helps that she's a natural coordinator. Combining spirituality with collaboration, she says, "When I get weary, the Holy Spirit somehow, through the ladies, helps the project continue as our friendships grow." This group serves as an extended family of increasingly close friends who support, share, and listen to each other and celebrate life's joys.

Virtually every personality type is represented among these ladies, and each gravitates toward their most comfortable roles. Acting within the characteristics of her type, an ESFJ made cutouts from magazines and cards, and organized them by subject into a system of file folders she developed. She said, "We are doing a good thing for the world and for ourselves." Others in the group bring their own creative style by taking on the role of hostess or quality control, or by contributing original artwork. For the SJs (Sensing Judgers), creativity comes from being part of a group with regular meetings and supporting established institutions, like our churches and armed forces. Sensors are fond of cutting, folding, and gluing cutouts to make tangible results, underscoring Project Boomerang's slogan: "God's Work, Our Hands." The SPs (Sensing Perceivers) are attracted to the exciting group dynamics and fun of combining paper and materials, as well as making a positive impact on our troops, who benefit from a little creative spirit from home.

Every one of the ladies contributes in her own way. Whether cutting, organizing, chatting, or supporting, the Scrappy Ladies are one of the finest examples of people bringing out the best in each other as they express love and scatter joy!

Gift from God

Each and every one of us is born with certain gifts, and as we go through life, many of us take our time unwrapping our special packages. Then, when our inborn gifts are accessed and appreciated, we become whole.

Some of your gifts are unwrapped during spiritual moments. Spiritual moments are all around, as are creative ideas; the challenge is to recognize them and use them to fuel our spirit. Otto, for example, was inspired to join the ministry by something that happened in college: One morning, he found himself with only a dime in his pocket. He went to a place where, if you got there early, you could drink coffee all day for a dime. It just so happened that a minister came by that day and treated everyone to coffee, so Otto's dime was returned. Later, Otto ran into a friend, who proceeded to take him to lunch; that evening, another friend invited him for dinner. Before bed, Otto reached into his pocket and found his dime. At that moment, he realized that God would always be looking out for him, and he would never again have to worry about material things; they would always be provided. Spirituality and inspiration are always around us, but they only become apparent when we are ready to accept them.

14

COURAGEOUS CREATIVITY

At this point, it's probably obvious that the most important thing you need to know about being creative is that we all aren't the same, and we all aren't creative in the same way. Knowing your creative differences gives you confidence, the same way you feel when walking into a party wearing perfectly tailored clothing. When you're acting creatively within your personality, it fits. You have the confidence to be yourself; you use your natural talents; and you stand in a position of strength, ready to take the necessary risks. Also, knowing the personalities of others helps you to understand mismatches and improve the way you learn, accept advice, and collaborate. For your own survival, it's more important than ever to use the strengths of our creative differences to join the creative economy.

There is so much pressure for us to conform. While conforming has the illusion of being safe, it actually poses the risk that what you produce can be done by anyone else. Making yourself indispensable requires you to be unique, and since there is nobody else in the world who is exactly like you, the best way to be unique is to act as your true self.

Other people's clothes may look great on them, but even if you are the same size, it's unlikely they'll fit you as well. Being creative isn't about doing what worked for someone else; it's about doing what's right for you. Your personality type lets you tailor ways to be creative that suit you best. Using your strengths allows you to contribute the most value as a team member, and knowing your weakness helps you gain balance by identifying the partners that complement you best.

Although we only have to be right once to produce a great innovation, part of being creative involves accepting that sometimes we'll be wrong. Sometimes we get dressed and go out without knowing if it will rain. Expect the rain as part of your creative process. By seeking sheltered areas to try out ideas, failing comes at low costs. In fact, failing teaches the lessons we need so, next time, we can boldly scale up what works.

Regifted

No matter how successful we feel in our lives, many of us sense there is something missing. Are you passionate about what you're doing, or are you just going through the motions without being fully engaged? Today, for our own survival, with competition coming from seemingly everywhere, we must act creatively—when we do so, we become engaged. Creativity is more than making art; creativity allows us to engage in whatever we're doing, leading us to greater career satisfaction, happiness, and overall well-being.

Many people say they just aren't passionate about anything, although they wish they were. Think back to when you were a child. What did you enjoy doing? Was it painting, singing in church, acting out dramas, writing stories, playing with clay, making crafts at camp, or something else? Why did you stop? It's time to take a second chance and try again! This time, you'll be trying from a position of strength. Now you know your creative style, how to use criticism to your advantage, and where to find the right audience. You have a wealth of accumulated experiences that you didn't have before.

Courageous Creativity

Some people are born with physical attributes that match well with their passions, like long fingers for playing piano or small bodies for jockeying racehorses. Though most of us may not be so lucky, we don't have to be held back. Height seems to be a prerequisite for basketball, but not too long ago, being female was a barrier too. One parent interviewed for the book has a daughter who lives and breathes basketball. Her height of five feet would discourage many from trying; it didn't stop her, however. With her parents' support, she plays on her high school's team, is having lots of fun, coaches, and was named to the All Conference team in one of the most competitive districts. Don't let obstacles or other people's preconceived notions discourage you or your children from following passion.

Have you tried to throw a baseball or swing a golf club for the first time and it felt completely natural, but you tried other things, like rollerblading, and it didn't? Remember what we said before: sometimes we must kiss a lot of frogs to find our prince or princess—we just can't tell if we don't try. Sometimes, what wasn't right long ago may work for us now. When was the last time you tried spinach or mushrooms or broccoli? Give them another chance! You may like them today.

We are most creative when we're freely acting within our preferred type, since it's what we enjoy most and where we've usually developed the most skill. However, just because we have an interest doesn't mean we had the opportunity to develop skills. Keep in mind, if you try drawing, or singing, or dancing, your drawing may be out of proportion, your singing out of tune, or your dancing awkward. Give it time; be patient. And find a teacher who resonates with you.

Seek to learn from great people who had a similar type as you, while remembering to be yourself. Don't try to paint like Monet or write like Hemingway, even if you discover that they had the same personality type as you. Instead, study them as people. Learn how they overcame obstacles, notice what they did particularly well, and choose to emulate what it is about them that inspires you most.

To express your ideas in the ways you want takes skill that comes with instruction and practice. Every dance starts with a single step, and it's not too late for you to learn a technique, or two, or three. You can never lose by broadening your palette. In fact, the more diverse techniques you learn, the more you can mix and meld them to produce something original. This small investment will, in time, open your mind to creative ways that pay significant dividends, as creative activities breed creative thinking.

If people in your early life told you that you weren't creative, think about those discouraging times and consider whether the people discouraging you were inadvertently talking through their own biases and misconceptions. Now is the time to revisit your passions and regift yourself with a second chance. Go draw, go paint; go sing, dance, or start a business; invent something new, and go with confidence!

You can become more creative just by changing the way you think about creativity. Give yourself permission to call yourself creative and do the things you love; if you consider yourself as creative, you will be. Discover your creative self by honoring your passions. Seek new experiences, try diverse activities, travel, be willing to fail, surround yourself with varied material, associate with open-minded people, and trust them to collaborate. Steve Jobs explained it well:

> Creativity is just connecting things. When you ask creative people how they did something, they feel a little guilty because they didn't really do it; they just saw something. It seemed obvious to them after awhile. That's because they were able to connect experiences they've had and synthesize new things. And the reason they were able to do that was that they've had more experiences or they have thought more about their experiences than other people.
>
> Unfortunately, that's too rare a commodity. A lot of people in our industry haven't had very diverse experiences. So they don't have enough dots to connect, and they end up with very linear solutions without a broad perspective on the problem. The broader one understands . . . the human experience, the better design we will have.[1]

This is only the beginning, and our hope is that these ideas open a dialogue about personality type and creativity that you can build upon. Be your natural self in order to be creative in your own way. Your creativity is as unique as your fingerprints and leaves an impression on whatever you touch. Knowing your creative differences gives you freedom—the freedom to express your ideas, the freedom to make your own decisions, and the freedom to be confident and courageous in whatever you apply yourself to.

ACKNOWLEDGMENTS

We are thankful for the generosity of many special people with different creative styles who added their own pieces of kindling needed to ignite our spark into a full blaze. This blaze has been a global effort, and we especially thank the following people, who reside on five continents.

This book would not have been possible without the support, encouragement, insights, and time of the wonderful Kellie Goldstein. We are thankful.

Words cannot express our gratitude for Linda Konner, our literary agent, for seeing the full potential of our ideas, and for her professional advice and assistance in turning our theories into something everyone can use. We're also grateful to Cynthia Black, the editor in chief at Beyond Words, for believing in our ideas, for her active participation and contributions, and for building a team to allow us to reach a wider audience.

We are grateful to Hile Rutledge, Pat Hutson, and all the people—past and present—at Otto Kroeger Associates for their support and help gathering necessary background information. Thanks to Jamelyn R. Johnson and Judy Breiner at the Center for Applications of Psychological Type for being so helpful in providing journal articles, and to

Acknowledgments

Sue Blair for providing enlightenment on children's learning styles. We also thank Cynthia Stengel Paris for her enthusiasm in promoting our ideas, and for her support and suggestions.

We thank Paul and Anne Goldstein for their endless support and encouragement to be creative. To Dr. Bobby Burchette and Christine Burchette, Jean K. Gill, Jim and Karin Sebolka, we appreciate your encouragement, your reading of drafts, and your suggestions.

This book couldn't have been written without two people who kept David's schedule clear to write: the amazing Megan North, who ran his company, and the attentive Olivia Rivera Rindos, who ran his household and took care of his son. We thank Gavin for his frequent interruptions (always with a smiling face), followed by his instructions: "Daddy, go back to work."

Otto especially thanks Yvonne Mellott for her support and laughter, along with his children: Amy Jane Kroeger, Stephen Kroeger, and Susan Major.

We're grateful for the friendship and generosity of so many in sharing stories of frustration and triumph from their own creative journeys, and for providing just the wisdom we needed to inspire us to keep going. Some of these people, in alphabetical order: Dr. Kendra M. Foltz Biegalski, Jaime Bowerman, Donna Brouda, Sara Brouda, Nikki Delport-Wepener, Scott Dingman, Dr. Charles De Seve, Lynn A. Doupsas, Tom J. Epps, David Feld, Marie Glass, Sam Guy, Vicki J. Haugen and all those in Project Boomerang, Mike Mikolosko, Joe North, Evelyn Novins, Claudia Lastella Overton, Tonya Peterson, Ann Pontius, Stacey Pritchett, Werner Schmitt, Mike Stahl, Lisa Schrum Talty, Lesley Turpin-Delport, and members of the Lake Barcroft community, among many others.

We are grateful to Joel Makower, Jane Cavolina, Victoria Klose, Sandi Klose, Lori Moreno, Andrea Lynn Colt, and Michael Ellsberg for your thoughtful directions in navigating our road to getting published.

We feel incredibly lucky for the good fortune of working with all the talented and collaborative people at Beyond Words, and extend special thanks to Dan Frost and

Acknowledgments

Anna Noak. We are grateful for the input from Rick Duff and are indebted to Joel Roberts, who shared a lifetime of his insights on how to create a message with impact. We also appreciate the developmental editing of Henry Covey, who used his way with words and ability to ask the right questions to bring clarity to our text.

We thank Lindsay Brown for managing all aspects of editorial and production with the assistance of Emmalisa Sparrow; copyeditor Jennifer Weaver-Neist for her tremendous attention to detail and her efforts to produce a consistent product; Devon Smith for design; and William H. Brunson for typography. And for all their efforts in marketing and promotion: Whitney Quon, Leah Brown, and Jessica Sturges.

For Dee Stafford and Gail Stafford, we appreciate your enthusiasm and laughter. David thanks Arion Maniatis and Dana White for early encouragement and great conversations about the possibilities, and Melinda Barrier Kroeze for teaching David how to blog while reminding him to laugh. Not least is his immense appreciation for lifelong advice and ongoing support from Richard Goldstein, Ken Busch, and Tom Stafford.

NOTES

Preface

1. Learn more about Jean K. Gill's work at: http://www.jeankgill.com/.

Introduction

1. Betty Edwards, *Drawing on the Right Side of the Brain* (New York: Putnam, 1989), 3.
2. Nikki Blacksmith and Jim Harter, "Majority of American Workers Not Engaged in Their Jobs," Gallup website (October 28, 2011): http://www.gallup.com/poll/150383/Majority-American-Workers-Not-Engaged-Jobs.aspx (accessed December 3, 2012).
3. Adobe, "State of Create Study: Global Benchmark Study on Attitudes and Beliefs about Creativity at Work, School, and Home" (April 2012), 3–9: http://www.adobe.com/aboutadobe/pressroom/pdfs/Adobe_State_of_Create_Global_Benchmark_Study.pdf.
4. Carl Jung first published his theory of psychological types in his book *Psychologische Typen (Psychological Types)* in Germany in 1921. The first English edition was published in the United States in 1923. The edition this book references is the sixth volume of the *Collected Works of Carl Jung* (Princeton, NJ: Princeton University Press, 1971).

Notes

Part I: Meeting Your Creative Self

Chapter 1

1. Academy of Achievement, "James Michener Interview," January 10, 1991, St. Petersburg, Florida.

2. Adobe, "State of Create Study: Global Benchmark Study on Attitudes and Beliefs about Creativity at Work, School, and Home" (April 2012), 3–9: http://www.adobe.com/aboutadobe/pressroom/pdfs/Adobe_State_of_Create_Global_Benchmark_Study.pdf.

3. Fredrik Ullén, Örjan de Manzano, Rita Almeida, Patrik K. E. Magnusson, Nancy L. Pedersen, Jeanne Nakamura, Mihály Csíkszentmihályi, Guy Madison, *Personality and Individual Differences* vol. 52, issue 2, (January 2012) 167–172: http://www.sciencedirect.com/science/article/pii/S0191886911004491.

4. Steven Leckart, "The Hackathon Is On: Pitching and Programming the Next Killer App," *Wired* (February 17, 2012): http://www.wired.com/magazine/2012/02/ff_hackathons/all/1 (accessed December 3, 2012).

5. Alice Calaprice and Freeman Dyson, *The New Quotable Einstein* (Princeton, NJ: Princeton University Press: 2005), 18.

6. Melissa Korn, "Top 'Innovators' Rank Low in R&D Spending," *Wall Street Journal* (October 24, 2011): http://online.wsj.com/article/SB10001424052970203752604576645401657833270.html (accessed December 3, 2012).

Chapter 2

1. Julia Child, *Julia's Kitchen Wisdom: Essential Techniques and Recipes from a Lifetime of Cooking* (New York: Knopf, 2000), 3.

2. Otto Kroeger with Janet M. Thuesen, *Type Talk at Work: How the 16 Personality Types Determine Your Success on the Job* (New York: Dell, 1992).

Chapter 3

1. C. G. Jung, *Psychological Types*, trans. R. F. C. Hull, revision H. G. Baynes, vol. 6, The Collected Works of C. G. Jung (Princeton: Princeton University Press), 4–6.

2. Isabel Briggs Myers, Mary H. McCaulley, Naomi L. Quenk, and Allen L. Hammer, *MBTI® Manual, 3rd Edition* (Consulting Psychologists Press, 1998). See also the Center for Applications of Psychological Type: www.CAPT.org.

3. Grace Glueck, "The Creative Mind: The Mastery of Robert Motherwell," *New York Times* (December 2, 1984).

4. William Grimes, "Jeanne-Claude, Christo's Collaborator on Environmental Canvas, Is Dead at 74," *New York Times* (November 20, 2009). See also Christo and Jeanne-Claude, "Most Common Errors: Conceptual Artists," ChristoJeanneClaude.net: http://christojeanneclaude.net/common-errors (accessed October 11, 2012).

5. Salvador Dalí, *Diary of a Genius* (Clerkenwell, UK: Doubleday, 1994), 124.

Notes

6. Peter Hassrick, *The Georgia O'Keeffe Museum* (New York: Harry Abrams Inc., 1997), 34.

7. Belinda Thomson, *Gauguin By Himself*, "Atuona, Hiva-Oa, 1903 to Avant Et Après" (London: Little Brown, 1993), 279.

8. Helen Hayes, "Quotes," official website: http://www.helenhayes.com/about/quotes.htm (accessed March, 17, 2011).

9. Alf Bøe, *Edvard Munch* (New York: Rizzoli, 1989), 15.

10. Roy Lichtenstein, "Lichtenstein: Paintings, Drawing Pastels" (MFA thesis, Ohio State University, 1949), 5.

11. Jung, *Psychological Types*, 289.

12. Myers, et al., *MBTI® Manual, 3rd Edition*, 157–158.

13. Isabel Briggs Myers and Mary H. McCaulley, *MBTI® Manual: A Guide to the Development and Use of the Myers-Briggs Type Indicator®* Palo Alto, CA: Consulting Psychologist Press, 1992), 248.

14. Lego Group, "About Us: Mission and Vision," Lego website: http://aboutus.lego.com/en-gb/lego-group/mission-and-vision/ (accessed October 11, 2012).

15. Richard Friedenthal, *Letters of the Great Artists—from Blake to Pollock,* trans. Daphne Woodward (London: Thames and Hudson, 1963), 256–257.

16. John D. Morse, "Oral History Interview with Edward Hopper," Smithsonian Archives of American Art (June 17, 1959): http://www.aaa.si.edu/collections/interviews/oral-history-interview-edward-hopper-11844 (accessed December 3, 2012). Hopper wrote "Notes on Painting" for the catalog of his exhibition at the Museum of Modern Art in 1933 and read it in the interview.

17. Julia Child, *Mastering the Art of French Cooking, 50th Anniversary Edition* (New York: Alfred A. Knopf, 2001), xv.

18. A. E. Hotchner, *Papa Hemingway: A Personal Memoir* (Cambridge MA: Da Capo Press, 1966), 128.

19. Larry Phillips, ed., *Ernest Hemingway on Writing* (New York: Scribner, 1984), 5.

20. Mike Wrenn, *Andy Warhol: In His Own Words* (New York: Omnibus Press, 1997), 24.

21. CNBC, "Biography on Henry Ford," video, January 8, 2010: http://video.cnbc.com/gallery/?video=1380597636 (accessed December 3, 2012).

22. Myers, et al., *MBTI® Manual, 3rd Edition.*

23. Myers and McCaulley, *MBTI® Manual*, 248.

24. James A. Michener, *The World is My Home: A Memoir* (New York: Random House, 1992), 314.

25. Genevieve Morgan, *Monet: The Artist Speaks* (San Francisco: Collins Publishing, 1996), 16.

26. Vincent van Gogh, "Letter to Theo van Gogh, The Hague, c. 4-8 August 1883, " Johanna van Gogh-Bonger, trans, Robert Harrison, ed., no. 309: www.webexhibits.org/vangogh/letter/12/309.htm (accessed December 3, 2012). See also www.VanGoghLetters.org.

27. Stephanie Terenzio, *The Collected Writings of Robert Motherwell: A Conversation at Lunch, November 1962* (New York: University of California Press, 1999), 136.

28. Jack Flam, "Looking at Life with the Eyes of a Child," an essay in *Matisse on Art* (London: E. P. Dutton, 1978), 149.

29. Myers, et al., *MBTI® Manual, 3rd Edition.*

30. William Safire, "John F. Kennedy, in Praise of Robert Frost, Celebrates the Arts in America," *Lend Me Your Ears* (New York: Norton & Company, 1992), 196.

Notes

31. Sir Isaac Newton, "Trinity College Notebook, 1661 to 1665," Cambridge Digital Library: http://cudl.lib.cam.ac.uk/collections/newton (accessed April 22, 2012).

32. *The Telegraph*, "Baroness Margaret Thatcher Portrait" (June 24, 2008): http://www.telegraph.co.uk/news/newstopics/nationaltreasures/2187363/Baroness-Margaret-Thatcher-portrait.html (accessed December 3, 2012).

33. Bill Ford, Q4 2005 Ford Motor Company Earnings (conference call transcript, NewsBank Access World News, January 23, 2006).

34. Michener, James A, *Caribbean* (New York: Fawcett 1990) 1.

35. Richard Kendall, *Cézanne by Himself* (New York: Little, Brown & Company, 1988), 29.

36. Wrenn, *Andy Warhol*, 16.

37. Mark Rothko, *Writings on Art* (New Haven: Yale University Press, 2006), 119.

38. Isabel Briggs Myers with Peter B. Myers, *Gifts Differing* (Palo Alto, CA: Consulting Psychologists Press, 1980), 3.

39. Vincent van Gogh, "Letter to Anthon van Rappard Nuenen, 2nd half of March, 1884": http://www.webexhibits.org/vangogh/letter/14/R43.htm?qp=art.influences.

40. John Richardson, *A Life of Picasso*, vol. 1 (New York: Pimlico, 1991), 3.

41. Jung, *Psychological Types*, 292.

42. Clara T. MacChesn, "A Talk with Matisse," *New York Times* (March 9, 1913).

43. Dr. Seuss, *My Many Colored Days* (New York: Knopf, 1996), 19.

44. Jung, *Psychological Types*, 296.

45. Brainy Quote. http://www.brainyquote.com/quotes/quotes/m/marilynmon386391.html.

46. Jack Flam, "Interview with Degand, 1945," *Matisse on Art* (London: E. P. Dutton, 1978) 159–165.

47. Richard Kendall, "Le Dimanche avec Paul Cézanne by Léo Larguier, 1988," *Cézanne by Himself* (London: Little, Brown & Company, 1988), 297.

48. Jack Flam, "Statements to Tériade, 1936," *Matisse on Art* (London: E. P. Dutton, 1978), 13.

49. Henry Ford, My Life and Work (Project Gutenberg: January, 2005), chap. 1: http://www.gutenberg.org/ebooks/7213.

50. Hiro Clark, *Picasso: In His Own Words* (San Francisco: Collins Publishing, 1993), 63.

51. Hotchner, *Papa Hemingway*, 23.

52. Marilyn Monroe, official website: http://www.cmgww.com/stars/monroe/about/quote.html (accessed October 11, 2012).

53. Dalí, *Diary of a Genius*, 49.

54. Wrenn, *Andy Warhol*, 20.

Chapter 4

1. Richard Kendall, *Cézanne by Himself* (London: Little, Brown & Company, 1988), 8.

2. Jennifer Conlin, "Detroit Pushes Back with Young Muscles," *New York Times* (July 1, 2011): http://www.nytimes.com/2011/07/03/fashion/the-young-and-entrepreneurial-move-to-downtown-detroit-pushing-its-economic-recovery.html?pagewanted=all (accessed December 3, 2012).

Notes

3. Otto Rank, *Art and Artist: Creative Urge and Personality Development* (New York: W. W. Norton & Company, 1932), 31.

4. Otto Rank, *A Psychology of Difference* (Princeton, NJ: Princeton University Press: 1996), 160.

5. Bente Torjusen, *Words and Images of Edvard Munch* (London: Thames & Hudson, 1989), 141.

6. Jack Flam, ed., "Notes of a Painter," *Matisse on Art* (Berkeley: University of California Press, 1995), 47.

7. Isabel Briggs Myers, Mary H. McCaulley, Naomi L. Quenk, and Allen L. Hammer, *MBTI® Manual, 3rd Edition* (Consulting Psychologists Press, 1998).

8. Isabel Briggs Myers and Mary H. McCaulley, *MBTI® Manual: A Guide to the Development and Use of the Myers-Briggs Type Indicator®* (Palo Alto, CA: Consulting Psychologist Press, 1992), 110.

9. A. A. Milne, *The Complete Tales of Winnie-the-Pooh* (New York: Dutton, 1994), 4.

10. David Keirsey, *Please Understand Me II: Temperament, Character, Intelligence* (Del Mar, CA: Prometheus Nemesis Book Company, 1998), 121.

11. Isabel Briggs Myers with Peter B. Myers, *Gifts Differing* (Palo Alto, Ca: Consulting Psychologists Press, 1980), 6.

12. Otto Rank, *Art and Artist: Creative Urge and Personality Development* (New York: W. W. Norton, 1932), 265.

13. Flam, *Matisse on Art*, 66.

14. Marci Segal, "Which Types Are the Most Creative," *TypeWorks* no. 39 (February 2001).

15. Myers, et al., *MBTI® Manual, 3rd Edition.*

16. National Gallery of Art, "Celebrating the Legacy of Paul Mellon": http://www.nga.gov/mellon/ (accessed April 22, 2012).

17. Helen Hayes, "Quotes," official website: http://www.helenhayes.com/about/quotes.htm (accessed March, 17, 2011).

18. Richard Kendall, "Le Dimanche avec Paul Cézanne by Léo Larguier, 1988," *Cézanne by Himself* (London: Little, Brown & Company, 1988), 297.

19. See note 14.

20. Henry Ford, *My Life and Work* (Project Gutenberg: January, 2005), Introduction: http://www.gutenberg.org/ebooks/7213.

21. Ibid.

22. Myers, *Gifts Differing*, 71.

23. See note 14.

24. Morse, "Oral History Interview with Edward Hopper," Smithsonian (see chap. 3, no. 16).

25. Myers, et al., *MBTI® Manual, 3rd Edition.*

26. Dr. Seuss, *If I Ran the Zoo* (New York: Random House, 1950), 3.

27. Keirsey, *Please Understand Me II*, 57.

28. Steven Naifeh and Gregory Smith, *Jackson Pollock: An American Saga* (New York: Clarkson Potter, 1989), 540.

29. Ibid., 27.

30. Mary Kissel, "Space: The Next Business Frontier," *The Wall Street Journal* (December 17–18, 2011), A13.

31. Claude Cernuschi, *Jackson Pollock: Meaning and Significance* (New York: HarperCollins, 1992), 107.

32. Paul Gauguin, *Nora Nora* (Mineola, NY: Dover, 1985), 7.

33. See note 14.

34. Thomas M. Inge, ed., *Charles M. Schulz Conversations* (Mississippi: University Press Mississippi, 2000), 63–75.

35. Salvador Dalí, *The Secret Life of Salvador Dalí* (Mineola, NY: Dial Press, 1942), 10.

36. Keirsey, *Please Understand Me II*, 32.

37. Ibid., 36.

38. Thomas M. Inge, ed., *Truman Capote: Conversations* (Mississippi: The University Press of Mississippi, 1987), 88.

39. Pablo Picasso, "Famous Quotes," PabloPicasso.org: http://www.pablopicasso.org/quotes.jsp (accessed February 16, 2012).

40. Dore Ashton, ed., *Picasso on Art: A Selection of Views* (New York: Da Capo Press 1972), 89.

41. Salvador Dalí, *Diary of a Genius* (Clerkenwell, UK: Doubleday, 1994), 95.

42. Pierre Schneider, *Matisse* (New York: Thames & Hudson, 2005), 98.

43. C. G. Jung, *Psychological Types*, trans. R. F. C. Hull, revision H. G. Baynes, vol. 6, The Collected Works of C. G. Jung (Princeton, NJ: Princeton University Press), 401.

44. Binnie Ferrand, "The Artist Georgia O'Keeffe, A Portrait of an Introverted Sensor," International Conference, Association for Psychological Type, 2001.

45. Robert Simon, "Jungian Types and Creativity of Professional Fine Artists" (dissertation, United States International University, 1979), 9.

46. Edward Hopper, Letter to Charles H. Sawyer (Andover, MA: Courtesy of Addison Gallery of American Art, Phillips Academy, October 19, 1939).

47. Francis Bacon, "Art Quotes," The Painter's Keys website: http://quote.robertgenn.com/auth_search.php?authid=2 (accessed February 16, 2012).

48. Vincent van Gogh, Letter to Theo van Gogh, Antwerp, on or about Thursday, 17 December 1885: http://vangoghletters.org/vg/letters/let548/letter.html.

49. Stephanie Terenzio, *The Collected Writings of Robert Motherwell: A Conversation at Lunch, November 1962* (New York: University of California Press, 1999), 136.

50. Ford, *My Life and Work*, ch. 7.

51. Dalí, *Diary of a Genius*, 34.

Part II: The Sixteen Creative Types

Chapter 5

1. Isabel Briggs Myers, Mary H. McCaulley, Naomi L. Quenk, and Allen L. Hammer, *MBTI® Manual, 3rd Edition* (Consulting Psychologists Press, 1998).

2. Henry Ford, *My Life and Work* (Project Gutenberg: January, 2005), ch. 1: http://www.gutenberg.org/ebooks/7213.

Notes

3. Isabel Briggs Myers with Peter B. Myers, *Gifts Differing* (Palo Alto, CA: Consulting Psychologists Press, 1980), 103.

4. Gail Levin, *Edward Hopper: An Intimate Biography* (London: University of California Press, 1996), 95.

5. David Keirsey, *Please Understand Me II: Temperament, Character, Intelligence* (Del Mar, CA: Prometheus Nemesis Book Company, 1998), 108

6. Mike Wallace, "The Private Side of Johnny Carson," *60 Minutes*, CBS, April 29,1979: http://www.cbs news.com/2100-500164_162-669087.html.

7. CNBC, "Biography on Henry Ford," video (January 8, 2010): http://video.cnbc.com/gallery/?video= 1380597636 (accessed on December 3, 2012).

8. Brian Kolodiejchuk, *Mother Teresa: Come Be My Light* (New York: Doubleday, 2007).

9. Myers, et al., *MBTI® Manual, 3rd Edition.*

10. Norman Rockwell, *My Adventures as an Illustrator* (New York: Harry N. Abrams, 1995), 35.

11. Samuel T. Williamson, "Homespun America, Illustrated," *New York Times* (February 14, 1960).

12. Richard Reeves, "Norman Rockwell Is Exactly Like a Norman Rockwell," *New York Times* (February 28, 1971).

13. Keirsey, *Please Understand Me II*, 115.

14. J. S. Bach, Quotes.net: http://www.quotes.net/quote/40610 (accessed September, 10, 2012).

15. Myers, et al., *MBTI® Manual, 3rd Edition.*

16. Neil Baldwin, *Edison on Inventing* (New York: University of Chicago Press, 1995), 104.

17. Richard Kendall, ed., *Cézanne by Himself* (London: Little, Brown & Company, 1988), 292.

18. Thomas Jefferson, "Meet Thomas Jefferson," TheJeffersonians.com: http://thejeffersonians.com/Meet%20 Jefferson.html (accessed April 22, 2012).

19. John Paczkowski, "Steve Jobs, in His Own Words," AllThingsd.com (October 5, 2011): http://allthingsd .com/20111005/steve-jobs-in-his-own-words/ (accessed January 13, 2013).

20. Ibid.

21. Myers, *Gifts Differing*, 109

22. Kendall, ed., *Cézanne by Himself*, 289.

23. John Rewald, *Cézanne: A Biography* (The Netherlands: Harry and Abrams, 1995), 275.

24. Myers, et al., *MBTI® Manual, 3rd Edition.*

25. "Gandhi Speech," YouTube video posted by IndiaVideo.org (September 24, 2009): http://www.youtube .com/watch?v=8yMcNubXqc4&feature=fvwrel (accessed December 3, 2012).

26. Ralph Waldo Emerson, Journals of Ralph Waldo Emerson: With Annotations (Boston: Houghton Mifflin, 1913), 549.

27. Vincent van Gogh, Letter to Theo van Gogh, Nuenen, October 1884: http://www.webexhibits.org/vangogh/ letter/14/381.htm.

28. Vincent van Gogh, Letter to Emile Bernard, Arles, April 9, 1888: http://www.webexhibits.org/vangogh/ letter/18/B03.htm.

29. Vincent van Gogh, Letter to Theo van Gogh, Arles, September 26, 1888: http://www.webexhibits.org/ vangogh/letter/18/541a.htm.

30. Keirsey, *Please Understand Me II*, 152.

Notes

31. Louis Fisher, *Gandhi: His Life and Message for the World* (New York: Mentor Press, 1954), 177.

32. Myers, *Gifts Differing*, 112.

33. "Life of Gandhi, 1869–1948," Real 31, Gandhiserve.org (1968): http://www.gandhiserve.org/video/mahatma/commentary13.html (accessed October 12, 2012).

34. Steven Naifeh and Gregory Smith, Jackson Pollock: An American Saga (New York: Clarkson Potter, 1989), 237.

35. Myers, et al., *MBTI® Manual, 3rd Edition*.

36. Naifeh and Smith, *Jackson Pollock*, 612.

37. Laurie Lisle, *Portrait of an Artist: A Biography of Georgia O'Keeffe* (New York: Washington Square Press, 1981), 180.

38. Mike Wrenn, *Andy Warhol: In His Own Words* (New York: Omnibus Press, 1997), 21.

39. Sarah Whitaker Peters, *Becoming O'Keeffe: The Early Years* (New York: Abbeville Press 1991), 8.

40. Myers, et al., *MBTI® Manual, 3rd Edition*.

41. Keirsey, *Please Understand Me II*, 71–72.

42. C. G. Jung, *Psychological Types*, trans. R. F. C. Hull, revision H. G. Baynes, vol. 6, The Collected Works of C. G. Jung (Princeton: Princeton University Press), 388.

43. Keirsey, *Please Understand Me II*, 72.

44. Thomas M. Inge, ed., *Charles M. Schulz Conversations* (Mississippi: University Press Mississippi, 2000), 153-157.

45. Charles Schulz, interview by Charlie Rose, *Charlie Rose Show*, May 9, 1997: http://www.charlierose.com/view/interview/5564 (accessed January 13, 2013).

46. Myers, *Gifts Differing*, 96.

47. George Sylvester Viereck, "What Life Means to Einstein," *The Saturday Evening Post 202*, no. 17 (October 26, 1929), 117.

48. Myers, et al., *MBTI® Manual, 3rd Edition*.

49. James Hamilton, *Turner* (New York: Random House, 1997), 56.

50. Alice Calaprice, *The Quotable Einstein* (Princeton, NJ: Princeton University Press, 1996), 199.

51. Myers, et al., *MBTI® Manual, 3rd Edition*.

52. Keirsey, *Please Understand Me II*, 159.

53. Ragna Thiis Strang, trans. by Geoggrey Culverwell, *Edvard Munch: The Man and His Art* (New York: Abbeville Press, 1977), 127.

54. Myers, *Gifts Differing*, 78.

55. Ibid.

56. Myers, et al., *MBTI® Manual, 3rd Edition*.

57. Myers, *Gifts Differing*, 94.

58. Myers, et al., *MBTI® Manual, 3rd Edition*.

59. Briggs Myers, *Gifts Differing*, 10.

60. Dwight D. Eisenhower speech, November 14, 1957, *Public Papers of the Presidents of the United States*, 1957, National Archives and Records Service, Government Printing Office, Washington, DC.

Notes

61. Meredith Fuller, "ENTJs: The Artist, the Headhunter & the Playwright," *Australian Psychological Review 5*, no. 2 (July 2, 2003).

62. Myers, *Gifts Differing*, 86.

63. Daniel Wildenstein, *Monet, or the Triumph of Impressionism* (Hohenzollernring Köln: Taschen, 2003), 345.

64. Ibid., 346.

65. Lawrence Groebel, *Talking with Michener* (Jackson, MS: University Press of Mississippi, 1999), 20.

66. Ibid., 20.

67. Academy of Achievement, "James Michener Interview," January 10, 1991, St. Petersburg, Florida: http://www.achievement.org/autodoc/page/mic0int-3.

68. Groebel, *Talking with Michener*, 48.

69. James A. Michener, *The World is My Home: A Memoir* (New York: Random House, 1992), 320.

70. Martin Luther King Jr., "Letter from Birmingham Jail," (April 16, 1963): http://mlk-kpp01.stanford.edu/kingweb/popular_requests/frequentdocs/birmingham.pdf (accessed January 13, 2013).

71. Ibid.

72. Myers, et al., *MBTI® Manual, 3rd Edition*.

73. Ronald Reagan, "Proclamation 5585: Walt Disney Recognition Day," December 5, 1986, The American Presidency Project website: http://www.presidency.ucsb.edu/ws/?pid=36786 (accessed January 13, 2013).

74. "Ronald Reagan, 1980," YouTube video posted by njloetz (October 2, 2008): http://www.youtube.com/watch?v=loBe0WXtts8 (accessed February 17, 2012).

75. Ronald Reagan, "Remarks at a Luncheon for Recipients of the National Medal of Arts," June 18, 1987, The American Presidency Project website: http://www.presidency.ucsb.edu/ws/?pid=38528 (accessed January 13, 2013).

76. Jack Flam, ed., "Sarah Stein's Notes, 1908," *Matisse on Art* (London: E. P. Dutton, 1978), 43.

77. Jack Flam, ed., "Looking at Life with the Eyes of a Child," *Matisse on Art* (London: E. P. Dutton, 1978), 149.

78. Larry Phillips, ed., "Letter to Edmund Wilson, 1952," *Ernest Hemingway on Writing* (New York: Scribner, 1984), 136.

79. A. E. Hotchner, *Papa Hemingway: A Personal Memoir* (Cambridge, MA: Da Capo Press, 1966), 198.

80. Myers, et al., *MBTI® Manual, 3rd Edition*.

81. Larry Phillips, ed., "By-Lines," *Ernest Hemingway on Writing* (New York: Scribner, 1984), 219–220.

82. Donald Trump and Tony Schwartz, *The Art of the Deal* (New York: Random House, 1987), 1.

83. Theodore Roosevelt, "Citizenship in a Republic," speech at the Sorbonne in Paris, France, April 23, 1910, Almanac of Theodore Roosevelt website: http://www.theodore-roosevelt.com/trsorbonnespeech.html (accessed January 1, 2013).

84. Hile Rutledge and Otto Kroeger, *MBTI® Introduction Workbook* (Fairfax, VA: OKA, 2005), 22.

85. Hotchner, *Papa Hemingway*, 52.

86. Myers, et al., *MBTI® Manual, 3rd Edition*.

87. Salvador Dalí, *Diary of a Genius* (Clerkenwell, UK: Doubleday, 1994), 123.

88. "Dalí Art a Mystery to the Painters Too," *New York Times* (February 22, 1939).

89. Keirsey, *Please Understand Me II*, 69.

90. Kroeger, Otto and Janet M. Thuesen, *Type Talk: The 16 Personality Types that Determine How We Live, Love, and Work* (New York: Dell, 1988), 263.
91. Myers, et al., *MBTI® Manual, 3rd Edition.*
92. Grace Glueck, "The Creative Mind: The Mastery of Robert Motherwell," *New York Times* (December 2, 1984).
93. Stephanie Terenzio, *The Collected Writings of Robert Motherwell: A Conversation at Lunch, November 1962* (NewYork: University of California Press, 1999), 43.
94. Bill Clinton, "Campaign Speech in California," audio, Investor's Business Daily, October 25, 1996: http://www.hark.com/clips/hltzdjzrms-the-constitution-said.
95. Myers, et al., *MBTI Manual, 3rd Edition.*
96. Will Rogers, "On Leon Trotsky Saturday Evening Post ," *Saturday Evening Post* (November 6, 1926).
97. Connie Robertson, *The Wordsworth Dictionary of Quotations* (Hertfordshire, UK: Wordsworth Editions, 1998), entry 9575.
98. Myers, *Gifts Differing,* 106.
99. Bill Clinton, "I Still Believe in a Place Called Hope," acceptance speech at the 1992 Democratic National Convention, July 16, 1992, Democratic Underground website: http://www.democraticunderground.com/speeches/clinton.html (accessed January 13, 2013).

Part III: Cultivating Courageous Creativity

Chapter 6

1. Steve Jobs interview by Daniel Morrow, transcript edited by Thomas J. Campanella, Smithsonian Oral and Video Histories, Computerworld Smithsonian Awards Program, April 20, 1995.
2. William Safire, ed., "Kennedy, in Praise of Frost," *Lend Me Your Ears* (New York: Norton & Company, 1992), 195.

Chapter 7

1. Otto Kroeger with Janet M. Thuesen, *Type Talk at Work: How the 16 Personality Types Determine Your Success on the Job* (New York: Dell, 1992).
2. Mary Ann Caws, *Robert Motherwell with Pen and Brush* (London: Reaktion Books, 2003), 82.

Chapter 8

1. Lawrence Groebel, *Talking with Michener* (Jackson, MS: University Press of Mississippi, 1999), 55.
2. Jack Cowart and Juan Hamilton, *Georgia O'Keeffe: Arts and Letters* (New York: National Gallery of Art, 1987), 137.
3. Ibid.

Notes

4. Helen Hayes, official website, "Quotes": http://www.helenhayes.com/about/quotes.htm (accessed March 17, 2011).

5. Salvador Dalí, "From May 12, 1956," *Diary of a Genius* (Clerkenwell, UK: Doubleday, 1994), 125.

6. Vincent van Gogh, Letter to Theo van Gogh, Nuenen, May 4–5, 1885: http://vangoghletters.org/vg/letters/let500/letter.html.

7. Vincent van Gogh Letter to Wilhelmina van Gogh, Arles, June 22, 1888: http://www.webexhibits.org/vangogh/letter/18/W04.htm?qp=lifestyle.appearance.

Chapter 9

1. Isabel Briggs Myers, Mary H. McCaulley, Naomi L. Quenk, and Allen L. Hammer, *MBTI® Manual, 3rd Edition* (Consulting Psychologists Press, 1998).

2. Roberta Smith, "Matisse, Drawing in Three Dimensions," *New York Times* (December 21, 2007).

3. Herbert Read, *Henry Moore: Sculpture and Drawing* (London: Lund Humphrise, 1946), xl.

4. Barbara A. Mowat and Paul Werstine, ed., *William Shakespeare's As You Like It* (New York: Washington Square Press, 1997), 83.

5. Isabel Briggs Myers and Mary H. McCaulley, *MBTI® Manual: A Guide to the Development and Use of the Myers-Briggs Type Indicator®* (Palo Alto: Consulting Psychologist Press, 1992), 244.

6. Ibid., 244–292.

7. *Grand Hotel*, directed by Edmund Goulding (Beverly Hills: Metro-Goldwyn-Mayer, 1932).

8. Myers and McCaulley, *MBTI® Manual: A Guide*, 248.

9. William Strunk, Jr. and E. B. White, *The Elements of Style*, 4th ed. (Needham Heights, MA: Allyn & Bacon, 2000), 21.

10. James A. Michener, *James A. Michener's Writer's Handbook* (New York: Random House, 1992), 18.

11. Myers and McCaulley, *MBTI® Manual: A Guide*, 132.

12. Vladmir Nabokov, *Strong Opinions* (New York: Vintage, 1973), foreword.

13. Myers and McCaulley, *MBTI® Manual: A Guide*, 132-3.

14. Strunk and White, *Elements of Style*, 70.

15. Ernest Hemingway, *Death in the Afternoon* (New York: Scribner, 1996), 3.

16. Larry Phillips, ed., "By-Lines," *Ernest Hemingway on Writing* (New York: Scribner, 1984), 217.

17. Lawrence Groebel, *Talking with Michener* (Jackson, MS: University Press of Mississippi, 1999), 55.

18. Fred Astaire, *Steps in Time* (New York: HarperCollins, 2008), 325.

19. A. E. Hotchner, *Papa Hemingway: A Personal Memoir* (Cambridge, MA: Da Capo Press, 1966), 114.

Chapter 10

1. Steve Jobs, Smithsonian Oral and Video Histories, 1995: http://www.cwhonors.org/search/oral_history_archive/steve_jobs/index.asp.

2. Henry Ford, *My Life and Work* (Project Gutenberg: January, 2005), ch. 5: http://www.gutenberg.org/ebooks/7213.

3. Ibid., ch. 1.

4. Vincent van Gogh, Letter to Theo van Gogh, Nuenen, Thursday, October 9, 1884: http://www.web exhibits.org/vangogh/letter/14/381.htm?qp=art.theory and http://vangoghletters.org/vg/letters/let465/letter.html.

5. "Art: The Silent Witness," *Time* magazine (December 24, 1956), 28, 36–39.

6. George Sylvester Viereck, "What Life Means to Einstein," *The Saturday Evening Post* 202, no. 17 (October 26, 1929), 113.

7. Zorana Ivcevic and J. D Mayer, "Creative Types in Personality," *Imagination, Cognition, and Personality* 26 (2006–7), 65–86.

Chapter 11

1. A. E. Hotchner, *The Good Life According to Hemingway* (New York: Ecco, 2008), 18.

2. Constantin Stanislavski, *My Life in Art* (London: Theatre Arts Books, 1924), 37.

3. Friedrich Kerst, *Mozart: The Man and the Artist, as Revealed in His Own Words*, trans. Henry Edward Krehbiel (New York: B. W. Huebsch, 1905), 12.

4. Lewis Funke and John Booth, *Actors Talk about Acting* (New York: Random House, 1961), 80–82.

5. Michener, The World Is My Home, 315.

6. Elizabeth Murphy, *The Developing Child: Using Jungian Type to Understand Children* (Mountain View: Davies-Black Publishing, 1992), 33.

7. Isabel Briggs Myers, Mary H. McCaulley, *Manual: A Guide to the Development and Use of the Myers-Briggs Type Indicator.* (Palo Alto: Consulting Psychologists Press, 1985), 247-8.

8. Isabel Briggs Myers, Mary H. McCaulley, Naomi L. Quenk, and Allen L. Hammer, *MBTI® Manual, 3rd Edition* (Consulting Psychologists Press, 1998).

9. Murphy, *The Developing Child*, 40.

Chapter 12

1. Isabel Briggs Myers, Mary H. McCaulley, Naomi L. Quenk, and Allen L. Hammer, *MBTI® Manual, 3rd Edition* (Consulting Psychologists Press, 1998).

2. Ibid.

3. Hile Rutledge and Otto Kroeger, "MBTI® Qualifying Workshop," December 5–8, 2005, Fairfax, Virginia. Visit OKA website to learn more about the Hile Rutledge's work: http://oka-online.com.

4. Sam Roberts, "A Founding Father's Book Turns Up," *New York Times* (February 21, 2011).

Chapter 13

1. Julia Cameron, *The Artist's Way, A Course in Discovering and Recovering your Creative Self* (London: Pan Books, 1995), xii.

2. Henri Matisse, *Jazz*, trans. Sophie Hawkes (New York: George Braziller, 1947, 1992).

3. Alice Calaprice, "Letter to a Child Who Asked If Scientists Pray, June 24, 1936," Einstein Archive 42-6001, *The Quotable Einstein* (Princeton, NJ: Princeton University Press, 1996), 152.
4. Roy M. Oswald and Otto Kroeger, *Personality Type and Religious Leadership* (Herndon, VA: Alban Institute, 1988), 22.

Chapter 14

1. Gary Wolf, "Steve Jobs: The Next Insanely Great Thing," *Wired* (February 1996).

GLOSSARY

Creative Preferences

Energy Flow

E Extraversion—Energized and focused externally/output focused outward.

I Introversion—Energized and focused internally/output focused inward.

Information Gathering

S Sensing—Prefer to look at the complete picture, gathering detail through the senses and creating by using what already exists.

N Intuition—Prefer to look at the big picture, gathering abstractions through the sixth sense and creating where nothing existed before.

Decision Making

T Thinking—Make decisions primarily with your head.

F Feeling—Make decisions primarily with your heart.

Outward (Public) Orientation

J Judging—Prefer to get things decided in dealing with the outside world, often seeking and promoting resolution. Tend to plan your creativity.

P Perceiving—Prefer to stay open to new information and options in dealing with the outside world. Are spontaneous about your creativity.

Creative Temperaments

NF Intuitive Feeler—Poetic, sensitive, and personal; creativity is largely an outlet for self-expression.

NT Intuitive Thinker—Experimental and complex; creations are theoretically minded and meaningful, though objective and impersonal.

SJ Sensing Judger—Realistic and traditional; don't see themselves as creative, even though they can be and often are; busting the myth that creativity has to be weird or wild, as they innovate through incremental improvements within systems.

SP Sensing Perceiver—Dramatic and flexible when inspired; unstructured, undisciplined, untraditional, action oriented, and spontaneous; creates excitement with innovations.

Other Pairs of Creative Preferences

NJ Intuitive Judger—A dreamer with a grounded side.

ES Extraverted Sensor—A super-Sensor who notices every little detail.

IN Introverted Intuitive—Seeks meaning and is sensitive to what goes unsaid.

EF Extraverted Feeler—People-oriented, inspiring, dramatic, and in touch with emotions.

IS Introverted Sensor—Has a constructive imagination; can sense the properties of items with a touch (as if by having an internal ruler, thermometer, or scale).

FP Feeling Perceiver—Rolls from style to style like a tumbleweed blowing in the wind in search of personal identity.

TJ Thinking Judger—Stays with a style that works and is slow to change.

NP **Intuitive Perceiver**—Abstract and flexible, an endless lightning storm of ideas.

IF **Introverted Feeler**—Empathetic and sensitive to interpersonal relationships, but prefers to be alone.

IP **Introverted Perceiver**—Has boundless imagination and prefers pondering over carrying out ideas to completion.

EN **Extraverted Intuitive**—Outspoken, seeks to find and promote new possibilities.

EJ **Extraverted Judger**—Tends to assert position and control the surrounding space, external objects, or other people.

EP **Extraverted Perceiver**—Fast and flexible, the most reactive to the surrounding environment.

IJ **Introverted Judger**—Contemplates with advanced plans and completes what they start.

Creative Types

ISTJ **Organizer** (Introverted, Sensing, Thinking, Judging)—Can be counted on to be austere, objective, realistic, and traditional; solving today's problems with practical solutions from tested, seasoned experience.

ISFJ **Facilitator** (Introverted, Sensing, Feeling, Judging)—Creativity comes through adhering to personal values; reflects on today's problems to solve them with practicality and a sponge-like memory of what has worked before.

INTJ **Visionary** (Introverted, Intuitive, Thinking, Judging)—An imaginative wizard who directs and controls from behind the curtain; always has a contingency plan.

INFJ **Inspirer** (Introverted, Intuitive, Feeling, Judging)—A contemplative visionary whose creative style is driven by the possibilities in people.

ISTP **Crafter** (Introverted, Sensing, Thinking, Perceiving)—Quickly sizes up the situation, surveys resources, and takes immediate action.

ISFP **Dreamer** (Introverted, Sensing, Feeling, Perceiving)—Reflective, action oriented, and aims to promote harmony; inspired by deep emotions and inner passion, but expression is limited without learning techniques.

INTP Idea Mill (Introverted, Intuitive, Thinking, Perceiving)—Theoretical, flexible, and responsive; adapts to immediate situation and future needs; least dependent on others and works best alone.

INFP Muser (Introverted, Intuitive, Feeling, Perceiving)—Has a vivid imagination, is autobiographical and poetic; generates endless ideas, especially related to possibilities in people; provides leadership by adhering to individual values.

ESTJ Realist (Extraverted, Sensing, Thinking, Judging)—Ingenious at solving real-world problems in practical, elegant, no-nonsense ways.

ESFJ Teacher (Extraverted, Sensing, Feeling, Judging)—Traditional, organized, people oriented; express creativity within the bounds of protocol and their values.

ENTJ Commander (Extraverted, Intuitive, Thinking, Judging)—Shows creativity by strategically executing plans to reach goals, becoming a leader in most fields.

ENFJ Persuader (Extraverted, Intuitive, Feeling, Judging)—Prefers to be with people, energized by the audience; their creative expressions come through stories; creativity is often intangible and based on ideology.

ESTP Adventurer (Extraverted, Sensing, Thinking, Perceiving)—Carefully collects all the aspects of the environment, objectively assesses the situation, and takes action, often on the spur of the moment; looks while leaping.

ESFP Entertainer (Extraverted, Sensing, Feeling, Perceiving)—Is active, enthusiastic, and empathetic; helps to inspire others; a super-Sensor who engages all senses to absorb everything in the environment.

ENTP Brainstormer (Extraverted, Intuitive, Thinking, Perceiving)—Aims to solve the unsolvable; technology-oriented and inventive; continuously pursues knowledge and gains competency.

ENFP Socializer (Extraverted, Intuitive, Feeling, Perceiving)—Creates and innovates through understanding people; collaborates and motivates friends and team members to be their best.

SELECTED BIBLIOGRAPHY

Berger, John. *Ways of Seeing*. London: Penguin Books, 1972.

Blair, Sue. *The Personality Puzzle*. Auckland, New Zealand: Personality Dynamics, 2007.

Csikszentmihalyi, Mihaly. *Creativity: Flow and the Psychology of Discovery and Invention*. New York: Harper Perennial, 1997.

Dalí, Salvador. *Diary of a Genius*. Clerkenwell, UK: Creation Books, 1994.

———. *The Secret Life of Salvador Dalí*. Mineola: Dover Press, 1993.

———. *The Unspeakable Confessions of Salvador Dalí*. New York: Quill, 1981.

Edwards, Betty. *Drawing on the Right Side of the Brain: A Course in Enhancing Creativity and Artistic Confidence*. New York: Tarcher/Putnam, 1999.

Evans, Joan. *Taste and Temperament: A Brief Study of Psychological Types in Their Relation to the Visual Arts*. London Jonathan Cape, 1939.

Flam, Jack. *Matisse on Art*. London: E. P. Dutton, 1978.

Ford, Henry. *My Life and Work*. Garden City: Doubleday, 1922.

———. *My Life and Work*. Project Gutenberg, January, 2005, http://www.gutenberg.org/ebooks/7213.

Groebel, Lawrence. *Talking with Michener*. Jackson, MS: University Press of Mississippi, 1999.

Selected Bibliography

Hirsh, Sandra K., and Jane A. G. Kise, *SoulTypes: Matching Your Personality and Spiritual Path*. Minneapolis, MN: Augsburg Books, 2006.

Hotchner, A. E. *The Good Life According to Hemingway*. New York: Ecco, 2008.

———. *Papa Hemingway: A Personal Memoir*. Cambridge, MA: Da Capo Press, 2004.

Jung, Carl Gustav. *Psychological Types*. Princeton, NJ: Princeton University Press, 1990.

Keirsey, David. *Please Understand Me II*: Temperament, Character, Intelligence. Del Mar, CA: Prometheus Nemesis Book Company, 1998.

Kendall, Richard. *Paul Cézanne by Himself*. London: Little, Brown & Company, 1988.

Kerst, Friedrich. *Mozart: The Man and the Artist, as Revealed in His Own Words*. Translated by Henry Edward Krehbiel. New York: B. W. Huebsch, 1905.

Killen, Damian and Garth Williams. *Introduction to Type and Innovation*. Mountain View, CA: CPP, 2009.

Kroeger, Otto and Hile Rutledge. *The 4 Temperaments Workbook*. Fairfax, VA: OKA, 2004.

Kroeger, Otto and Janet M. Thuesen. *16 Ways to Love Your Lover: Understanding the 16 Personality Types So You Can Create a Love that Lasts Forever*. New York: Dell, 1994.

———. *Type Talk at Work: How the 16 Personality Types Determine Your Success on the Job*. New York: Dell, 1992.

———. *Type Talk: The 16 Personality Types that Determine How We Live, Love, and Work*. New York: Dell, 1988.

Lawrence, Gordon. *People Types & Tiger Stripes*. Gainsville, FL: Center for Applications of Psychological Type, 2009.

———. *Looking at Type and Learning Styles*. Gainesville, FL: Center for Applications of Psychological Type, 1997.

Loomis, Mary and Eli Saltz. "Cognitive Styles As Predictors of Artist Style," *Journal of Personality* 52:1, March 1984.

Michener, James A. *The World Is My Home: A Memoir*. New York: Ballantine Books, 1992.

Murphy, Elizabeth. *The Developing Child: Using Jungian Type to Understand Children*. Mountain View, CA: Davies-Black Publishing, 1992.

Myers, Isabel Briggs and Mary H. McCaulley. *MBTI® Manual: A Guide to the Development and Use of the Myers-Briggs Type Indicator®*. Palo Alto, CA: Consulting Psychologist Press, 1985.

Myers, Isabel Briggs, Mary H. McCaulley, Naomi L. Quenk, and Allen L. Hammer. *MBTI® Manual 3rd Edition*. Palo Alto, CA: Consulting Psychologists Press, 1998.

Selected Bibliography

Myers, Isabel Briggs, with Peter B. Myers. *Gifts Differing*. Palo Alto, CA: Consulting Psychologists Press, 1980.

Naifeh, Steven and Gregory Smith. *Jackson Pollock: An American Saga*. New York: Clarkson Potter, 1989.

Oswald, Roy M. and Otto Kroeger. *Personality Type and Religious Leadership*. Herndon, VA: Alban Institute, 1988.

Rank, Otto. *A Psychology of Difference*. Princeton, NJ: Princeton University Press, 1996.

———. *Art and Artist: Creative Urge and Personality*. New York: W. W. Norton & Company, 1932.

Read, Herbert. *Education Through Art*. New York: Pantheon Books, 1945.

Rockwell, Norman. *My Adventures as an Illustrator*. As told by Tom Rockwell. New York: Harry N. Abrams, 1995.

Rutledge, Hile and Otto Kroeger. *MBTI® Introduction Workbook*. Fairfax, VA: OKA, 2005.

Safire, William. *Lend Me Your Ears: Great Speeches in History*. New York: W. W. Norton & Company, 1992.

Stanislavski, Constantin. *My Life in Art*. London: Theatre Arts Books, 1924.

Terenzio, Stephanie. *The Collected Writings of Robert Motherwell: A Conversation at Lunch, November 1962*. New York: University of California Press, 1999.

Wildenstein, Daniel. *Monet, or the Triumph of Impressionism*. Köln, Germany: Taschen, 2003.

Worringer, Wilhelm. *Abstraction and Empathy: A Contribution to the Psychology of Style*. New York: International Universities Press, 1953.

Wölfflin, Heinrich, trans. M. D. Hottinger. *Principles of Art History: The Problem of The Development of Style in Later Art*. Mineola: Dover, 1950.

Wrenn, Mike. *Andy Warhol: In His Own Words*. New York: Omnibus Press, 1997.

Zichy, Shoya. *Career Match: Connecting Who You Are with What You'll Love to Do*. New York: American Management Association, 2007.